The Pursuit of Wow!

EVERY PERSON'S GUIDE
TO
TOPSY-TURVY TIMES

Also by Tom Peters

In Search of Excellence
(with Robert H. Waterman, Jr.)

A Passion for Excellence
(with Nancy Austin)

Thriving on Chaos

Liberation Management

The Tom Peters Seminar

The Pursuit of WOW!

EVERY PERSON'S GUIDE
TO
TOPSY-TURVY TIMES

by Tom Peters

VINTAGE BOOKS
A DIVISION OF RANDOM HOUSE, INC.
NEW YORK

A Vintage Original, First Edition
November 1994

Copyright © 1994 by Excel, / A California Partnership

Library of Congress Cataloging-in-Publication Data
Peters, Thomas J.
        The pursuit of wow!: every person's guide to topsy-
turvy times / by Tom Peters—1st ed.
        p.   cm.
        "Vintage original."
        ISBN 0-679-75555-1
        1. Organizational change—Management. 2. Career
Development. I. Title.
HD58.8.P482   1994   94-37660
658.4'06—dc 20   CIP

Book design by Ken Silvia Design Group

Excerpt from *The Paradox of Success* by John O'Neil, copyright
© 1993 by John O'Neil, reprinted by permission of The
Putnam Publishing Group/Jeremy P. Tarcher, Inc.

Excerpt from *The Rise and Fall of Strategic Planning:
Reconceiving Roles for Planning, Plans, Planners* by
Henry Mintzberg. Copyright © 1994 by Henry Mintzberg.
Reprinted with permission of The Free Press, a Division
of Simon & Schuster.

Manufactured in the United States of America
10 9 8 7 6 5 4 3 2 1

for
Robert and Sarah

What recommends commerce
to me is its enterprise and
bravery. It does not clasp
its hands and pray to Jupiter.

–Henry David Thoreau

Contents

Foreword

This book is about generating yeasty responses — personal and corporate — to these very yeasty, and frequently frightening, times. I've called it *The Pursuit of Wow!*

"Wow" might sound a bit frizzy. I think not. I'm repeatedly struck by the parade of "new" cars that look like every other car, by how many newly opened French restaurants or just-launched PCs or software packages fail to zap you, by how one Big Six audit service resembles all the others. And I'm also struck by how timid most people are in fending off staleness. Then they wonder why they become a statistic in the continuing middle management and senior professional blood bath.

In preparing this book I've looked back on my ten years of writing syndicated columns, had lengthy conversations with dozens of successful entrepreneurs — and convened a session of FedEx employees to talk about diversity. But mostly I've let my daily exposure to business over the last 25 years lead my mind where it will: I wondered why I feel compelled to go to London to buy chubby Ball Pentel Fine Point R50 pens. Wondered why thank you notes are always appreciated. Why success (personal, business) invariably leads to hardening of the arteries. Thought about why certain delis (and churches), in a world full of delis (and churches), reach out and suck you in instantaneously — while so many others only give you a case of the blahs. And why any employee would put up with mistrustful firms that practice random drug testing, unannounced call monitoring, and the like.

All in all, you'll find 210 numbered observations, from one line to several pages in length and loosely collected by topic in 13 more-or-less chapters.

The common bond is . . . WOW: stepping out (individuals at all levels in a firm and independent contractors) and standing out (corporations and other organizations) from the growing crowd of look-alikes.

Being average has never had much appeal. Better to fail with flair in pursuit of something neat. While I think that's an idea for the ages, right now it takes on great urgency.

India, China, Argentina, Mexico, Brazil, Chile, the Philippines, Malaysia, Thailand, Indonesia — and more — are coming online. They're chock-a-block with hundreds of millions of talented, well-educated workers — and already producing sophisticated, high-quality goods that are often the equal of the best from the monster U.S., Japanese and German economies.

To stay on top of this fermenting global brew will require people and companies to paddle like never before; will require — again — personal and corporate WOW. (And the renewal thereof — in perpetuity.) I hope the ideas from these pages will help you strip off the blinders (the crazy past is soon going to look like mellow prelude) and move yourself toward bold and daring action.

I've had a ball pulling all this together. And now I hope you'll have a ball reading it. I say "had a ball" on purpose and without apology. I think work and business can be creative and exciting. A hoot. A growth experience. A journey of lifelong learning and constant surprise. But, to be honest, I think such rewards will only be yours if you learn to approach your career and enterprise with the strategy I call . . .

. . . THE PURSUIT OF WOW!

Good luck!

حظ سعيد

好 運 氣

โชคดี

행운을 빕니다

शुभाषीश

শুভ কামনা !

がんばって!

Viel Glück!

Buena Suerte!

Bonne Chance!

STARTERS

1 One-Minute Excellence

One-minute excellence. I can sense the curling of your lips. While such a catchphrase makes me shudder, too, it contains a gem waiting to be discovered.

How do you go on an effective diet? How do you stop smoking? How do you stop drinking?

In short, you do it and it's done. Then you work like hell for the rest of your life to stay on the weight-maintenance, non-smoking, or booze-free wagon.

A while back, I came across a line attributed to IBM founder Thomas Watson. If you want to achieve excellence, he said, you can get there today. As of this second, quit doing less-than-excellent work.

The idea is profound.

Suppose you're a waiter and, for your own future's sake (not because of pressure from the clowns who run the restaurant), you decide to set a matchless standard for service. How? You do it. Now.

Sure, you'll be clumsy at first. You'll get a lot of it wrong. You'll need to read up, listen to audiotapes, take classes, tune in to on-line electronic chat rooms, visit other restaurants to collect clues. And you'll need to keep doing such things to maintain your edge (as an opera singer or professional athlete does) until the day you hang up your corkscrew.

Nonetheless, you can become excellent in a nanosecond, starting with your first guest tonight.

Simply picture yourself, even if it's a very fuzzy picture, as the greatest waiter ever — and start acting accordingly. Put yourself in lights on Broadway, as a galaxy-class waiter; then perform your script with derring-do.

Does it sound wild? Silly? Naive? Maybe, but it isn't. The first 99.9 percent of getting from here to there is the determination to do it and not to compromise, no matter what sort of roadblocks those around you (including peers) erect.

The last 99.9 percent (I know it adds up to more than 100 percent — that's life) is working like the devil to (1) keep your spirits up through the inevitable storms, (2) learn something new every day, and

"Nordstrom" it. "Motorola" it.

(3) practice that something, awkward or not and no matter what, until it's become part of your nature.

What holds for the waiter also holds for the manager of the six-person department or the chief executive of the 16,000-person firm.

How long does it take you, as boss, to achieve world-class quality? Less than a nanosecond to attain it, a lifetime of passionate pursuit to maintain it.

Once the fire is lit, assume you've arrived — and never, ever look back or do anything, no matter how trivial, that's inconsistent with your newfound quality persona.

Suppose you commit to achieving new heights in quality or service here and now. In your own mind, you're an instant Nordstrom (retail) or Motorola (manufacturing). But your next task — dad-blamed real world — is to go through your boring in-basket.

What an opportunity! Respond to the first item that turns up as you imagine a Nordstrom or Motorola exec would.

A memo from a frontline worker complaining about a silly impediment to improvement? A request to change office-supply vendors? An irate note from a customer or distributor? "Nordstrom" it. "Motorola" it. Act out, in a small way, your Nordstrom-Motorola fantasy of matchless quality.

Sure, if you keep it up for even a few hours, people all over the organization will start looking at you oddly. You want them to, because you've achieved your first tiny victory. You, Ms. Planet-class Quality, are living a new life. Their misfortune is that they haven't figured it out for themselves yet.

Does all this amount to a quarter-baked pep talk better delivered under a revival tent? Hardly. (And if you don't believe me, ask a friend in Alcoholics Anonymous, perhaps the most effective change program on earth today.) You see, the deeper point is that you'll either change in a nanosecond — or never. It's true with booze, smokes, fat, and world-class quality. The determined shift of mind-set is an all-or-nothing deal.

In case you can't tell, I'm fed up to my eyebrows with execs (and folks of every other rank) who talk about how l-o-n-g it takes to achieve change. That's pure rubbish. It takes forever to *maintain* change ("One day at a time," according to AA); but it takes just a flash to achieve change of even the most profound sort.

One morning in Houston almost six years ago, I changed. I was a nonexerciser. But that day, for a lot of not very significant reasons, I went out at 5 A.M. and took my first, bumbling speed walk. Eleven minutes later (OK, more than a few nanoseconds), I was hooked. True, every day since then I've fretted that I'll renege. Exercise is a lifetime pursuit, which causes pain some days (e.g., as I write, it's unseasonably cold, rainy, and getting late). But as of that morning, I was a no-baloney, world-class, rudely dogmatic exerciser.

Change *is* that simple. Honest.

2

"Honor your errors. A trick will only work for a while, until everybody else is doing it. To advance . . . requires a new game. But the process of going outside the conventional method . . . is indistinguishable from error. . . . Evolution can be thought of as systematic error management."

Kevin Kelly
*Out of Control: The Rise
of Neo-Biological Civilization*

When, oh when, will we learn to honor error? To understand that goofs are the only way to step forward, that really big goofs are the only way to leap forward?

Bosses who don't support the importance of failure are public nuisance No. 1 in my book.

3 Attentiveness

The poet Mary Oliver, in her touching *Mockingbirds,* tells of an impoverished old couple who responded to the knock of strangers at their door. The poor folks had no worldly goods to offer the unexpected visitors, only "their willingness to be attentive."

The unbidden guests turned out to be gods — who surprised their hosts by treating their attentiveness as the finest gift mere humans could have made.

I suspect that the story, with its small but grand revelation, resonates with most of us, and, paradoxically, especially so in these topsy-turvy times. Overwhelmed by new technologies, new competitors, new everything, we hold the gift of human attention — from the sales clerk or nurse who looks you directly in the eye, rather than conversing while staring blankly at the computer screen or medication tray in front of her or him — to be the most munificent of blessings.

> **70 percent of lost customers hit the road not because of price or quality issues but because they didn't like the human side of doing business with the prior provider of the product or service.**

But can we do more than nod our heads and mutter "Amen"? For starters, we can bring hard, cold statistical evidence to bear on this topic that might better seem the province of poets or Zen masters.

Consider research done by the Forum Corporation, which analyzes commercial customers lost by 14 major manufacturing and service companies. Some 15 percent of those who switched suppliers did so because they "found a better product" — by a technical measures of product quality, such as a greater mean time between failures or a lower defects score. Another 15 percent took off because they found a "cheaper product" somewhere else. Twenty percent of the lost customers hightailed it because of the "lack of contact and individual attention" from the prior supplier; and 49 percent left because "contact from old supplier's personnel was poor in quality."

It seems fair to collapse the last two categories into one, after which we could say:

- 15 percent left because of quality problems
- 15 percent scooted because of price
- 70 percent hit the road because they didn't like the human side of doing business with the prior provider of the product or service.

Which brings us directly back to the impoverished old couple and their "small" gift of attentiveness. In the age of e-mail, supercomputer power on the desktop, the Internet, and the raucous global village, attentiveness — a token of human kindness — is the greatest gift we can give someone: anyone, including our American or Japanese or German customers for paper clips, ham and cheese sandwiches, jet aircraft engines, or $10 million lines of credit.

4

Ellen Langer, a leading social psychologist, begins her book, *Mindfulness*, with a story about elderly nursing home residents who were given houseplants to care for and allowed to make some other minor decisions about their daily routine. "A year and a half later," she writes, "not only were [the plant minders] more cheerful, active, and alert than a similar group in the same institution that were not given these choices and responsibilities, but many more of them were still alive. In fact, less than half as many of the decision-making, plant-minding residents had died as had those in the other group."

What do nursing home residents have to do with business success? Everything. Langer offers a dramatic tribute to the power of personal engagement. It was good for the plants; it was even better for the people who got involved in their care. Well, people-nurturing has two good sides, too — one for the nurtured and another for the nurturer. The phone call, the small courtesy, the warm words, are all modest acts of engagement that make customers feel good. That may not extend your life, but it will surely boost your business and make you feel a lot better about yourself — which, come to think of it, is probably a pretty good life-extending therapy.

5

Terry Neill, managing partner of Andersen Consulting's worldwide change practice, translates an old French saying as, "Change is a door that can only be opened from the inside." He buttresses this assertion with the philosophy of Notre Dame football coach Lou Holtz, "It's not my job to motivate players. They bring extraordinary motivation to our program. It's my job not to *de*-motivate them."

Empowerment, Neill concludes, is not the things you do *to* or *for* people, it's the impediments you *take away*, leaving space for folks to empower themselves.

So what, exactly, have you done today to remove obstacles to success from the path of the would-be heroes at the front line?

6

Nothing is carved in stone. *Nothing.* Everything is written in sand and is likely to be erased or unrecognizably altered by the next wave or wind that sweeps over it. With that disclaimer out of the way, let me offer a few tentative truths that I've squeezed out of my life's adventure:

■ **Unintended consequences outnumber intended consequences.** I'm always amused, amazed — and frustrated — that audiences think I'm exaggerating when I say, "I don't know anything." Well, dammit, I don't. The world is a complicated place. Strategies rarely unfold as we imagined. Intended consequences are rare.

■ **Fiction beats nonfiction.** Avoid nonfiction! It's too unrealistic. Lately I've reveled in Paul Bowles, Heinrich Böll, Julian Barnes, and Max Frisch, among others. Nothing conveys the richness of life in quite the same way as a great novel.

■ **Success begets failure.** If you (or your company) luck out and find something that works, you're in trouble. You'll most likely try to make history repeat itself, which can hardly ever be made to happen. (The times that it does happen are when you most want it not to.) Circumstances change, and the strengths that led to your first success often become weaknesses.

■ **Democracy and markets are untidy, but effective.** American democracy is an eternally unfinished, messy experiment. Markets are far too complex to comprehend; their evolution is not pretty. But despite — or because of — their messiness, American democracy and markets both work. Beware the champions of order who would clean them up!

■ **Vermont farmers have a lot to teach us.**  I live among rural Vermonters much of the time. They can do a million things. The average "hick" in my neck of the woods is a crafty, multiskilled networker/trader/entrepreneur. Many of my neighbors are degreeless and diplomaless, but they could outwit the average corporate manager without raising a sweat.

■ **Lighten up.** I despise stuffed shirts! It's pure prejudice, I know, but I like and trust people who put their feet up, spout an occasional four-letter word, and laugh at their own screwups.

■ **Smile if it kills you.** The physiology of smiling diffuses a lot of anger and angst. It makes your body and soul feel better — not to mention the bodies and souls of those around you.

■ **Each day is a miracle.** The sun rises over the eastern mountain on my farm. Fog settles into its shoulder. The goats eat (everything). The sheep bleat. The mare and her foal trot across the field. Each breath of wind, each flurry of snow, each bit of good news, is miraculous. Savor them. You won't be here forever.

■ **Reject simple explanations.** According to the press, I'm a "guru." (Should I put on a saffron robe and start chanting?) No, no, a thousand times no! I just make observations and try to confuse people. Still, an awful lot of people come to my seminars looking for answers. Thanks for coming, but there are no answers. Just an awful lot of questions that need to be asked and, at best, a few guesses at answers that might be worth trying.

7

"The only security we have is in our ability to fly by the seat of our pants."

Brad Blanton
Radical Honesty

8

"How do I work? I grope."

Albert Einstein

9

"Hey-heggggggggggggggggggghhhhhhhhhhhhhhhh!"

So goes the sixth line of dialogue in Tom Wolfe's *The Bonfire of the Vanities.*

And so go I. And you too, I bet, when you have to deal with an unresponsive behemoth of a company. But let me start the story at the beginning.

Several years ago my wife, Kate, and I built a guest house on our Vermont farm. The phone lines were installed when we were away, and we returned to find two open switch boxes inside the house, with a spaghetti tangle of loose wires dangling from each.

I called to get the wiring job done. The approximate conversation with GTE, in abbreviated form, adds new meaning to the concept of Catch-22 (and to the word hey-hegggggggggggggggggghhhhhhhhhhhhhhhh):

ME: I'd like to have some phone work completed. Could you send a service person out?

SHE: Exactly what do you want done?

ME: I'm not sure, because I don't know what was installed. I'd like a service person to help me sort it out.

SHE: You'll have to tell me exactly what you want done.

ME: But I can't. I don't know.

SHE: Then I can't initiate an order.

ME: Why can't you send a service person out?

SHE: It would be inefficient.

ME: OK, I'll make something up to get us started.

SHE: You're being sarcastic.

ME: No, just desperate.

On it went. I ended up talking to a supervisor and placing a "pretend" order for something I didn't want. Then it was time to schedule the visit (a.k.a. adding insult to the injury already sustained).

ME (on a Thursday): Can you get someone out here on Friday or Monday? I leave for the Far East on Tuesday, and a guest is arriving for a long stay as soon as I get back.

SHE: I think we can send someone out on Monday or Tuesday.

ME: Tuesday won't help.

SHE: We can try for Monday.

ME: OK, what time?

SHE: Excuse me?

ME: What time?

SHE: Monday.

ME: But what time on Monday?

SHE: I could put down morning, but I certainly can't guarantee anything.

ME: My wife and I work, and we can't hang around all day.

SHE: I can't help that.

ME: But we can't give up 16 combined hours of working time on the off chance that the service person will show up.

SHE: Sorry.

ME (to myself): Hey-hegggggggggggggggggghhhhhhhhhhhhhhh!

Oh, if only we could see ourselves as others see us, comprehend the ways we dehumanize, demean, and demoralize our customers.

The good news for some companies is that such insane — literally — behavior makes the teeniest affirmative expression stand out in bold relief.

A while back, I bought an Odwalla fresh fruit drink. As I was knocking back the last, luscious drops, I noticed the expiration date: "Enjoy by March 12."

Why fuss over "Enjoy by" instead of the normal "Expires on"? Simple. It's the very essence of humanness, of connecting with the customer — and a strong indicator of superior service and quality. "Enjoy by" brought a smile to my face and an "ahhh" to my lips — and that "ahhh" could mean hundreds of dollars of lifetime business for Odwalla from me, plus ten times that via word of mouth or the power of print (thanks to this book, for instance).

The choice is yours: Ahhh! or hey-heggggggggggggggggggghhh-hhhhhhhhhhhh!

10

Retail guru (and Wal-Mart board member) Bob Kahn tells this great story of business integrity and goodwill:

In a 72-page sales catalog, the Bon Marché in Seattle (part of the Federated Stores combine) made an error on the price of a Sony five-disk carousel CD player — the regularly $199 item was to be discounted to $179, but $99 appeared in print. Long lines awaited the store's opening, fueled in part by e-mail about the sale circulated at nearby Microsoft.

"What would you do under those circumstances?" Kahn writes in his newsletter, *Retailing Today*. "Run a small ad the next day professing a mistake had been made? Tell the customers that common sense would indicate that the price was wrong?

"Here's what the Bon did: It sold all the players in stock for $99. In addition, it took orders for another 4,000 units at $99! . . .

"Could any other expenditure of $200,000 [5,000 units times $40 — the $99 price was $40 below cost] have done as much to establish the Bon's integrity? I think not."

Among other things, Kahn notes, the $200,000 netted a feature story in the *New York Times* that was also circulated around the nation via the *Times'* wire service.

Hats off to the Bon Marché. More pertinent, would you have reacted the same way?

11 I Love Retail!

Frito-Lay marketer? Chief information officer at a $6-billion-asset bank? Staff accountant at a Fortune 500 company? Dress shop owner? Nurse, doctor, teacher, auto-mechanic, or, like me most of the time, seminar presenter?

Whatever we do, most of us are retailers of one sort or another. And I, for one, love it!

Retail as practiced by Wal-Mart or Barneys calls for sophisticated information systems, skill at finding the right location at the right price, and, of course, artful selection of merchandise.

But given all that (and they aren't small things), the essence of retail is theater. Retail, in the classroom or showroom, is performance art.

Have you ever walked onto the field of a Big Ten football stadium in July? It's eerie in its stillness. And yet, especially if you're an alum or former player, you can feel the emotion of the 80,000 fans who will gather there 60 days hence.

A shop, or especially a big retail store, feels the same way at 6 A.M. Still. Dark, except for the glow of security lights. The merchandise casts long shadows on the empty floors. But, as with that football arena, you can sense the energy that will soon be set in motion.

If I'm scheduled to speak to 17 or 1,700 people in Miami or Timbuktu, I like to sneak down to the slumbering meeting room around 1 A.M. the night before. Usually I can sense the spirit of the group that will assemble there eight hours later, which invariably motivates me to go back to my bedroom and review my material one more time, perhaps make a few changes. In fact, such stealthy visits to deserted meeting spaces frequently have prompted total revision of my remarks.

Sure, I count on the seminar organizer to bring in a good crowd, select an adequate facility, and get a hundred logistical details just so. Likewise, the store clerk counts on the powers above to choose a location that attracts customers and to provide merchandise that sings.

Still, once the stage is set, it's *my* show, or *your* show. The auditorium opens, the auto body shop's garage door clanks upward, or the class bell rings, and we are absolutely, positively in charge. It's our stage. Literally, not figuratively. That classroom or showroom is as much a stage as any found at Carnegie Hall.

It's up to us to invest the script (a play by Ibsen, food by Chef Whomever, chapter seven of the U.S. history textbook) with life. To perform. To build the emotional links among ourselves, the

Great = having the imaginatio

material, and the audience.

Retail is a connection business. Relationships are forged, one at a time, whether the audience is 2,000 people in a darkened ballroom or a single auto-repair customer who suffered a fender-bender yesterday afternoon.

The best bosses understand what the people on stage are trying to do. They're collaborators with them. They are retailers, too. They're out and about, nudging and cajoling, chatting and listening, and cheering. The worst bosses are wholesalers. They hide behind secretaries and assistants, memos and videotaped speeches to the masses. They don't connect or emote.

Retail also allows — no, requires — continuous reinvention. Actors and actresses will tell you that every audience is different. So is every day in the classroom, restaurant, or surgical suite.

For great actors and actresses, each performance is a fresh opportunity to experiment with a new approach — in fact, to experiment with nothing less than a new persona. Who are you going to be *today*? How are you going to connect? Every day the

nd zeal to re-create yourself daily.

play begins anew. On *this* day, how will you perform it?

I said *great* actors and actresses, because some are average and lousy — just as some bellhops and teachers and surgeons are. The difference between great and average or lousy in any job is, mostly, having the imagination and zeal to re-create yourself daily.

The best aspect of retail for you or me, however, is that it is management-proof. Sure, managers make you abide by thinner or thicker rule books. Some bosses hover, and some give you space. But at 10 A.M. sharp, it's your store (or at least your 75 square feet). You are absolute master, ruler, czar. You alone bring that 75 square feet, or those five restaurant tables, to life. Ninnies or saints, fearful or fearless, management can't hold you back.

If I sound off the wall on this topic, it's because I am. I'm in love with the boundless, though often squandered, potential of retail.

12

O'Hare, 6:05 A.M., September 14, 1994. Weary and bedraggled from a San Francisco to Chicago red-eye, I mosey into a concourse shop to grab a few newspapers.

As I approach the register, the clerk chirps, "$3.25 please." I ask her how she knew from afar, and she says she's watched me picking up the papers, knows all her prices, and likes doing the addition in her head.

Compared to famine, war, and pestilence, it's a small thing. At 6:05 A.M. at O'Hare, it was one *big* deal.

I recalled anew the ability of a spirited employee, using a clever trick or two (e.g., long-distance addition), to change the course of the day — literally — for her customers. That's what happened to me in this instance.

The tiny, spontaneous (which is clearly how this one felt), human act has enormous power. Folks like Southwest Airlines' Herb Kelleher, who encourage (demand, for all practical purposes) such regular expressions of individual personality, find that most people *are* up to it — and the payoffs are enormous.

Q: **With employees having greater access to profit-and-loss statements, becoming subcontractors, etc., do you see them as a potential threat — e.g., by taking their knowledge to, say, a competitor?**

A: That's the wrong way to think about it. I run a small company. The last thing I worry about is folks departing with proprietary knowledge. *My* concern is creating an environment where good people want to hang around. On the other hand, if they find an opportunity that's better than anything we can offer them, I'm all for their taking it and advancing their careers. If they leave, I assume they'll behave honorably — I wouldn't have hired them in the first place if I didn't think so. And besides, the trick for my company (for any sensible company!) is to keep topping itself — so any "stolen" secrets are secrets to *yesterday's* success.

I'm not alone. A pal in a Silicon Valley high-tech company has a fabulous reputation for attracting talent. One key: When he comes across a job outside his company that one of his good folks might fill (and it's better than anything he can provide), he tells her or him about it. To say he has a superb reputation throughout a huge network of peers in many companies is understatement; and his company, of course, is the long-term beneficiary of the goodwill he's accumulated and the top talent he's attracted (even if it wasn't for life).

14 And the Winner Is . . .

Six key ideas are animating business transformation. Moreover, there is a pecking order among them:

No. 6 — Total Quality Management. No doubt about it, superior quality is a must for competitive success these days. The hitch is, everybody's doin' it (the Indonesians, Thais, Argentines, et al.). Topnotch quality is a must, but it's no more than a pass to the players' entrance to the stadium. Those who put all new management ideas under the TQM banner are making a big mistake. TQM is not about life writ large, it's about products that work unerringly. A big deal? Yes. The whole deal? Hardly.

No. 5 — Reengineering. Today's reengineering proponents match the religious zeal of yesterday's quality fanatics. And the idea *is* damned important. Decimating hierarchies via slash-and-burn strategies is one (big) thing. Reengineering — linking up activities horizontally and reinventing key business process-es — is quite another. It's even revolutionary, as the reengineer-ing gurus claim.

But it ain't the main game — at least the way reengineering is being played by most companies. Like most quality programs, reengineering is mostly internally focused busywork — i.e., streamlining. While another necessary item in today's manage-ment arsenal, it is far from the whole story.

No. 4 — Leveraging knowledge. Brains are in; heavy lifting is out. That's the essential nature of the new, knowledge-based economy. Therefore, the development of knowledge is close to job No. 1 for corporations.

Maybe one company in 10 (and I'm being very generous) understands this, and of those that do, only one in 10 is doing it right. The challenge is only 5 percent bits and bytes (a spiffy e-mail system that spans continents, for example); it's 95 percent psychology and sociology — an organization that dotes on shar-ing information rather than hoarding it.

No. 3 — The curious, cannibalistic corporation. In an increas-ingly crowded, noisy global marketplace, innovation is not optional. Corporations need an appetite for adventure, a pas-sion for bold leaps into the unknown. That means hiring the adventurous and the bold, even when they set your teeth to grinding and break a lot of china. It means a passion for lobbing an exciting new product onto the market, even if its success will dry up your current "cash cow." It means cherishing your fail-ures — especially the granddaddies. And it means chopping your company into firewood before the competition does.

No. 2 — **The virtual organization.** It's the real thing, the big umbrella that captures entirely new ways for human beings to work together across time and space.

The virtual corporation is a colleague of mine, engaged in dozens of globe-spanning adventures, who brags about not having visited his own headquarters in the last five years. It's "big" companies, booking billions, with, literally, only a handful of full-time employees. Mostly, it's the idea that to own resources is a mistake. Instead, you need instant access to the best resources from wherever, whenever, to get the job done.

Business and management have long been about control, job descriptions, organization charts, headquarters towers, structures that are changed reluctantly every five years, and linear careers that rise up "ladders." Now impermanence and improvisation are markers for success.

No. 1 — **Empowerment.** My last book (*The Tom Peters Seminar: Crazy Times Call for Crazy Organizations*) included, heaven forbid, pictures — e.g., Virginia Azuela, a housekeeper at the Ritz-Carlton Hotel in San Francisco. One of reengineering's most visible advocates said to one of my office mates, "Why in the world did he do *that*?"

He (I) did it because all this highfalutin "stuff" about running companies boils down — surprise! — to the folks who actually do the work: ad copywriters, movie cameramen, nurses, technicians, teachers. And hotel housekeepers.

"People," "they," "them" always were important; they always were "our most important asset," as so many annual reports mindlessly proclaim. But now "they" really *are* important.

Hierarchies are going, going, gone. The average Mary or Mike is being asked to take on extraordinary responsibility. He or she may be on the payroll or, at least as likely, an independent contractor. In any event, the hyperfast-moving, wired-up, reengineered, quality-obsessed organization — virtual or not — will succeed or fail on the strength of the trust that the remaining, tiny cadre of managers places in the folks working on the front line.

It's not that the other five main ideas pale in comparison to this one. It's just that we get so caught up in reengineering, knowledge-management schemes, TQM, and virtual organizations that, as usual, we end up downplaying, shortchanging, and glossing over that one person who actually makes it happen.

VIRGINIA AZUELA

Back to Virginia Azuela. The Ritz-Carlton, 1992 winner of the Malcolm Baldrige National Quality award, has given her enormous autonomy to serve her guests as she sees fit (e.g., the ability to spend up to $2,000, on her own, to solve a customer problem). While Ritz-Carlton may be a top flight practitioner of all the arts enumerated here and then some, it still comes down to Virginia Azuela's frame of mind. Why did I put her picture in my book? Because, for crying out loud, she's the star of the new economy!

15 Values for the '90s?

One small ($10 million revenue) service business strives to live by these values:

❶ Do fabulous work and be known around the world for our innovativeness.

❷ Attract exciting people — more than a few of whom are a little offbeat.

❸ Raise hell, constantly question "the way things are done around here," and never, ever rest on our laurels. (Today's laurels are tomorrow's compost.)

❹ Make sure that those who leave us, voluntarily or involuntarily, can testify to having learned a lot, having had a special experience, and having made fast friends while they were here. (Ye shall be known by your alumni!)

❺ Have a collegial, supportive, yeasty, zany, laughter-filled environment where folks support one another, and politics is as absent as it can be in a human (i.e., imperfect) enterprise.

⑥ Ensure that no question or innuendo ever surfaces about our ethics.

⑦ Dot the "i"s, cross the "t"s, answer the phones promptly, send out errorless invoices, and in general never forget that the devil *is* in the details.

⑧ Work with exciting customers (and other partners) who turn us on and stretch us, from whom we can learn, and with whom we enjoy associating (and who pay their bills on time, too).

⑨ Take in substantially more money than we spend (where spending includes above-average compensation and a very high level of investment in the future).

⑩ Grow via quality services and customers, not via growth for growth's sake.

I think such aspirations fit the 1990s to a tee, for the $10 million or $10 billion outfit. Agree? And if you do, how do you measure up?

16 Just a Drop in the Bucket

Ho-hum, just a 24-point headline topping a tiny article on page three of *The Australian*, July 20, 1994: "Beijing to Issue 200mn Credit Cards."

By the end of the decade, China, as part of its effort to modernize its financial sector, will spew out 200 million new credit cards. Conclusions: (1) Ye gads. (2) How'd you like to be in the ATM business? (3) It's Asia, stupid.

17 What Diversity "Problem"?

"Dealing with the Diversity Problem." "Clearing the Diversity Hurdle." "Assimilating the Rainbow within the Workplace."

You've read dozens of business-journal headlines like that, right? And do you agree with me that they're silly?

Diversity *problem*? *Hurdle*?

Diversity creates one and only one thing: opportunity.

Business, in the mad global marketplace, needs a rush of serious creativity. Creativity is, invariably, a byproduct of sparks, new views, juxtaposed interests, etc. How does a company acquire those assets? Diversity!

All other things being equal, which company (car maker, textile producer, bank) is going to create the more interesting products or services?

This one?

The 17 members of the executive group of Company A file into the boardroom. All U.S. born (whoops, sorry, one Canadian). Fifteen are white males, best guess at average age: 47. One female. One Japanese-American. Dress: suits, suits, suits as far as the eye can see.

Or this one?

Company B's 16-person top team noisily straggles into the boardroom attired in everything from Brooks Brothers to Calvin Klein to Banana Republic to Venice Beach leftovers. Six of the 16 are white males, four are women (two white, one African-American, one Hispanic), plus two Indian-born males, two African-American males, one Chilean-born male, and one British-born male. Average age: about 42, with two or three who are clearly on the low side of 32.

It's a no-brainer: Company B by 20 furlongs.

Sure, I'm oversimplifying. Or am I? It seems obvious to me that Cacophony, Inc., a wild mixture of colors, sexes, styles, and ages will almost automatically generate and pursue more interesting ideas than Homogeneity, Inc. My argument is a simple statistical one: The variety of experiences, from birth onward, captured in a Company B executive meeting is immensely greater than in a similar meeting at Company A. An unusually high level of curiosity among Company A's OWMs (old white males) makes virtually no difference; Company B's folks bring hundreds of years of, um, diverse perspectives to bear on everything from soup to software.

Is Company B a sea of tranquility? Of course not. Diversity

implies clashes, subtle and overt. People (men and women, London born and L.A. born, 20-somethings and 50-somethings) will bridle at what they feel are bizarre — and dumb — views held by others from time to time. The Company B top team (and the rest of the company, too, assuming its makeup mimics the top) could probably benefit from a hefty dose of sensitivity training. But the point of such training is not to "clear a hurdle" or "solve a problem." On the contrary, it's to help the company reap maximum possible strategic leverage from its diversity *advantage*.

(Incidentally, the fact that purchasers of most goods and services — Uzis being a possible exception — are themselves diverse contributes to the practicality of diversity. Why should we expect an OWM top team to design cars that send women into fits of ecstasy? We shouldn't. They don't.)

18 Nanosecond Nineties to Terabit Twenties

Not so long ago, in 1985, the standard memory chip held 1M bits — one megabit, or a million bits — of information. By 1994, that number had increased to 16M.

Projections for the standard, garden-variety memory chip of 2005: 4G — four gigabits, or four billion bits. And 2030? Sure, it's raw speculation, but one guess is 16T. T, as in terabit — or trillion bits of information.

That's right: 16 t-r-i-l-l-i-o-n.

Translation: We ain't seen nothing yet.

19

Not subscribing to *Computerworld* or *Informationweek*? Even if you're determinedly nontechnical, you need one of the two to keep up — weekly — with the *feel* of the changes being wrought by the information industry. Just 10 minutes spent flicking through each is enough — but essential.

20 Not That One Again!

Oh Lord, there it is again. *The* question: "What kind of business should I start?" Incidentally, it has a twin that also sets me off: "What should I specialize in during the second year of my MBA studies?"

Sorry, but those are two of the most profoundly upsetting questions anyone can ask — upsetting because the answer should be obvious: Do what turns you on, not what the statistics say is best.

Business, life itself, is damned hard work if you wanna be good at it. Actually, that's precisely wrong. Business ceases to be work when you're chasing a dream that has engorged you. ("Work should be more fun than fun" — Noel Coward.) And if the passion isn't there, then biotech and plumbing will be equal drags.

To give a nod to contrarian thinking and take a poke at conventional wisdom, the best advice anyone could offer might be to go to where the apparent hot spots aren't. Cognetics boss David Birch, who knows as much about what businesses are growing and declining as anyone around, discovered a disproportionate share of growth companies in the (thought to be) dullest industries (e.g., paper products manufacture, rubber and plastics, insurance, nondurable wholesaling).

In slugabed industries, slugabed competitors tend to dominate — and to leave gaping holes for agile, turned-on folks to slip into.

Hmmm.

21 Doing Something about Nonsense That Makes Me Mad

Want to develop a killer managerial or corporate philosophy? Start by making a list. On the left side of (several?) pages, enumerate things that have really pissed you off in business over the years (especially in your first couple of jobs, if your memory's keen). On the right side, write counterpoints. E.g.:

26. Executive parking spaces	No assigned slots
27. Too many memos	More face-to-face communication
28. Bosses who have secretaries get coffee for them	Get your own coffee!

The right-side list becomes, de facto, your managerial philosophy, credo, or vision (if you must). You can get others to produce their own lists. An amalgam gleaned from the broader exercise is a good rough draft (kept rough in perpetuity) of "the way we mean to do things around here." But hold on to your own for the duration, since this is a philosophy for your professional career.

Hats off to Bob Townsend (*Up the Organization*, Avis's "We Try Harder" campaign, etc.), who gave me the seed of this idea. I've gotten dozens of managers to elaborate and implement the above, and it always works or at least gets their ball rolling.

22 Double Knots for Your Shoelaces?

Call me a spoilsport, but I had problems with a paper on Total Quality Management that came my way from the ordinarily sensible Graduate School of Business at the University of Chicago.

It carries TQM to the executive suite and touts the use of personal checklists as a vehicle for doing so. A computer-based defects-measurement scheme used by a vice president at a large corporation is featured. I happen to know that this fellow's company has a massive agenda for change; nonetheless, I can nearly forgive his choosing "on time for meetings" as the top item on his personal quality-evaluation list. (Nothing wrong with the big cheese being courteously prompt.) I get a little queasy over "clean desk," though; and "haircut," "shoes shined," and "clothes pressed" (three of 12 supposedly critical items) drive me to the wall. What drives me up and over the wall, however, is his practice of plotting these "defects" graphically.

Somehow, I don't think this is what the late Dr. Deming had in mind as he crisscrossed America, well into his nineties, preaching the quality gospel.

Gimme a break.

23

Now I know what's wrong with management. For $139, the venerable American Management Association will let you attend a 6-hour course, "How to Legally Fire Employees with Attitude Problems." The skills you'll exit with, according to an article in *Harper's*, include:

■ Finally! A way to catch and document employees who badmouth you behind your back.

■ Three rules for dealing with hypochondriacs who abuse — but don't violate — your sick leave policy.

■ How to take the guilt out of firing an employee with an attitude problem.

Do people really attend such courses?

Firing anyone is awful. I hate it. You are screwing up people's lives in a big-league way, even if it honestly is for the long-term good. You are also acknowledging that you did: (1) a rotten recruiting job, (2) a rotten development job, or (3) both. "Both" is most likely the correct answer.

Letting someone go, secretary or vice president, *always* gives me days of chest pains, sometimes hives. The day firing becomes easy ("guilt-free") is the day to fire yourself. Period.

Design is important. Vital. For products, sure. But, paradoxically, design is more important for services.

Harvard marketing guru Ted Levitt tipped off those who took the trouble to listen years ago: If your product is tangible (plane, boat, car, penknife), distinguish yourself from the herd by emphasizing intangibles (e.g., service). If your  product is intangible (banking services, travel services), distinguish yourself from the masses by emphasizing the tangible — to wit, design.

FedEx offers timely delivery service. Its on-time statistical record attests to that. But the company also stands out on the tangibles. Tangibles? Sure, such as spiffy — and clean — trucks. (Why, for God's sake, don't companies realize that trucks are a fabulous/awful form of advertising?) And easy-to-use forms. (Why, once again, don't most businesses understand that forms are part of their signature and therefore great/awful advertisements for their businesses?)

So if you're in a service business, worry a lot if you're not *specifically* working on the tangibles. (One small hint for the independent contractor: You can't spend too much time on calling-card design!)

25

"He who fears corruption fears life." By that, '50s and '60s political organizer Saul Alinsky wasn't championing cynicism, selfishness, and contempt for one's fellows. He was urging that we push the bounds hard. And when you enter the fray with vigorous enthusiasm, you're likely to break the always tetchy establishment's rules and risk its ire. (Name a real reformer who doesn't have an arrest record. I can't.)

Epitaph for those with a hummingbird's appetite for life: "Whatever became of, um . . . whatshername?"

26

"You better start swimming or you'll sink like a stone."

Bob Dylan

GETTING THINGS DONE

27

Power. Libraries have been written about its use and abuse. It has motivated the great (and the greedy) throughout history. It has been called the ultimate aphrodisiac. But what is it? A dirty word that connotes backroom politics, conniving end-runs, and secret deals? Or a normal part of everyday life? Both, no doubt. But I'm mightily predisposed to the latter definition.

Like it or not — and often we don't — power is a pervasive phenomenon. From midnight decisions in the Oval Office that risk the lives of young Americans to quarrels over the kitchen table, power is part of every human equation. Yes, it can be — and often is — abused, in business as in all arenas of endeavor. But it can also be used to do great good for great numbers. And as a career-building tool, the slow and steady (and subtle) amassing of power is the surest road to success.

There's nothing earth-shattering about the following observations. They amount to reflections on 51 years of life, making every possible mistake in the development and nurturing — and occasionally severing — of relationships.

Don't forget your thank-you notes! You just read the most important piece of "advice" in this book. If you take it to heart, you can throw this little volume in the nearest trash can and still have gotten ten times your money's worth (make that ten thousand times). The power of a thank-you (note or otherwise) is hard — make that impossible — to beat.

Years ago I worked for a Type A boss. Analytic to a fault. Tough, and proud of it. But every evening when Walt finished his daily whirlwind, he'd sit down with his Dictaphone (circa 1972) and bat out fifteen thank-you notes. Most would run no longer than a sentence or two: "George, that was a terrific idea you had. Hope you follow up on it. Let me know what's going on. Walt."

It's barely an exaggeration to say that Walt had people eating out of his hand. There were a lot of reasons for that, but I'm convinced those thank-you notes weren't far from the top of the list.

Then there was the recently retired 3M exec who attended one of our seminars. A stickler for expressing his appreciation, he recalled his retirement party: "Several people came up to me, one or two with tears in their eyes, and thanked me for a thank-you note, sometimes one I'd written 10 or 15 years before!" People don't forget kindness (do a quick sweep of your memory bank — I bet you'll find that car mechanic who saved the family vacation or the bakery clerk who always has a warm twinkle in her eye).

My experience (and psychological literature) bears out the potency of this simple tool. Positive reinforcement goes a long way; and most people don't give (or get) much of it. Further proof if you need it: I write a syndicated column and a couple of years ago, plumb out of ideas, mindlessly dashed one off on thank-you notes. I received far more responses than for any other column I've written in 10 years.

What about a phone call? Good, do it, but lifting up a phone is pretty easy. Writing a note demonstrates a level of effort, and is permanent. Typed or handwritten? Handwritten by a country mile. A two-line, largely unreadable scrawl beats a page and a half spit out by the laser printer.

Recognition, or Mary Kay knows. Farmer, senator, salesperson, engineer, janitor, CEO, you, me, and the kid who mows your lawn — everybody loves being recognized, in any way, large or small. Mary Kay knows! Tupperware knows! And if you're wise, you'll join the parade.

Appreciation, applause, approval, respect — we all love it! Balloons, badges, prizes, our picture in the company newsletter — wonderful! Can't get enough!

A few years ago, we passed out "You Made My Day!" notepads at my office. The idea was to send one to a colleague who'd given you a hand — with anything, mundane or monumental. Well, cubicle walls were soon plastered. Folks treasured each and every one. (Me, too.)

Still, I've had people say, "But if you pat people on the back every day, you'll wear it out." I suppose there's some truth to that. And a phony pat is just that — phony — and counterproductive. Like a jerk I worked with years ago who thought he could make up for Neanderthal behavior by delivering loads of flowers the morning after his latest tirade; he only succeeded in deluding himself — he was shocked when I gave him the lowest grade possible on "staff relations."

I have been bountifully blessed and gotten many times more than my fair share of recognition, but I assure you that I am anything but jaded. Each note that comes in is to be cherished — truth is, I save them, large and small, handwritten, typewritten, e-mail (which I save and print), whatever.

Remind people (gently) of how much you've done for them. If you can't get recognition from others, at least recognize yourself! I'm only half kidding. A Chicago-area cardboard box manufacturer specializes in delivering tough orders on time — the firm hasn't missed a single deadline in 10 years. A few years ago, the boss added a performance box score to the monthly

OUACHITA TECHNICAL COLLEGE

invoice. It lists date requested, date delivered, and the difference between the two; of course, since everything is either on time or a bit early, the company ends up advertising a sterling grade. Though long renowned for timeliness, after adding this little reminder the firm's business jumped.

Obviously, you can go too far with self-promoting and come off the arrogant ass. But don't hide your light (if it's shining) under a bushel either — done right (that is, subtly, very subtly), this is a potent tool.

Potlatch works (mostly). Potlatch is the ancient practice of overwhelming a person with gifts. In some tribes, people literally gave away all their wealth — and their status rose proportionately. Guess what: It still works. Continuous generosity creates an aura of altruism. More crudely, it ain't a bad idea to maintain a positive "balance of favors" with a large number of people. I'll be honest: It's precisely what I try to do. Hey, it's nice to have a big stash of chips to call in when "the time comes" — and the time does come.

There is such a thing as an embarrassment of riches, so don't overdo it. (As I have a couple of times.) Kept within bounds, however, potlatch has its place.

Skinner was wrong. The psychologist B. F. Skinner demonstrated the potency of positive reinforcement. He was also adamant that negative reinforcement (punishment) is a loser. It doesn't stop people from doing bad stuff, it just gives them encouragement to hide it. I pretty much agree. But . . .

There is an argument for making it clear to people who step out of line that they'll suffer consequences. Lyndon Johnson was a master of this. He did it in subtle ways — no longer sending the handwritten note of thanks. And he did it in grand ways — no invitations to White House dinners or bill-signing ceremonies, no visits to your district when you were in the midst of a tight reelection campaign. On the other hand, Bill Clinton (hardworking and bright though he is) seems to suffer from being too good a guy: He can't seem to bring himself to "punish" those who step out of line.

Punishment is a real art form. General rule: Praise in public, punish in private. Also make sure that the dressing down has been heard: I've seen people (and committed this sin *many* times) who are so punishment-averse that they coat the negative in so many positives that the punishee walks out of the meeting thinking he's just been given a promotion, rather than threatened to within an inch of his life.

Give EVERYONE credit. Some people are real misers. They act as if giving others credit will somehow diminish themselves. What rot! Put simply (and somewhat coarsely), giving credit costs you nothing, and nets you big-time. I believe in long acknowledgments sections in my books; it doesn't hurt a bit, and it's the first time that most people mentioned have seen their name in print.

Truth is, that guy you had a five-minute chat with six months ago, who casually mentioned, "Mary, pogo sticks are due for a huge comeback," thinks he and he alone is responsible for the killing you subsequently made in bongo drums. In his mind he was the one who gave you the critical clue at just the right moment. So, give him credit for having done precisely that! First, he has a (very tenuous) point; but mostly, the stroking costs you nothing and offers an inordinate gain.

Showing up. There's a Woody Allen one-liner I love: "Eighty percent of success is showing up." (I reckon 85 percent.)

The president of a women's college was faced with a paltry endowment. Women's issues were hot at the time. She decided to play her potential power for all it was worth. She tenaciously sought appointments with Fortune 500 chairmen (almost exclusively chair*men*), and managed to wrangle audiences with several hundred of the Big Boys Club — and gained pledges from most of them. She hung in there. She showed up. She won.

Showing up redux, or 3,000 miles to "do" lunch. Mark McCormack, agent, entrepreneur, potent force in professional sports, offers this advice: Fly 3,000 miles for a five-minute meeting. I think he's even more on target than Woody Allen. In fact, I've practiced what he preaches. Yes, it's the age of e-mail and virtual meetings, but showing up, getting the body there, making it clear that you did fly 3,000 miles to close the deal, or celebrate the anniversary, or whatever, is a very, very potent tool indeed.

Is it a pain in the butt? You bet it is! Nobody said that power comes cheap.

Stand behind people in times of stress. This is yet another way of driving home the importance of "showing up"; but like the thank-you, it deserves to be said in as many ways as I can dream up. When people are facing a battle, a board meeting, or a big sales pitch, having you, the leader, show up for a few minutes is crucial life-support.

You're a partner in a consulting company. Your four-person team is making a presentation to the client tomorrow. You've got a fabulous team leader, and you want to give her all the autonomy in the world. Fine, don't interfere with the "substance" — but do show up at the office at 1 A.M. to drop off a pizza. Your trivial yet noble act will become lore, or something close to it, for months to come — if not years.

It's the little stuff. A while back I gave a speech to newspaper publishers, and criticized the *San Jose Mercury News*, a paper I like, for not getting its product in my driveway early enough. (I'm an early bird, and "pretty early" is unacceptably late.) Later that day, the publisher, Jay Harris, and I participated in a panel discussion.

The next morning, about 18 hours later, my paper arrived at 5:05 A.M. — early enough even for me. Harris had a thousand things on his mind, yet he took the time to deal with one newspaper hitting a doorstep at the rooster hour. No matter what the *Merc* does to me

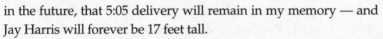

in the future, that 5:05 delivery will remain in my memory — and Jay Harris will forever be 17 feet tall.

The best congressional offices go light on policy staffing, heavy on the folks who help constituents with "little" stuff. Except that late Social Security check ain't so "little" to the old man who depends on it to meet his bills. Likewise, that "little" vacation-schedule juggle you arrange for one of your people so he can make it to that family reunion earns you credit "big"-time.

Remember, too, it's the "little stuff" that torpedoes the big stuff. As one software pioneer put it: "How does a major project get to be a year late? One day at a time." As a boss, the best way to gain the undying loyalty of subordinates is to clear the tiny (to the boss) hurdles out of the way. Getting a team extra space, an extra PC, a refrigerator — this is where you, Ms. or Mr. Big, can really earn your pay.

Accumulate the "small wins." "Small wins" are a large plus. Call them favors owed, chits in the bank, whatever. Then-vice president George Bush campaigned for every Republican from senator to selectman, flying around the country like Superman on steroids. Did these candidates remember him? Is water wet? When 1988 arrived, and other Republicans sought their party's nomination, they ran into a wall of Bush-league loyalty that had

been built one (red-eyed) brick at a time.

Search out the hidden levers. Al Smith, legendary governor of New York during the Roaring Twenties, began his career as a state legislator. As a young bachelor in the colorful capital of Albany, he declined to join his rowdier colleagues in their pursuit of booze and bimbos. Instead, he holed up in a cheap rooming house and proceeded to study every line of the New York State budget (an imposing document even in those somewhat simpler days).

This conquest of minutiae launched a wildly successful career mastering the legislature, and then the state of New York itself. (And almost the United States — had his Catholicism not cost him the 1928 presidential election.) Power often lies in the details. Al Smith's experience is mirrored in my own. As a young and powerless Pentagon naval officer, I tried my damnedest to master my little corner of the defense budget; I managed to absorb more of the arcane details than most of the significantly more senior people who surrounded me. Though I didn't end up in the governor's mansion in Albany, I did achieve dramatic local success. Moral: The tenacious and time-consuming pursuit of hidden levers that most don't bother with can pay off enormously.

Obsess on the "little stuff." "Details Jimmy" Carter was infamous for scheduling the White House tennis courts. While I suppose that demonstrates anything can be overdone, in general obsessing about details is important. No, you don't want to get a reputation as a prissy worrywart, but worrying about details in private isn't a bad idea at all.

Truth is, process beats substance. That is, the way people are handled is all-important. You may think you're the world's greatest speaker with a message of the utmost urgency, but if the auditorium's air conditioner is on the fritz and the sound system is singing static — well, forget it.

Don't forget the "little people." My use of "little people" is not meant to be condescending, merely descriptive in the misbegotten argot of the day. (In truth, some of the "littlest" — as in small-minded, small-hearted, small-souled — people I've known have been Fortune 500 luminaries.) But what I'm about to say is rather crude, and that is what I mean: I've seen a lot of fast-track men and women have their dreams dashed because they left a trail of (rightfully) resentful folks in their condescending wake.

The little people will get even, which is one of a thousand reasons why they are not little people at all. If you're a jerk as leader, you will be torpedoed. And usually it won't be by your vice presidents; it will be on the loading dock at 3 A.M. when no supervisors are around.

All this was brought home to me about a decade ago. The given-to-arrogance McKinseyites I worked with were often less than thoughtful to the "little people" (so-called support staff). While I give myself no points for saintliness, truth is I enjoyed hanging out with those folks more than my self-important fellow consultants. No matter the motivation, it paid off in one of those strange ways that life has of getting even.

One of our report-preparation people (about as low on the totem pole as you could get) called me four years later — as a writer for a major magazine assigned to do a cover story on yours truly. I'm not telling you the story turned out well because of what had gone down at McKinsey, but then . . .

Sticking with the consulting world: When digging for intelligence (of the CIA variety) in a client company, the "little people" are, by far, the best sources. They're the ones who know where the skeletons are buried, who understand the humble origins of the grand half-truths. Your intelligence — as leader, consultant, investment banker, securities analyst — will, in general, be directly proportional to the number and depth of your relationships with folks six levels "down," who have access to the real data, unexpurgated.

Rolodex power. Your power is almost directly proportional to the thickness of your Rolodex, and the time you spend maintaining it. Put bluntly, the most potent people I've known have been the best networkers — they "know everybody from everywhere" and have just been out to lunch with most of them.

One reason (among many) that women may well take over in the world of "virtual enterprises" is that they seem to have a greater instinct for networking. And the unfettered-by-machismo males who have taken to networking will do better than those who shun it as "sissy stuff." But, truth is, it has always been the age of "networkers"; and in an era where organizations depend more and more on tenuously connected outsiders to get the job done, it will only become more so.

People give to friends, not causes. Though Bob Farmer, Michael Dukakis's 1988 campaign finance chairman, hardly had the most scintillating candidate to shill for, Democrats for the first time in recent memory matched the GOP at fundraising buck for buck. At a seminar during the Democratic Convention in Atlanta, Farmer revealed his success secrets — the most important being The Network. That is, find a friend to go after a friend. Farmer swears that if you make an appointment with a powerful pal and show up at her office, you have infinitely bettered the odds of wheedling big bucks out of her. Moreover, the cause itself is mostly irrelevant!

Go to cocktail parties. Maybe you love cocktail parties. Maybe you hate cocktail parties. It doesn't matter. Go to cocktail parties. Bon vivant or hermit, you can strike gold over Johnnie Walker Black or Perrier. And, sexist as it is, a lot of deals still get done in the men's room. (Remember the boys peeing together in the TV movie of *Barbarians at the Gate*?)

While chairman, John Sculley said he seriously considered moving Apple Computer's headquarters from Northern California to Manhattan. The reason: The entertainment industry was going to play an increasingly important role in his business strategy, and he felt he needed to be near the action — meeting and mingling daily with a wide (and wild) variety of people. And for that constant bumping into someone, there's no place like crazy Manhattan (in many ways the city of the future, but that's another book).

Cocktail parties. The men's room. Increasingly, the women's room. The golf course. The Decathlon Club in Silicon Valley. This is where a lot of the serious action takes place. And this goes double (or more) in the rest of the world, particularly Asia and the Middle East.

Don't waste a single lunch. When I was at McKinsey & Co. in San Francisco, our boss used to get down on bended knee and beg us not to waste lunches eating alone. We were buried in our analyses, and they were important. On the other hand, market development is as much a lunchtime activity as an analytic one.

Think about it: 49 working weeks a year, subtract a few holidays — 225 mid- **THINK ABOUT IT!** day opportunities to develop relationships. You'd be wise to tally your batting average using 225 as a denominator. (Or 450: Power-breakfasting is clearly a growth market.) Even if it means Maalox, Mylanta, or an extra trip to the gym, don't waste those meal slots.

Work the phones! Remember the pictures of Bill Clinton prior to the NAFTA vote? On the phones, hour after hour after hour. Well, it's not just our Commander in Chief. I've been in a corner or two in my life, desperately needing support. Sometimes it means getting on the plane and flying 3,000 miles for a five-minute meeting; more often it means working the phones, hour after hour, day after day.

By nature, I'm not much of a phone person. Don't like 'em. But I recognize the importance of gluing myself to the horn. If face-to-face is impossible, then voice-to-voice and voice-to-voice and voice-to-voice is a reasonable second best.

Study your butt off. In his first book, Harvey Mackay, author, entrepreneur, management guru (the shark man!), saved the best for last — the Mackay 66. He offered 66 questions you should be able to answer about your clients — including spouse's birthday. Mackay is right on the money. Know more about your client (or coworker) than the next person, and you've got a leg up.

Years ago I crossed paths with the fellow who ran Boeing's defense-related helicopter business. He had a rule of thumb: One hour of preparation for every minute of a client meeting. If he got a twenty-minute slot with one of the senior folks in the Saudi government, that meant studying for about twenty hours — from defense capabilities to the many-branched royal family tree.

Amen.

Building credibility from the outside in (and avoiding internal politics in the process). Tired of internal power plays? Backside sore from being bitten? Well, forget it. (Mostly.) Become so indispensable to outsiders that the insiders dare not lay a glove on you. That was my strategy at McKinsey, and it worked for a while — unfortunately, I was only 3,000 miles away from head-quarters. With a 9,000-mile gap, the strategy worked miracles for McKinsey superstar Kenichi Ohmae, who long headed the company's Japanese operations.

Oh, yes, and the fact that Ken was much more established in Japan than I was in the United States. He's written a dozen or more books; he's at the very epicenter of Japanese politics; he is, according to polls, the country's most-respected commentator on economics and management and most everything else. McKinsey couldn't have fired him if it wanted to. He goes his own sweet way. (And in 1994 he left McKinsey to enter politics. Prime Minister Ohmae? Don't bet against it.)

No, I'm not suggesting that you irritate everyone (or anyone) in your organization. I am suggesting — especially in today's world, where outside relationships are at least as important as internal ones — that you can insulate yourself from a lot of hassle by building up external credibility. It gives you, at the very least, the power to be more or less left alone. And that's no small thing.

Build credibility in the field. What works with outsiders also works inside the company. You're a junior staffer. You've got a hot idea. Your boss is busy with what she considers more important ideas. How do you boost yours up the priority ladder?

Don't keep nagging the boss, for heaven's sake. (It's self-defeating and gets you nowhere.) Instead, steal the time, by hook or by crook, and get out into the field. Make friends with people, sell them on your idea, induce them to test it — and give them all the help you possibly can. Then let them sell your idea to your boss. Your credibility becomes their credibility — and theirs is typically better than yours.

Sure, they take the credit. Now it's their idea. (That's the point.) What, then, is the payoff for you? The grapevine never fails: People know it was you who sparked the fire, and eventually that information finds its way to the top.

People can smell emotional commitment (and the absence thereof) from a mile away. When I was in a relatively junior job in and around the White House, I seemed to get an inordinate amount done (that's what people said, anyway, which is what counts). The secret was my bulldog-like persistence on issues that mattered to me — I'd wear the bastards down. That was about it. The "bastards" had their own agendas, and the

> **People can smell emotional commitment from a mile away.**

things I was working on usually weren't at the top of them. Given my tenacity, they'd usually let me have my way rather than waste a lot of time fighting.

Go back to the economics classroom: The perception that you will do whatever it takes to get something done (and waste an inordinate amount of others' time in the process) amounts to a fabulously effective "barrier to entry." People can smell serious emotion, commitment, energy from a mile — make that 10 miles — away.

Bob Kriegel, author of (with Louis Patler) *If It Ain't Broke —* *Break It!*, recalls working with Hewlett-Packard project managers. He'd have them score potential tasks on "importance" (substance) and their "level of commitment." If a project didn't bag a commitment score of at least 7 (on a scale of 1 to 10), then it shouldn't be pursued.

I reiterate: It's not just that commitment counts in the "real" sense of your willingness to go the extra mile, it also counts in others' perception of your willingness to battle on (and on . . .) — they wisely choose another piece of turf to fight over.

Return phone calls, fast. Credibility comes from being a gal/guy "you can count on." There are a lot of ways to earn that reputation, but perhaps none better than by returning phone calls. When I put in a call to the secretary of labor, and his secretary says, "He's in a meeting with the president [i.e., Bill] right now, but he'll be out in a half hour and call you from his car phone." Well, when (if) he does, you'd better believe I'm more or less his slave for life. The late Sam Walton returned his phone calls instantly, without the buffer of a secretary. And you can get through to Bruce Nordstrom, president of $3.5 billion Nordstrom, with no muss or fuss.

There seem to be two kinds of people in this world: those who return their phone calls with dispatch, and those who don't. Funny thing, it seems to have little to do with rank. Walton, worth billions, found a way to return his phone calls — to anybody and everybody — fast. Others — both high and low, no matter who the caller — don't.

To be honest, I've pretty much survived in life without scoring close to a perfect 10 (or imperfect 5) on this. I just hate the phone. It makes me sad because it's impolite and has doubtless cost me in ways I'm unaware of. (And a few I'm very aware of.) But learn from my mistakes — return your calls pronto.

"I was just in the field" — a showstopper of an answer. When I was working in Washington in 1973, and "my" issue (international narcotics control) was moving up the agenda, I'd almost invariably do the contrarian thing — get out of town. Hop on a plane, fly over to Thailand or down to Mexico, and have a conversation with the critical parties there. I didn't really expect to pick up much new information. But I knew that when I got back to Washington, I'd be able to say, "Well, just last week I was in Thailand talking with the ambassador." "When I asked the CIA station chief, he had a different take. . . ." How the hell was anyone going to top that?

Yes, it means racking up tens of thousands of frequent flier miles, but it works almost unfailingly. It's a variation on the 3,000 miles for a five-minute meeting theme: This is about logging those miles to increase your stature and credibility as the person who "talked to the real people in the field . . . *yesterday*."

Perception is all there is — manage it! There is no reality. There is only perceived reality. Jeff Greenfield was an advance man for Bobby Kennedy and other pols. He offers this advice: If you think your candidate can only draw a crowd of seven, hold your next event in a phone booth; when the press pix hit the streets, they'll show people clawing to get in.

Greenfield has a point. A big one. In my life as a speaker, I pay close attention to it — trying to book auditoriums that hold significantly fewer than the number of folks expected. Sure, it means you leave a few bucks (or more) on the table, but there's nothing quite like the word getting around that people are scalping tickets for twice their price — hey, this dude must be something!

Write the agenda. Pay attention to something and it's perceived as important. That's a no-brainer. But it also suggests that the agenda-writer has inordinate power. She decides what gets on that list (and what gets left off). What gets handled first (and last). Sure, she has to yield to those above — but a lot of honchos don't appreciate the importance of writing the agenda, and will let our smart cookie do her own thing.

For a boss, one of the most effective ways to move an issue to the top of the agenda is via repetition. Roger Milliken, chief of the peerless textile firm that bears his name (Milliken & Company), went gaga over quality in 1980. Every question he asks (to this day) manages to include a quality angle. Every agenda starts with quality. He turned around a huge organization quickly by changing the very nature of the internal language: Everyone learned to speak quality — fluently.

One more: Stanford professor Jim March suggests that he who (re)writes history has significant power. That is, leap at the opportunity to be the "mere" recorder of a meeting's minutes. Again, there are limits. But within the bounds of propriety, even narrowly defined, the ability to make a meeting come out right after the fact is a piece of cake for the masterful minuteer.

Dress for success. This one just about makes me sick to utter. I like to hang around in shorts or sweat pants — in fact, when I got canned by McKinsey, one of the charges against me was that I came to work in shorts.

Sad truth is, the bad guys got us on this one. Like it or not, there is a "look and smell of power." It's not that "some got it, some don't" — it's that some work at it, some don't.

On the one hand, the power suit can be taken to the off-putting extreme of slick or pretentious. On the other hand, the nation didn't much take to President Jimmy Carter talking about global affairs in his cardigan sweaters.

It's not a simple issue — what's right at your office may be wrong at their office. Bottom line: Be yourself, develop your own

distinctive sartorial style. Show care, show confidence. Those who walk with their chin a little up, keep their backs straight, and wear exquisitely tailored clothes will find that people pay more attention to them. If you don't believe me, ask the best lawyer you know what advice she gives her clients on courtroom attire — where "dress for success" takes on *real* significance.

Don't be obsequious. Saying thank you, being decent — incredibly important. On the other hand, there's the fawning, too-nice, obsequious person — who, de facto, assumes a victim's posture. Big mistake.

It's not that nice guys finish last (they often finish first). It's that "weaklings" (not the physical variety) leave an awful lot on the table.

Join Toastmasters. Oral communication skills count. Enormously. A lot of managers aren't bad at public speaking. But "aren't bad" ain't good enough, not if you're wise — and especially these days, when jawing with the same old gang from year to year is becoming rare. Height and hair color may be in the genes. Public speaking isn't. It's a skill that can be studied, polished, more or less perfected. (Look at Bill Clinton, who went from putting the nation to sleep at the 1988 Democratic Convention to winning bipartisan kudos for his forceful 1993 inaugural address.) You can not only get good at it, you can get damn good at it. And it makes a heck of a difference.

I give a lot of talks and seem to have become more than pretty good at it. Let me tell you about powerful public speaking: If you have any sense of humility at all, it scares the hell out of you. There have been times when I held an audience in my hands. That's real power. Churchill's sonorous eloquence was an indispensable tool in steeling the British people during the darkest days of World War II. His adversary across the Channel was an awesome speaker himself, that former paperhanger, Adolf You-Know-Who.

One (good) answer to the public speaking problem/opportunity is Toastmasters. They do a fabulous job of helping people shape up their communication skills. If you've got any questions about your speaking ability (and if you don't, you've probably got a problem), think about joining Toastmasters.

(And if you're the boss think about getting *all* your employees in Toastmasters or Dale Carnegie — plumber Larry Harmon does the latter, as you'll read in item No. 76.)

Mind your manners! The next several items are mostly defensive, rather than offensive. To get things done you often need to be aggressive, touting a point of view that may not be popular. One of your best allies is keeping your crude side (assuming you have one — most of us do) under wraps.

When I began working on the project at McKinsey that led to *In Search of Excellence*, I got some good advice from one of the firm's senior partners: "You're going to be pushing some ideas that are beyond what people around here want to confront. So make sure you're beyond reproach on 'the little stuff' — show up for meetings on time or early, dress conservatively, and so on." Fantastic advice. I successfully followed it for several years.

Since I knew that my message bugged a lot of people, I worked overtime at being a good soldier, particularly when one of my "enemies" felt I had something to offer his client (and therefore conveniently ignored our adversarial status). I'd move heaven and earth to get where he wanted me to be, ahead of time, prepared as hell, to work with that client. By doing those things, which were the very heart of McKinsey partner-to-partner etiquette, I could keep shoving pretty darn hard, and pretty darn far, with my own baby — which was what really mattered.

(Note: Eventually the price of dealing with folks for whom I was losing respect became too high: Knowing when to cut and run is also part and parcel of the power practitioner's arsenal.)

Don't be a smart-ass; don't EVER embarrass folks in public. I know too many consultants and MBAs who have blunted their effectiveness by relentlessly parading their brains (a.k.a. being a smart-ass), and, especially, by publicly embarrassing people — even clients! — who are more talented than they are (though perhaps not quite so quick, IQish, or analytic). They just don't seem to be able to contain themselves. This fatal (condescension is a killer) flaw is much more common than you might think.

Learn to hold your tongue. Whenever you go into a meeting, repeat this mantra: I will not be a smart-ass. I will not be a smart-ass. . . .

If you behave even half decently, you can avoid a lot of shit in this life. Nice guys (and gals!) may or may not finish last. Assholes eventually get their just desserts.

Yes, I'm using crude language. But I'm using it for a good reason: To drive home my point. If you're championing stuff that's off the wall (hey, they laughed at the Wright Brothers), you have 2.76 strikes against you to begin with. But if you are decent, if you at least behave decently, your battle is half won.

I make my living "selling" unwelcome messages. And I genuinely like the people I work with (thanks to my mom and dad, probably); I sympathize, empathize, feel for, am at one with them — and they sense I'm on their side and am delivering the bitter pill because I think it's important, not because I take pleasure in it.

If you aren't half decent, at least fake it — though I don't really think that's possible. People tend to develop pretty reliable bullshit detectors by age 14.

You CAN get away with all sorts of crap when things are going well — resist the temptation, because it'll come back to haunt you (or worse) when things go sour (as they will). In his autobiography, Norman Schwarzkopf told of getting promoted to brigadier general. Overnight, he said, everyone started laughing at his lousy jokes.

When you're top dog, you can bark and people will go into hysterics. Problem is, it goes to your (swelled) head — you start believing you're Robin Williams.

Jokes, of course, aren't the issue here. Don't let success pump you full of hot air. Skip the tiny arrogances of power. First, they make you a pain in the butt, and less respected. Second, when the yogurt hits the fan, "they" will get even.

People have long memories. Very long memories. Infinitely long memories. If you slight them or pull some childish prank, they'll remember. They'll torpedo your policies. They'll get you when you're down. They're not creeps, just normal, garden-variety human beings — who don't like to be put down.

Be magnanimous in victory, even more so in defeat — tomorrow is another day. Be especially nice when somebody is hurting — simple human kindness has power beyond measure. And spread around the glory when you luck out (and any victory is largely a matter of luck — don't ever forget it).

There are NO right answers — don't press your case too hard. The problem with McKinsey and BCG consultants, the problem with many MBAs, is that they believe there are right answers. And since they know that the angels have furnished them with those answers, they push their case far too hard. They run roughshod over the 49-year-old (when they're 26) who has been in the war zone for decades. Sorry: Despite the staggering price tag on that MBA, and the fact that McKinsey/BCG accepted you into the priesthood, there are no right answers. Period.

(Lighten up, you say. OK. Look, I'm not saying that the 49-year-old is necessarily right. I'm saying "go easy." He's had his experiences. He does have wisdom. He's seen the likes of you come — and go — before. And I am saying, I repeat, that

THERE ARE NO "RIGHT" ANSWERS.)

Remember: We are all centers of our own universe — you, and EVERY person whom you address. Every person is the star of his own movie. Every person values his ideas (and ideals). Every person who ends up buying into *your* idea does so by changing it into *his* idea (even if it still looks a lot like your idea).

If you always remind yourself that the other person is at the epicenter of his world, you'll be a lot better off. Let his star shine — he will literally love you for it.

It is ever so easy to slight an individual. Five people are on the welcoming committee. You believe in thank-you notes. (Hooray!) You send four follow-up thank-you notes. Whoops. Major whoops.

The only way not to slight people is to be careful. Very careful. Very, very careful. Take notes, check, then check again, and then check a third time to make sure that you've got a completely accurate list of the people who helped you out. Then check on the spellings of their names. Check once. Check twice. Check three times. Check their titles. Once. Twice. Three times. (Maybe four.)

Remember that business is a human game, and it is so easy, so very easy, to unintentionally slight someone. Again: The key is hard work. (And taking such "little" items seriously.)

Maintain one good friend who revels in telling you that you're full of hooey. When you get to the top of the heap, nothing you hear is true (or, at least, the whole truth). Keeping things in perspective is very, very difficult. The difficulty is directly proportional to the size of the heap you're sitting atop.

The best defense is one good, no-bullshit buddy. It can be a spouse. It can be a college roommate you talk to three times a year. But somewhere, somehow, you've got to keep in touch with reality. A person who can laugh at you. More than that: A person who takes pleasure in laughing at you — and making you laugh at yourself. When Roman senators addressed the masses, they'd have an underling stand behind them whose sole job it was to lean over and repeat: "Remember you're mortal." You are too, and had best be reminded of it often — and bluntly.

Quite simply, no matter how hard you try, no matter how "open" you are, you'll end up being surrounded by "yes people." It's hard not to believe people who are repeating your own ideas. Resist the temptation.

Move slightly prematurely — and fast. Timing is everything. There is such a thing, to be sure, as moving prematurely, before you've built your network of support. On the other hand, waiting too long is perhaps the bigger sin. "They" will never be ready for the revolutionary move; hence, moving a little bit prematurely and doing the "dirty work" (for example layoffs) fast is imperative.

When I look at the careers of the best turnaround executives, such as the late Mike Walsh at Union Pacific Railroad and Tenneco, that's the story. Walsh listened intently to the long-timers. He got to know the lay of the land, made friends among the troops. He communicated, communicated, then communicated some more. But, a little bit before people expected, he made his big move. Walsh followed the old Chinese proverb: "It is not wise to leap a chasm in two bounds." He leaped his in one.

The street is often left bloody. But at least it was a clean cut. The Walshes tell you what they're going to do. Then they do it. Once. Fast. Then it's over. And time to build.

Knowing when to retreat is as important as knowing when to advance. The best military (and business) leaders agree that a good offense beats a good defense. Being an attacker, an innovator, especially in today's crowded markets, is critical. But whether you are Napoleon, Hannibal, or Harry of Harry's Hot Dogs, there are times when the other guy gets you dead to rights. In which case, get the hell off the field — you'll save some troops (as at Dunkirk) and live to fight another day. Knowing when to take your losses is an essential part of eventual success.

Persist. Wear the buggers down! I came across an article on the success of Sunkist Growers, the American firm that enjoys huge exports to Japan. The company has even developed great relationships with Japan's often touchy farmers. The CEO was asked his secret. It's simple, he said in effect; I've been going over there regularly for 30 years.

I liked that. I loved it. Want to succeed in the "tough"

Japanese market? No sweat: Just keep going over, just keep hanging out. And sure enough, within a few decades, you may make a dent.

In short, victory tends to go to the most resilient. Almost nothing, small or large, was ever accomplished without setback after setback after setback. A lot of people cut and run. (And sometimes it makes sense — see above.) But others take their lumps, fall down, bounce back, get knocked down again — and hang in there.

> **Today's triumph (or setback) is just one step in a long journey.**

Stand back and admire the (long) view. We tend to get hopelessly involved in today's deal, today's victory, today's loss, today's whatever. And an exceptional level of involvement is certainly needed, given the number of potholes that mar any road worth traveling. So, on the one hand, be serious, be passionate, be committed. On the other hand, realize that today's triumph (or setback) is just one step in a long journey. Try to put it in perspective. Be accepting in loss, magnanimous in victory — because there are still lots of innings, lots of games left to play.

The big cheese usually understand this (hey, they made it to the top). Hence, they place great importance on the way up-and-comers handle setbacks. "The professional pouters," one executive told me, "aren't long for the fast track." Remember those words.

Beware the middle-ground compromises; losses and (insufferable) delays can be more valuable than mushy outcomes — in the long run. A lot of things end up "in the middle," so it's often tempting just to split the difference and skip the fight. On the other hand, once more: Remember the long run. This is only one round. The mushy compromise could be a mistake. Maybe it's better to get your nose bloodied, become a martyr. Accept the (maddening) delay, because it allows you to retreat to your corner, build up your muscles (and bolster your squad), and go after the big victory tomorrow, or the day after, or the day after that. . . .

Take the crummy little job, out of sight, where you're left alone to do your own thing. Staying close to the center of power — taking that job as the honcho's assistant, say — is tempting. And can often pay off. On the other hand, quickly building a substantive track record is essential, too. And going for the glamorous job, which puts you in or near the spotlight, can make it harder to do your own thing, collect your own wins. With all that light shining on you, you're less likely to take quirky risks; plus, you've got your boss breathing down your neck every step of the way.

Answer: Amaze your peers. Take the rotten little assignment in the boondocks that no one wants. Then do it well. Do it very, very well. Innovate, create, make your mark.

A software designer who attended one of my seminars worked for a company that didn't pay much attention to customer service — which was his (mostly secret) passion. But he was a rising star in the spotlight. We talked and I encouraged him to follow his instincts. He went back to work, demoted himself (literally), and took over the customer-service operation. He went to town and had a ball, turning a backwater into the firm's principal competence. And turning himself into a force to be reckoned with.

Goals are (mostly) stupid; seize the day. Having a vision. Not a bad idea. In fact, a pretty good idea — it motivates you and inspires those around you. Just make sure that "vision" has some give and take. In fact, create a vision that can become a very different vision — if something exciting pops up on your radar screen. Opportunism isn't a dirty word, any more than power is. If a window of opportunity appears, don't pull down the shade because it doesn't fit into your long-term plan. Such a response, ironically, turns visions into blinders.

Fact is, I'm sugarcoating this. I've long felt goals are rather stupid. The notion, in the midst of life's turbulent flow and fabulous cacophony, of following one currently shining star (to the exclusion of the rest of the galaxy) makes little sense to me.

Instead, look at each day as a new canvas on which to paint. Hey, what works for me may not work for you. But at least think about it my way. . . .

Build bridges with friends, rather than burn them with enemies. I hate conflict. Avoid it like the plague. But it's not just my disposition — I don't think conflict makes much sense. Your scintilating personality and brilliant analytic skills rarely turn enemies into allies. And win or lose, you waste a hell of a lot of time training for the battle and cleaning up the mess.

Forget your enemies. Work around them. Work instead on developing friends, turning people who agree with you (a little bit or a lot) into passionate advocates and adherents. That is, surround your enemies with your friends.

Head-on fights are stupid. Well, that's not always the case: Sometimes they serve a symbolic end, showing people you're tough, or some such (crap). In general, though, they're to be avoided. Fighting drains an enormous amount of emotional energy and usually makes you look like a jerk. Moreover, it doesn't necessarily gain you supporters — which is the whole point.

Make that call NOW: Solve the problem before it festers. It's obvious, at least in retrospect: Every big problem was at one time a wee disturbance. If only . . .

If only you had nipped the damn thing in the bud. The simple truth is (and I've been found wanting on this more often than not): A single, four-minute phone call (240 seconds) right now may save you a $2 million lawsuit 18 months down the line. (**Hint:** Ignore your lawyers when they tell you not to make the call.)

Look, I don't know how to deal with this except in a very personal way. Usually I avoid the four-minute calls. Though I haven't suffered any $2 million lawsuits (yet), I've caused a lot of pain and agony (to myself and others). But, from time to time, I have made the call. And there is one thing I can tell you: Not once has it failed. In fact, at the end of the four minutes — or the 14 minutes it usually stretches into — you frequently find that you've actually made a friend. (Most people are surprised when someone makes the effort to deal promptly with a bruised feeling or misunderstanding.)

Believe me on this: Most of the mistakes that you will make in your career (and probably in your personal life) will come from having avoided that four-minute phone call that could have stopped the farmhand from letting out the cow that kicked over the lantern that started the fire that burned down the barn. . . .

Being a brawler is not necessarily the answer. Tough guys don't always finish first. Two very different presidents, Ronald Reagan and Bill Clinton, are famous for avoiding conflict. Sure, you can go too far in avoiding harm's way; both of them have gotten in trouble for doing precisely that. On the other hand, they both made it to the White House — and you and I didn't. So steering clear of the big imbroglios, the big bloodlettings, isn't necessarily a design for disaster.

Tell people to buzz off from time to time, including your boss — process IS important, but you also gain power from results, which come from narrowly focusing on the outcome. It's important to send your thank-you notes. It's important to return your phone calls. And sometimes it's important to be rude.

About every 18 months I write book. All the other "good stuff" that comes my way rides on the back of those books. So when it's time to write, I write. I can't write a book and do other things. So, I don't. I become rude.

I don't return phone calls. I don't respond to mail — sometimes for days, weeks, months, a year! Anything other than an emergency gets dumped in the "later" basket. To be sure, my life is not the ordinary life. Or is it? I think it is. Return your phone calls and answer your mail, if you want, but when you're working on your main event, slam the door on distractions.

So that's my little screed on power. Very personal. Very idiosyncratic. Offered with a grain (or a 25-pound block) of salt. It's not your normal take on the issue. It focuses on thank-you notes and not being a jerk, instead of negotiating skills. Which brings me to football . . .

Football games are often lost in the last 30 seconds because of an unlucky bounce, a referee's bad call, whatever.

But I have no sympathy with those who complain of the bad bounce, the bad spot of the ball. If you'd been ahead 27-7, then a fumble in the last 30 seconds wouldn't have cost you the game.

These musings are mostly about building up 27-7 leads. If you consciously keep these "minor" items — have you fed your Rolodex today? — on the front burner, you can (usually) avoid the showdown, the big battle that hinges on chance.

That's what the accumulation and exercise of power is all about to me.

28

Beware of easy solutions and "rules" laid down by management gurus, starting with yours truly.

Milk, Cookies, and Managing People

29 Putting Customers in Their Place

CEO Hal Rosenbluth chronicled the incredible success of his travel-services firm, Rosenbluth International, in. . .

The Customer Comes Second.

Love that title!

Who comes first? Don't be silly, says King Hal; it's employees. That is — and this, dear Watson, is elementary — if you genuinely want to put customers first, you must put employees more first.

You get it, right?

30 Rites of Spring

A Vermont winter is always long, but especially 1993-94's snowy record-breaker. And then . . . spring bursts upon the scene. In a flash, literally, life returns. It is noisy, glorious, raucous. We and our neighbors are transformed. As I contemplate a late April sunrise, I think I can move mountains!

Such rebirth seldom occurs in corporations. Checkout clerks face another umpteen customers today (and then tomorrow), claims adjusters another raft of problems, chambermaids another passel of fetid bath towels and bed linens. And what holds for claims adjusters holds for execs, too. Every day brings, on average, 5.27 meetings with 48.1 more transparencies per meeting. Right?

No wonder we become cynical, or at least stale.

What if we managers put rebirth near the top of our agendas? As the marketplace becomes more and more demanding, the pace more and more relentless, it becomes especially important to bolster the renewal process. Hence, these suggestions:

■ **Take a serious daily break.** I'm worried about my new, high-speed Canon copier. What will I do now for a break? I find — seriously — that many of my best ideas have come while I stood by my old copier, feeding in 75 pages, one at a (slow) time. Planned coffee breaks are one (good) thing, but I'm talking about something else, a *real* pause to refresh or redirect our brain waves.

■ **Do something different.** One company gives its telemarketers a whole day "off" each week to work on productivity-improvement projects. In addition to rekindling energy for the primary job, project payoffs have more than covered the costs of the extra staffing required. I can imagine such an approach applied almost anywhere.

■ **Call "time out."** Hey bean-counter, why not take the accounting department team to the movies this afternoon? Or to see one of the members' kids perform in a play?

■ **Change the scenery.** When the weather turns warm in Worthington, Ohio, designers at Fitch RS take their work outside to picnic-table settings. In general, changing location makes an enormous difference. (I routinely work in two or three places a day, even when confined to an office; and I sometimes just drive my truck somewhere, and sit in the front seat and work for a couple of hours.) If you can, locate several picnic tables near the office — or keep a few bikes handy. Then, when you're in search of a productive meeting, the whole group can hop on the bikes and head for the park!

■ **Celebrate.** Most weeks (days?) bring *something* worth celebrating. How about MBDA, or Managing By Donuting Around? There's no better investment in renewal than donuts, muffins, and balloons. To aid the cause, set up a "crazy money" fund that gives everyone access to $25 for a spur-of-the-moment bagel or pizza party.

■ **Put on a show.** You'd be amazed by your colleagues' off-the-job talents. So why not give them bragging space and learn more about them in the process? To wit, a performing arts week, capped by a formal-ish evening program for employees and their families.

■ **Curl up with a good book.** One company shuts down the factory for two hours a week, and employee-boss teams work through a chapter of a book on quality, customer service, reengineering. In other firms, informal reading groups of execs, engineers, and whomever tackle a novel or a play a month. Nice.

■ **Do some spring cleaning.** Replay your mom's (my mom's, anyway) spring cleaning blitz. For two days, everyone dons 501s and specially printed T-shirts and cleans house — toss out old files, clear the fridge, do whatever it takes to induce the feeling of a fresh start.

■ **Head for spring training.** Every April, Chicago Cubs fans dream anew of a World Series title. Why not our businesses? This goes beyond the cleanup/clean-out affair above, and toward something even more fundamental. Maybe it's a two-day, all-hands effort (call it The Rites of Spring) in which you examine "wins" and "losses" and recommit, perhaps formally, to each other and the unit's vision and values.

If your heart's not in it, any tactic can backfire. Even a tiny "celebration" can be a dud. And there's nothing special about my list. It's only intended to get you focused on renewal per se, on that life-giving phenomenon most farmers (and part-time farmers like myself) experience each year, but which most companies overlook entirely. In an economy that begs for spirited responses, and usually gets the opposite from firms large and small, this is a strategic opportunity.

31

"Equilibrium is death. . . . Seek persistent dis-equilibrium."

Kevin Kelly
*Out of Control: The Rise
of Neo-Biological Civilization*

Hooray!

32 The Magic Number 153

I know it wasn't E. F. Schumacher. (To be honest, I *still* haven't read *Small Is Beautiful*.) And it wasn't my disposition: I was long disposed to the potency of big enterprises.

Maybe it was Ren McPherson, who made it into *Fortune*'s Business Hall of Fame (next to Henry Ford, Cyrus McCormick, and other Babe Ruths of enterprise) for his pioneering, people-first approach to the 1970s at auto-parts maker Dana Corporation. He liked his plants small, he told me when I was doing my initial research for *In Search of Excellence* in 1979. If they go over a couple hundred folks, he said, they tend to lose their spirit. (Dana plant bosses were called "store managers," in keeping with the overall concept of spirited intimacy.)

People-first is probably the wrong description for Emerson Electric's Chuck Knight, a hardheaded, no-nonsense efficiency nut. Yet Chuck, too, likes to keep energy high — and, therefore, unit size low. (Emerson was another *In Search of Excellence* stop.)

Though I gradually became more and more interested in the disproportionate success of middle-size businesses and business units, the size bug didn't really become a preoccupation with me for another 10 years. Then, with competition getting hotter and hotter (and hotter) in the late '80s, I started stumbling over more and more (and more) examples of folks and enterprises that swore by moderate size.

ABB Asea Brown Boveri's Percy Barnevick (*Liberation Management* and *The Tom Peters Seminar*) blasted a 200,000-person enterprise into 5,000 units averaging just 40 people each. Though Barnevik is engineering trained, his logic was as unconventional (by engineering standards) as McPherson's or

Knight's: Constant innovation and customer concern, musts in every crowded market in which he competes, come only from a "spirited, obsessed, energetic" unit, he told me. Hence, the tiny unit size. Ben Lytle of the successful financial-services outfit, The Associated Group (*Liberation Management* and *The Tom Peters Seminar*), used the same reason to explain why he split his (big) joint up into 100-person units — and split them again when success took a unit's numbers above 200.

What are the upper and lower boundaries of these inchoate musings? Richard Branson (Virgin Group) is another small-unit, split-'em-when-they-grow-big guy; he says that if you get above 50 or 60, folks get "lost in the corridors of power." So there's one peg: 50, give or take. Mike Walsh, when leading a remarkable turnaround at the Union Pacific Railroad, defined intimacy as 600. Though Walsh was logical to a fault, his reason for cracking the huge railroad into 600-person bits had a strictly personal basis: Unit managers (Top Guns, as UPRR called them) must know *all* their employees and major customers by name.

About 50 on the low end, 600 on the high. But is there more to this "size thing" than gut feeling (even if it's from some very wise guts)?

There is.

Antony Jay, in his landmark 1972 book, *Corporation Man*, carefully examined unit size. "I had a feeling . . . there was a grouping of great importance, even if I could not understand why," he wrote. "It lay somewhere around 400 or 500." His hunch was borne out in studies of the Australian outback, Paris suburbs, and numerous schools and entrepreneurial firms.

"A unit of 500 . . . is something you actually feel a part of," Jay explains. "You know that if you leave, everyone will notice the gap you have made. . . . This is profoundly important in a community, if only because it so radically affects what you can get away with. . . . Imagine trying to conduct a matrimonial intrigue in a village of 600 people: You could reckon that the time lapse between one person suspecting and the whole village talking would be a maximum of 12 hours."

More recent research pegs the magic number at 150 (153 on the dot, according to one analysis). Groups of 100 to 230 "turn up everywhere," Britain's *New Scientist* magazine reported:

> In most modern armies . . . the smallest independent unit normally [numbers] 130 to 200. . . . Sociologists have known since the 1950's that there is a critical threshold in the region of 150 to 200, with larger companies suffering a disproportionate amount of absenteeism and sickness. In 1989, Tony Becher of the University of Sussex published a survey of 12 disciplines in both the sciences and the humanities. . . . Once a discipline becomes larger than [200 researchers] it fragments into two or more subdisciplines. . . .
>
> Neolithic villages from the Middle East around 6,000 BC typically seem to have contained 120 to 150 people. . . . The Hutterites, a group of contemporary North American religious fundamentalists who live and farm communally, regard 150 as the maximum size for their communities. . . . They find that when there are more than about 150 individuals, they cannot control the behavior of the members by peer pressure alone.

Bedrock beneath these wide-ranging observations comes from research labeled the "social intelligence hypothesis." Primate groups max out at 55. The reason: "Social grooming," the main mechanism used to cement relations between individual monkeys, can only be done one on one. Thus, according to *New Scientist*, the upper limit to the number of monkeys in a close-knit group is a function of the finite time available for mutual licking, fussing, and bug-picking.

Social grooming, via language, preoccupies humans. "Conventional wisdom has always supposed that language evolved to enable humans to exchange information about food sources and . . . hunting," *New Scientist* continues. "But it is difficult to see why humans should be any more in need of this than other primates. . . . A more plausible suggestion is that language evolved to enable humans to integrate a larger number of individuals into their social groups." And language, the research suggests with precision, is three times more efficient than nonverbal grooming: "The sizes of conversation groups in a student [dormitory], for example, consist of an average of three to four individuals. . . . Larger groups fragment into smaller conversation subgroups. . . . Thus the characteristics of speech seem to be closely tied to the size of the interaction group required to maintain cohesion."

Arguably, we got away with violating this limit during the age of mass production and hyperspecialization, when the traditional craftsman's imagination was subordinated to machine logic. Now, brains, imagination, craft, and whole jobs are once again the order of the day and 150 people, give or take, may again be the right group size. McPherson, Barnevik, Lytle and Branson think so. And Microsoft's Bill Gates, wrestling with dramatic growth, has latched on to 200 as an ideal unit size.

33   2-3-9

2-3-9. Two-three-nine. Two hundred and thirty-nine.

Can you imagine? 239. I'm out for my daily power walk, while visiting my Mom in Annapolis. I happen by the headquarters (I assume) of the Anne Arundel County Board of Education, mid-morning, Friday, September 23, 1994. It is a vast sea of automobiles.

I am stunned. I stop and count. 239. That was it. And I didn't include the cars in visitors parking or obvious service vehicles (a phone company truck, etc.).

I'm going to make some absurd assumptions: No carpooling. Everyone came one to a car. No one was absent that day. So that's 239 people in HQ. Ludicrous.

Call me Ishmael or call me arrogant, I can see no reason for a county school's HQ (even Manhattan!) to have a staff of more than 50. That is, let the principals run the damned schools!

Yikes, what a bureaucracy. In closing, you'll be pleased to know that the slot closest to what appeared to be the front door was reserved for the Superintendent. Wouldn't want him to wear out his tootsies or get rained on, would we?

So let's talk about the education "problem." I've got a great idea for a place to start our discussion. . . .

34 A Boost for Dairy Farmers?

Carl Schmitt is founder and chairman of the wildly successful University Bank & Trust (Palo Alto, California). In a speech to fellow bankers, he took a leaf from Robert Fulghum, author of *All I Really Need to Know I Learned in Kindergarten*, and suggested our business enterprises might run more effectively if we took a regular afternoon break for cookies and milk.

Knowing Carl, I think he was being only slightly facetious. This is a bank, after all, that offers free shoeshines, balloons for kids — and sends customers a huge bag of Walla Walla onions every August.

So what are you waiting for? Get out your baking pan and milking stool and . . .

35 "Small e" entrepreneurship

The prospect of a downsizing/layoff looms. The probability of hiring on someplace else for comparable money not good. So what about IT? The BIG E? ENTREPRENEURSHIP?

How scary, you think. I'm not Microsoft's Bill Gates, CNN's Ted Turner, or Blockbuster's Wayne Huizenga. I'm just a fairly talented, 34-year-old Jane or Jake.

If not Bill Gates's variety of entrepreneurship, what about starting an Italian restaurant? Great idea, except that you can't even separate an egg without turning the kitchen into a war zone.

Well, you may or may not have IT in you, but so far you're considering a false choice (Gates or Italian chow). Turn your mind instead to "small e" entrepreneurship. Consider taking your 12 years of experience in training (marketing, finance, whatever) and converting it into a one-person professional service firm/consultancy. Maybe it grows to 40 (or 400!) people in 10 years, maybe it doesn't grow at all and you hook up with a middle-size client (back on someone's payroll). Or maybe you are the next Gates-Turner-Huizenga. But in any event, start thinking in modest terms. At least it will cut your Maalox-Librium bill.

Many professionals who can imagine getting the ax are panicked because they can't imagine running a Pizza Hut or Midas or Sir Speedy franchise, or opening that Italian eatery. That's the common definition of entrepreneurship, and it is intimidating. (It intimidates me, and I can separate eggs with the best of them.)

Don't get me wrong: Starting a one-person shop is no walk in the park. You've got to lay the groundwork, figure out what makes you special, cope with a hundred details (office at home, business cards, letters of announcement, etc., etc.). But you will at least be dealing with familiar predicaments that you mostly understand; and you'll be able to think of the transition as a largely manageable, one-step-at-a-time process. (With luck you'll have a fistful of clients — or at least one or two — lined up before you leave the corporate cocoon.)

"Small e" entrepreneurship can be remarkably rewarding. I practiced it for a couple of years before other opportunity knocked at the door of my office-in-the-home enterprise. In fact, I often look back fondly on my simpler, one-man-band days.

On the other hand, if you are a star at the stove and do have a better menu idea, start that restaurant — and send me an opening-night announcement!

36

Excited about the three-day training course you're scheduled to attend next week? Can't wait to acquire a few more skills? Great, but have you thought about the Monday after next week's training? You'll come back to work to find your phone log full, your in-basket overflowing, and your schedule overbooked with meetings. Until I catch up, you say to yourself, I'll put those grand new skills on hold.

Don't! Solid research reveals that the chances of your *ever* applying training lessons that are not applied on the first day back range from low to nothing.

The remedy: Use the plane trip home from the course, or three or four hours on Saturday, to review the high points of what you learned and figure out exactly how you're going to start to put them into practice on Monday.

Don't be unrealistic. Playing catch-up is going to make Monday a bear of a day in any case, but to get the new skills to stick, you've got to start nudging them onto your agenda posthaste. If you can't practice all of your new tricks on Monday, consciously try one or two more on Tuesday — without fail. Also spend half an hour a day reviewing those skills you haven't had a chance to put into immediate use. New skills need gentle, persistent nurturing.

Tip: Exchange phone numbers with several colleagues at the course and agree to act as support for one another. That practice you mastered in the classroom won't work quite the same way back at the office. Chances are your fellow-trainees are having similar problems, and their colleagues back at work are also looking at them as if they are alien creatures. It helps (a lot) to have an empathetic ear to talk to.

37 Three Rs for the '90s

The new three Rs, says a colleague, are Reputation, Résumé, and Rolodex. Showing up on time, being of good cheer, and clearing the in-tray by 5 P.M. no longer ensure job security. Nothing, in fact, ensures job security in the one-company-for-life sense of the term that was yesterday's expectation.

Today you are as good as those who swear publicly by your work (Reputation), the skills and results you can confidently and concisely brag about (Résumé), and the number of contacts you maintain in your professional sphere of interest (Rolodex).

Does this week's calendar reflect the above? That is, are you specifically and conscientiously working on your three Rs?

38 1,000 People, 1,000 Careers

While wandering through Munich's grand art museum, the Alte Pinakothek, in pursuit of the paintings of Pieter Brueghel the Elder, I thought about several friends and imagined what they might have done with a free Sunday 3,000 miles from home.

One would doubtless have mounted a birding expedition, and would be hefting 100 pounds of photography equipment through the nearby Alpine foothills. Another would probably have played anthropologist, proceeding from coffeehouse to public house and striking up conversations in his passable German. And a couple might have headed for Oktoberfest. (I've logged some heavy-duty time there myself.) My musings reminded me that each of us, though pals engaged in somewhat similar professional pursuits, is very different from the others. So what?

The age of mass production is fading fast. The emerging economy is based on knowledge, imagination, curiosity, and talent. What if we could learn to tap the wonderful, rich differences among people? Wouldn't a corporation that could exploit the uniqueness of each of its 1,000 employees (or 10 or 10,000) be phenomenally powerful? Put negatively, isn't a corporation that doesn't figure out how to use the special curiosities of each of its people headed for trouble?

Hence, the idea of 1,000 people, 1,000 career paths. Peter Drucker hinted at something like this when he declared, in the September-October 1992 issue of the *Harvard Business Review*, that "the relationship between knowledge workers and their organization is a distinctly new phenomenon." The grand viziers of this concept are University of Virginia professor Ed Freeman and Bucknell professor Daniel Gilbert. In *Corporate Strategy and the Search for Ethics*, the authors propose "the personal projects enterprise strategy." The corporation, they write, is a "means to facilitate the realization of the projects of corporate members. . . . Persons are only passing through corporations on the way to their respective ends. . . . Corporations are fictions that stand for the interests of the members." In a world where success depends upon brainpower and curiosity, the self-managed growth of the individual becomes paramount, and the wise corporation wittingly turns itself into a tool for fostering individuals' growth. Both the firm and its temporary constituents benefit.

How might a company pursue a personal projects enterprise strategy? A couple of general notions quickly come to mind:

■ Organize everything into projects, and allow members to assign themselves to those projects. This is the congenital style of the professional service firm, and as giant firms like Arthur Andersen and EDS demonstrate, there's no limit to the size of a "projectized" firm. More and more traditional organizations are getting the idea.

■ Allow careers to unfold as they will. At ad agency Chiat/Day, a secretary might decide to get into the creative side of things — and if she's willing to put in the hard labor, she can then proceed to move in that direction. Why not? Allowing — and encouraging — literally everyone to go where their passion and curiosity take them is important.

I have one nit to pick with Peter Drucker. "Knowledge worker" — his phrase — underplays an important point. "Curiosity is more important than knowledge," Albert Einstein once said. So how about "curiosity worker" instead? It's a bigger, and more important, idea.

Question du jour: Are you tapping the special skills of everyone in your group? Yes? Are you sure? (E.g., what *are* their special skills?)

39   Never treat a temp like a temp!

The fastest-growing segment of the American workforce is temporary workers. These days everybody's using them. Temporary work offers both companies and workers often-desirable flexibility. But as their use has grown, problems have cropped up. How do you instill loyalty and the company's culture in someone who's only going to be with you for a few months? How do you get people to put out 110 percent when they know they're only involved for the short term?

Answer: Never treat a temp like a temp!

Treat temporary workers just as you would a permanent employee — welcome them into your company, show them respect and trust, give them real responsibilities, *and* hold them to the same high standards. This is the secret to success at places like Disney, where turnover is enormous. Training and reward systems (and bosses) treat the 90-day employee just the same as if he or she were going to be a 20-year member of the Disney team.

40 It's Services, Stupid!

How dominant are "services"? Would you believe 96 percent of us ply service trades? Seventy-nine percent of us work in the official service sector (transportation, retail, entertainment, professional services, etc.). *And* 90 percent of the 19 percent employed in so-called manufacturing do service work (design, engineering, finance, marketing, sales, distribution, purchasing, etc.). So 79 percent plus 90 percent of 19 percent equals 96 percent.

Capital investment per employee in the service sector runs higher than in manufacturing, and value added per employee is equal in both sectors. The fact is, the awesomely sophisticated service-sector leaders (e.g., Wal-Mart), with more information than manufacturers (though accounting for 75 percent of GDP, the service sector racks up 85 percent of information-technology investments), are now calling the shots — and virtually dictating manufacturers' strategies.

The world's two most competitive economies — the U.S. (No. 1) and Singapore (No. 2) — displaced longtime leader Japan in 1994, according to the acclaimed World Economic Forum annual survey. Two big reasons for our high marks: An enormous edge in services productivity, and an awesome positive balance of services trade.

So why do we continue to bad mouth the services? Real men may or may not eat quiche, but practically *all* men *and* women are performing service activities — let's organize and compensate accordingly. Hey, maybe Washington will even figure it out someday, and start concentrating on services-friendly policymaking.

41

Q. We run three shifts at the plant I manage. The night shift has some morale and productivity problems. Any suggestions?

A. I suspect the basic problem is that the night shift feels left out — and probably is! It never sees top management (not from one year to the next, some of my third-shift friends tell me — and not *all* bad), it's not part of day-to-day affairs; but, mostly, it senses it's operating in an unappreciated, isolated no-man's-land.

In filmmaking, when special lenses are used to shoot night scenes during the day, it's called "day for night." What your company needs is the opposite: night for day. You can use special measures to make third-shift work as bright as first.

Start at the top. Have senior management around for the night shift with significant regularity. Then consider putting 10 percent of your accounting, personnel, and clerical staff on a de facto night shift. Also try to create a little magic, a little excitement — celebrations and recognition events, special foods in the canteen, awards that recognize the rigors of being a night owl — make it a hoot (sorry, couldn't resist). Poor punning aside, the whole point is to make the night gang feel as special in positive ways as they now do in a negative way.

42

The Sound of (Not So) Distant Thunder: More U.S. workers are now employed by women-owned companies than by the entire Fortune 500.

43

Do you ever have the feeling that you're drowning in information — newspapers, television, magazines, software, Internet, e-mail, this book? That it's coming at you from all sides faster than you can possibly digest it, let alone make sense of it? That you're out of control on the information superhighway? Do you ever want to throw all the papers and magazines away, pull the plug on the radio and TV, dump the videotapes, and cancel the mail?

<u>Don't.</u>

Let the files grow thicker and pile up. Hold on to the item you clipped from that local paper when you were out of town. Videotape that program that sounded so interesting but that you won't be home to watch. Squirrel away the fax on North Dakota's top three tourist attractions. Did you guess? I'm a pack-rat and I devoutly believe in pack-ratting. I can't tell you how many times some little nugget of information — buried deep in my overloaded brain and in some folder someplace — will occur to me and provide the missing link that ties together everything I'm working on.

I figure the efficiency of this process is about 2 percent, but that's all right. I like to keep a lot of information around, and I don't mind the messiness. Super-tidy systems end up, in my opinion, being hopelessly ineffective. You spend so much time being neat and orderly that you lose the power of the information — oddball connections, a little bit of this mixed in with a little bit of that. Information overload is useful, and unavoidable anyway, so have fun with it.

44 **Toward "Do"-Manuals**

I'd rather read just about anything than a company policy and procedures manual. Inevitably such manuals are collections of "don'ts." And "don'ts" stop initiative, squelch innovation, stymie creativity. When I see a thick manual, I know I'm looking at a slow company, one that's struggling under a lot of "Halt, who goes there"- ism and excess baggage.

Get out the red pen. Be a *ruthless* editor. Ask this about *every* sentence, *every* rule, *every* "don't": Does this need to be in there? Is it going to help our company one bit, whit, or iota as it struggles to hustle and achieve towering competence in an upside-down world? No? Tear it out. Crumple it up. See that wastebasket? Practice your hoop skills.

Better yet, dunk the whole frigging Don't Manual and replace it with a Do Manual. That's what David Armstrong, inventor of MBSA, or "Management by Storying Around," did. (He even wrote a book about it.)

> **When I see a thick manual, I know I'm looking at a slow company, one that's struggling under a lot of excess baggage.**

Armstrong, whose calling card offers "Story-teller" as his title, runs his company by telling and retelling stories about how real people in the trenches at Armstrong International have effectively handled dicey situations — irrational customers, personal conflicts, and so on. These "do" stories are not de facto rules to be mindlessly applied next time a problem crops up. To the contrary, they are vignettes that almost always demonstrate a flexible, innovative response to today's issue (as all adults know, *every* situation is different). These stories set a distinct tone, but it is *anti*-by-the-book.

No kidding, Armstrong's collection of stories *is* his policy and procedures manual. And there ain't no other.

45 That's Gonna Cost You (and Me!), Bud

Looking for a Boboli pizza shell. (They're s-o-o good; does anybody make their own anymore?) Not where they usually are. There's a clerk at hand (from the butcher's counter, next to where the Boboli used to be). "Could you tell me where the Bobolis are?" I ask.

"They moved 'em," he replies, then walks away.

OK, it had been a stressful day. And I'm not that keen on the store. (His is the standard scintillating response.) So . . . so I pretty much lost it.

"They. They. . . .'They' moved it? Who be they? What be they? Where be they? Can *w-e* ask *t-h-e-y*?" (The decibel level was not especially low.)

So what? Another crappy service experience. But it did get me thinking about t-h-e-y. Ted Turner, it's said, fines CNNers who use the word "foreign" (we're all in this together, as he sees it); and if I were running a grocery store, restaurant, whatever, I'd fine any employee $5 who I *ever* caught explaining *anything* to *anyone* in terms of "they."

There's one catch: I'd fine the employee's supervisor $50 and myself $500 for creating an environment where "they" use "they."

CHAMPION COMPETITIVENESS:
HELP STOMP OUT "THEY"-ISM!

46 The Bumping-into Strategy

Case. My giant *Random House Dictionary of the English Language* used to sit on a bookshelf. I used it a couple of times a month. Then I moved it to a hall table that I pass a dozen times a day. Now I use the dictionary at least once a day.

Case. We kept our bikes in the garage at our seaside home. We went bike riding every two or three days. Then we moved the bikes outside, next to the back door. Now we go riding a couple of times a day.

These two vignettes tell you most of what you need to know about life. Honest.

I call it the "bump-into factor."

Want your 20 employees to become more "business mind-ed"? Start by giving all of them subscriptions, sent to their homes, to *Inc.*, *Fortune*, and *Success*. They won't be able to help themselves: They'll thumb though them — and read more and more as time passes.

Want to increase customer-service consciousness? Forget barking orders. Or issuing a "Customers First" vision statement (plasticized, of course). Instead:

■ Prominently post customer-service statistics all over the place.

■ Distribute *all* good and bad customer letters to *everyone*. (Do mark over any offending employees' names in the latter — public humiliation is hardly the point.)

■ Plaster pictures of customers (buyers, products, facilities, etc.) all over the walls.

■ Invite customers to visit any facility, any time; urge salespeople to bring customers through the plant, distribution center, accounting office.

■ Start making weekly awards for "little" acts of customer heroism.

■ Use a customer-service story (good or bad — 90 percent good) as the lead story in *every* company/department newsletter.

■ Hold an all-hands, half-hour "wins and losses" meeting on new orders and lost orders every Thursday at 8 A.M.

The list could include 100 more items. The idea is dictionary in the hall, bikes by the door: Make it impossible for people not to trip over customer "stuff" several times a day. That's the essence of long-term attitude change.

The psychologists (at least the ones I respect) agree: Behavior changes attitude, not the reverse. That is, if employees are inundated with practical customer information rather than vague exhortations, they won't be able to keep their distance. They'll begin to "think customer" — and, maybe, even start to dream about customers.

(Incidentally, honcho, begin by playing this trick on yourself. To get yourself more quality-, service-, innovation-, whatever-conscious, put pertinent material in places where you walk past it — or find it on your screen — 10 times a day.)

47

TGI Friday's wants pizzazz to mark its restaurant-pubs. How do you recruit pizzazz? Easy: You look for pizzazz.

When Friday's was about to open in London, it had job applicants, in small groups, go off and create an improvisational skit
— and then perform it in front of Friday's personnel and fellow
job candidates.

Lessons: (1) You get what you ask for. **(2)** Nice.

48 The Lesson of a Lifetime

"A minute with the CEO is worth a month with the guy or gal
two levels down." That's the conventional wisdom. And there is
some truth to it.

But not much.

I learned a big lesson working in Washington 20 years ago.
"Somehow, find a way to get through the Praetorian Guard and
to the congressman, even if it's only for 30 seconds" — that's
what I was told and taught.

Sometimes I did get through, get my 30 seconds, or even a
minute. It was heady, but usually not that productive. He (she,
very rarely those days) was invariably dis-
tracted. . . . And then there was that glazed
look in the eyes.

Mostly by accident I figured something else
out: The congressman/woman was going to
vote on my issue (not at the top of the national
agenda) based mostly on the advice of a
junior, 26-year-old aide who would brief the
Big Guy/Gal at the right moment.

I also learned that I could easily get a half
hour, not just 30 seconds, with that hungry-
for-information aide; and that if I shot straight,

> I've paid most
> of my precious
> attention to
> the people with
> access to the
> people who
> actually move
> the ball down
> the field.

didn't overplay my hand, and had something to say, she or he
would usually pay close attention.

From those days onward I've paid most of my precious attention (time is all we have) to the people with access to the people
who actually move the ball down the field.

Take a situation with a joint-venture partner. I'm boss of my
outfit. He's boss of his. We get along swimmingly, like and

respect one another. We return each other's phone calls promptly. (In this case, I really do.)

Still . . . I took the time to get to know, as pal and professional, one of his chief line operatives — the fellow most intimately engaged with our venture on a day-to-day basis. Over time, I got this "real" person fired up as the devil about our group's work together. And as I did so, things really started popping.

It was a lesson well worth relearning. Now that I'm the big cheese (relatively speaking), it's easy to deal "top to top" — but not necessarily all that valuable.

Invest in players with day-to-day responsibilities for the nitty-gritty, invest in the junior aide who will tell the politico, as she heads for the House floor to cast her ballot, "Vote 'yeah' on the Peters bill." Your ego might not get stroked as much this way, but your record for implementation will likely soar.

49 It's Only the Most Important Force in the World

The annual August Perseid meteor shower got me to thinking about stargazing. About Ursa Major and Ursa Minor, Cassiopeia and Orion. And man's unslakable need to know. To create meaning, often from whole cloth, whenever confronted with the incomprehensible.

The Greeks knew little of the way their world worked by the standards of Copernicus or Newton, let alone Einstein. Yet they developed a system of meaning as finely articulated as any you'll find in a modern quantum mechanics text.

Keeping customers informed may be the premier element of good service.

The translation to everyday life is clear. When confronted with anything unusual, from a new ache or pain to a new boss, we try to build a theory of how things are going to work out. And, says experience and psychological research, the less we know for sure, the more complex the webs of meaning (mythology) we spin.

The business lesson is obvious. Keeping customers informed may be the premier element of good service. Explain the delay and update your explanation — even if you have nothing new to say — every three or four minutes. Estimate the waiting time for the theme-park ride, the customer-service rep, or the bank teller (Disney, Microsoft, and First Chicago, respectively, are great at doing this).

What works for customers also works for employees: Discuss in excruciating detail with them the new unpaid leave policy, the new health plan, the meaning of the big customer we lost (or gained) last week, the announcement of a new chain-store competitor opening a block away six months hence. You don't have to have all the answers. (Or even *any* for-sure answers.) Just making the effort to discuss things openly, vigorously, and repeatedly is itself a good thing to do.

The idea of "keeping people informed" (customers, suppliers, franchisees, employees, bankers, securities analysts) is hardly novel. My point is that the issue is of overarching significance, that it is tied directly to perhaps the primary human psychological drive: to achieve the perception of control through information and explanation.

Does it seem absurd to assert flatly that NOTHING is more important than keeping people informed? There's plenty of good research to bolster my contention. What an opportunity we waste by keeping folks in the dark, or irregularly informed!

50 The Wrong Stuff

Why do we always emphasize the wrong stuff? During the two years I spent getting an MBA at Stanford in the early 1970s, I probably crunched a million numbers. (It certainly felt that way.) But I never had 30 seconds' worth of counsel about interviewing techniques.

My subsequent experience as a management consultant leads me to conclude that lots of people can crunch numbers and do problem analysis effectively. Damn few, however, are excellent interviewers — the Mike Wallaces, you might say, of the business world.

I'll be blunt: For youthful analysts in finance and for VPs of marketing alike, little (nothing?!) is of greater importance than interviewing skills. Who cares how good your analytical skills are if the information you're analyzing is skimpy or misleading?

Second-rate interviewers follow a checklist of questions (hey, it's a start) but rarely burrow beneath the surface. They pride themselves on the number of interviews "completed" in a day or a week. (Some idiots I worked with at McKinsey bragged about doing a half-dozen interviews in a day.)

Interviewer divas have that solid checklist, too, but mostly they follow their noses. Two interviews a day that yield paydirt (a real surprise, for instance) are incredible output to this bunch. The top questioners leave an interview encounter looking as wrung out as if they'd played all 48 minutes in a tight National Basketball Association game.

My point here is not to offer tips for interviewing (though offering tips is a good idea), but to suggest that interviewing is a phenomenally important activity; and that, as with golf, tennis, or differential equations, we can get better at doing it if we take it seriously and work incessantly at honing our skills.

51 Digging Tools

OK, OK. Offering some interviewing tips *is* a good idea. Hence these, culled from 25 years of interviewing and, more important, watching superb interviewers at work (e.g., a former 60 Minutes director I worked with on several PBS television shows):

■ Don't overschedule. I repeat, this isn't a horse race. Three solid interviews of an hour or more duration are a hell of a day's workout. If all your senses are really tuned into the person on the other side of the table, you'll be exhausted by a single interview, let alone three.

■ Save the Big Guy/Gal till last. Don't start by interviewing the CEO. She (or he) is likely to be impatient, and you don't know a damn thing yet. Save your most important interviews for a time when you know the lay of the land.

■ Find a comfy setting. The more pleasant, casual, and neutral the setting, the better. The worst: Your chair on the far side of his desk. The best: It varies, but winners include a two-hour walk along the beach or a plain, cozy room with a few arm-chairs, a chalkboard, a coffee machine, and refrigerator with Cokes and tomato juice — and no phone.

■ Try small talk (maybe). I favor chatting a bit about last night's ballgame, loosening up the interviewee (not to mention myself); mostly it works. But there are two caveats: If you are lousy at small talk, don't try to fake it. Also, there are a lot of execs who abhor small talk (I'm convinced it's part of their self-constructed persona; but no matter the reason, they hate it); get a quick take on your subject, and if she's the "Let's get down to business" sort, well, let's get down to business.

■ Prepare. Read everything you can, for example. (But try to avoid preconceptions — you're there to be surprised, not con-firmed in your speculative beliefs.) Go into the interview with three or four pages of questions, from the general to the specific. Will you get through such an imposing list? Heaven forbid! But it will give you a sense of security, guide you — and, no small thing, give the impression that you are prepared. Most folks you interview are busy (or think they are), and "Let's just chat about the weather" may send a very bad opening signal. (And open-ings are all there are. . . .)

■ **"Please give me an example."** These are the five most important words in the interviewer's arsenal, and they can't be used enough. There is nothing worse than walking out of an interview and finding an extraordinary comment in your notes — for which there is not a shred of supporting evidence.

When she says, "We've experienced some problems with cus-tomer service lately," that should *automatically* trigger a whole line of questioning: "Give me a corroborating example from something that's happened within the last 72 hours." "Who else can I talk to to get the details on that?" "Would you mind if I called the offended customer?"

MOST OF THE PURPOSE OF AN INTERVIEW IS TO GATHER STORIES — PRACTICAL ILLUSTRATIONS OF PRECISELY HOW THINGS WORK (OR DON'T). MEASURE YOUR EFFECTIVENESS BY THE NUMBER OF "SAGAS" THE INTERVIEW PRODUCES.

■ Think small. It's the details you are after. "Walk me through the process, please." "Here, let's sketch it on the chalkboard." (Now you see why I want a chalkboard in the room.) "No, try it on me again. . . . At this point purchasing gets involved, right? . . . But what *level* in the engineering organization does the requisition go to? . . . Can you show me the *exact* form they use? . . . You really mean they actually don't fly it by operations at that point?"

■ Get to the front line. The devil is in the details, and the details are usually at the front line. I know a lot of consultants and marketing staffers who from one year to the next don't conduct front-line interviews. (Or customer interviews. Or supplier interviews.) DON'T MEASURE YOUR INTERVIEW EFFECTIVENESS BY THE SENIORITY OF THOSE YOU'VE TALKED WITH. MEASURE IT BY JUNIOR-ITY.

■ Don't stop burrowing until you understand. The best interviewers ask the dumbest questions. In any interview, you are, by definition, a foreigner: You don't understand the lingo, the culture, the details. When something isn't clear (and it rarely is at first), go back over it and over it and over it — until you get it straight. REMEMBER, YOU'RE BEING PAID TO ASK STUPID QUESTIONS.

■ Forget generalizations. "Our products are blah." "We have screwups with quality on a regular basis." "Engineering doesn't talk to purchasing." These are important conclusions, but they are suspect, to say the least, until you've got hard evidence. Interviews are for evidence-gathering.

■ Seek out "the way we do things around here." Yes, I've just panned generalizations. But at the *end* of an interview, it can be helpful to get the interviewee to write down (better than talk about) 10 statements that characterize the corporate culture —

i.e., what's most/least important. In a related vein, you might bring your best cut, culled from previous interviews, of 10 such descriptive statements ("Spare no expense when it comes to customer service"; "Engineering wins all debates"; etc.) — and have the interviewee react to them, even score them on a 10-point, agree-to-disagree scale.

■ "Take me through yesterday." You are usually trying to figure out how the place works. What better example than yesterday? How, exactly, did the interviewee spend the day? This one's a no-brainer (assuming yesterday wasn't a vacation day): It invariably uncovers leads worth chasing.

■ Don't let your notes age. Schedule time immediately following the interview to (1) collect your thoughts (instantly write down a half-dozen impressions; they will never be more pure than this) and (2) make a first pass through your notes, to fill in holes while your memory is fresh. (You should always ask the interviewee for a time, tomorrow, when you can call her back for 10 minutes to clarify points that you find confusing upon reflection.)

■ Practice (and observation) makes better. Tag along on interviews with great interviewers in your firm; try not to focus on the content (that's hard to do), but on how the interviewer is playing her hand. Likewise, assess your own performance each day, after your two or three interviews: What did you miss? Fail to follow up on? How could you have gotten out of there with so few concrete illustrations? Etc.

FINAL WORD: FEW THINGS SET ME OFF FASTER THAN REVIEWING SOMEBODY'S INTERVIEW NOTES AND FINDING A DEARTH OF "EVIDENCE" — CONCRETE EXAMPLES AND MINUTE DETAILS THAT ILLUSTRATE THE "BIG" POINT.

52 Do-It-Themselves Strategy Sessions

On October 21, 1993, $300 million Rockport Co. (a Reebok subsidiary) shut down entirely to conduct an all-hands strategy retreat. Bold, eh? Now add in the fact that there was no agenda for the "open space" meeting, as consultant/guru Harrison Owen calls it.

All the Rockport employees gathered in a warehouse. They sat in a circle. Owen, as reported by Professor Srikumar Rao in an article called "Welcome to Open Space" in *Training* magazine, stepped into the center of the circle and told them, in effect, to invent their own meeting:

> One by one, each person who wished to do so would step into the center of the circle. He would announce his name and a topic about which he felt passionate — passionate enough, at least, to take responsibility for convening a break-out session. He would then write the topic on a large sheet of paper and stick it to the wall with masking tape. On it he would post a sticker . . . indicating what time the group would meet and where.
>
> This would continue until nobody had any additional items to post. Then the "marketplace" would open. Everybody would examine the wall, which became a "community bulletin board," and sign up for as many issues as desired. Participants who posted issues would be responsible for convening groups, facilitating discussion, and recording minutes of the proceedings on one of the dozen or so computers set up for the purpose.

The event, Owen added, would be guided by four Zen-like principles:

> *Whoever comes is the right people.*
> *Whatever happens is the only thing that could have.*
> *Whenever it starts is the right time.*
> *When it's over, it's over.*

There was also, Rao reports, "a large poster with a crude, hand-drawn depiction of two footprints with the heading, 'The Law of Two Feet.' That illustrated the voluntary nature of participation. If anyone was bored, not learning anything or felt she had nothing to contribute, then she was honor-bound to use her two feet to walk away."

After a few, seemingly endless moments of shuffling, one Rockport employee tentatively stepped forward. An hour later, Rao recalls, "An energized group had posted dozens of issues on the wall: distribution, on-time delivery, customer service, excess raw material." The upshot: The meeting, which encompassed some 66 sessions with 5 to 150 participants each, was a smashing success, according to even the most ardent skeptics (and there had been more than a few); and follow-up led to practical actions as well as a major (and positive) shift in overall attitude.

The bottom line: Do-it-themselves beats do-it-for- (to-) them, regardless of the topic. Got the nerve to try this for your next all-hands strategy session? ☜ **THINK ABOUT IT!**
(You do have all-hands strategy sessions, don't you?)

53

To run a new-fangled virtual organization (or an old-fangled one, like a consultancy where 80 percent of the consultants are on the road at any point), is hard work.

That is, you've got to talk, a lot, about what you're up to — i.e., "What's important around here (and what isn't)." Then you've got to keep talking. And talking.

Considering telecommuting, computer industry guru Patricia Seybold puts it this way: "If you can succeed in creating a shared mental model of your work together, you'll be successful in bridging the obstacles of telecommuting."

Shared mental model. I like that. Translation: Talk, talk, talk . . .

54 A Thirst for Change

Change is a pain. As I write, the powers that be are fixing a road between my home and office. That means I have to detour, and I've been taking the same route for 10 years. The detour really upsets me.

That detour is peanuts compared to the introduction of self-managing teams or a new performance-evaluation scheme. Still, it illustrates how the smallest disruptions can irritate in a big-league way.

Lesson: We all need constancy in our lives. Wise managers spend a lot of their time helping employees find new constancy in the midst of perpetually stormy commercial seas. (Which describes most every commercial sea, these days.)

But that's not the end of my little screed. Most people would stop here: (1) Change is a pain. (2) Help people cope.

That is *exactly* one-half of the story. A ton (literally, probably) of solid psychological research says that we humans need stability . . . and equally we need stimulation. The change-is-a-pain activists ("They don't want it," "They can't handle it," etc., etc.) ignore the other half.

Did you return to the same vacation spot this summer as last? Did you go to the same restaurant last Friday as the Friday before? Did you re-read John Grisham's *The Firm* instead of getting a new book for your last plane ride? See my point? In tiny ways (those I just listed) and much bigger ones (new project, new hobby, new night-school course, new job searches), we seek stimulation while we also value stability.

Messages: *Don't* treat change with kid gloves. *Don't* assume that "they" (or you) can't cope with it. *Do* realize change is as normal as breathing, and that we want *lots* of it (along with *lots* of constancy).

55

Hollywood's powers-that-be went into collective shock a few months back when they opened *Daily Variety* and saw that the highest-grossing picture of the week was an independently produced, $2 million-budget British film called *Four Weddings and a Funeral*. Sure, it was soon knocked from its perch by Hollywood's latest

$40 million-budget action juggernaut, but it has gone on to gross a highly respectable — and highly profitable — $50 million. (A $40 million picture, by contrast, doesn't even hit black until its gross reaches $80 million.) What propelled this quirky romantic comedy to the top of Hollywood's notoriously greasy pole? The same thing that has made stars of quirky little products (and conventional big products) since time immemorial, the greatest advertising medium there is — word of mouth.

One satisfied customer's telling a friend, an acquaintance, a cousin, a bus driver, a total stranger how happy he is with your product or service is worth its weight in gold (or five times its weight in advertising dollars). An associate of mine is fond of recounting what he considers the ultimate word-of-mouth experience. Some years back, he was sitting in an airport minding his own business when a woman a few seats down turned to him and pressed her copy of *The Exorcist* into his hand. "I just finished this. My heart is pounding. You've got to read it." He knew right then and there that Mr. Blatty had written one heck of a book.

How do you generate word of mouth? Excellence, of course. First, last, and every place in between. But, say you've got your excellent product or service — is there some way to stimulate that priceless good word? Yes. If you really believe in that product, put your money where your faith is. Give it away. That's right, let people try it for free. Whether it's salad dressing, software, or Saturn, offer tastings, tryouts, and test drives. First, no one can be happy with your product until they've tried it. Second, you'll convey your passion about the product. Remember, passion is contagious — spread from person-to-person, mouth-to-mouth.

56

There are two bookstore salespersons. Joe Doaks. Jane Blivens. A customer comes to Joe's register to check out. "Hey, I saw the book *Ike and Monty: Generals at War* on your shelf," he says. "I'm reading it. It's really great." Joe looks at him glassily, keeps working the register, and mutters, "Uh huh" in total and final acknowledgment.

Jane Blivens is at the register. Same customer. Same line, *Ike and Monty*, etc. Jane responds, "That's great. What did you like about it?" The customer gives a 45-second description, completes the transaction, and leaves.

What has Jane done? She's lit up the customer by paying attention. At least as important, she's picked up some valuable intelligence. When a customer comes in looking for a good, new nonfiction book (perhaps an older male, into World War II and war in general), she's got a lead, "Well, one of our customers just told me he liked . . ."

And Joe? I suppose he responds to the second customer with another of his trademark grunts.

This story is aimed at retailers (hire the Jane clones, fire the Joe look-alikes; encourage clerks to be chatty, not officious, distracted automatons). And aimed at could-be Joes and could-be Janes: Regardless of the company rules and regulations, you have enormous power, on your own, to grow — or shrivel.

Incidentally, the Joe half of the story (though I don't know the guy's name) recently happened to me in the Chartwell bookstore at 52nd between Madison and Park in Manhattan. I don't intend to go back.

57

Q. No way will my company ever install any form of profit-sharing. And why should we? Can't workers be satisfied with a fair day's pay for a fair day's work?

A. Workers cannot and should not be satisfied with a "fair" day's pay, because there is no such thing as a "fair" day's work. Every day is a challenge; we must constantly cope with machines that break, colleagues who are out sick or distracted by a breakfast table fight, unexpected deadlines. Nobody goes home thinking he or she did a "fair" day's work. Instead, egocentric as we humans all are, we think of the hassles we had to confront and the "unfair" burdens that seemingly fell on our shoulders today. Without constant positive feedback, access to continuing training, *and* various team and individual incentive schemes, we consign ourselves to getting mediocre results — not the routine "above and beyond the call of duty" that's necessary if a product or service is going to stick out in an increasingly crowded global marketplace.

58

Where would you expect greater loyalty? At Real Corp.? Or Virtual Corp.? No contest, says a friend in the movie business. Virtual Corp. is the hands-down winner

If an independent contractor (cameraman or gaffer or make-up person) fails to show for 5:30 A.M. crew call, it's safe to say, says my friend, that "She'll never work in this town again." Word-of-mouth reputation and "You're as good as your last assignment" is the alpha, omega, and all stops in between for the Virtual Corp.'s independent contractor.

It's also safe to say that that's a lot more accountability than you'll generally find with an on-the-payroll employee of Real Corp.

Whence springs loyalty? To whose back does the monkey of accountability cling most tightly?

59

"Reward excellent failures. Punish mediocre successes."

Advice from Phil Daniels
seminar participant
Sydney, Australia, July 28, 1994

60

"Control is an illusion, you infantile egomaniac. Nobody controls anything."

Nicole Kidman to Tom Cruise
in Days of Thunder

61

Reflections upon the excesses of the go-go '80s have had the effect of turning business ethics into a hot topic — as it should be. Unfortunately, this heightened ethical awareness has in turn created a spate of mindless "do good, be good" writings and speeches. Dealing with ethics ain't quite that simple. Having accepted an invitation to speak on the topic at a University of Virginia business school conference, I had no choice but to grapple with it — over many a restless night. The following observations are one byproduct of the tossing and turning:

■ Ethics is not principally about headline issues — responding to the Tylenol poisoning or handling insider information. Ethical concerns surround us all the time, on parade whenever we deal with people. How we work out the "little stuff" will determine our response, if called upon, to a Tylenol-size crisis. When disaster strikes, it's far too late to seek out ethical touchstones.

■ High ethical standards — business or otherwise — are, above all, about treating people decently. To me that means respect for a person's opinions, privacy, background, dignity, and natural desire to grow.

■ Diversity must be honored. To be sure, it is important to be clear about your own compass heading; but don't ever forget that other people have profoundly different — and equally decent — ethical guidance mechanisms.

■ People, even the saints, are egocentric and selfish; we were designed "wrong" from the start. Any ethical framework must take into account man's (and woman's) inherently flawed character.

■ Corporations are created and exist to serve people — insiders and outsiders. Period.

■ By their very nature, organizations run roughshod over individuals. They produce powerlessness and humiliation for most participants with more skill than they produce widgets.

■ Though all men and women are created equal, some surely have more power than others. Thus, a central ethical issue in the workplace (and beyond) is protection and support for the unempowered — especially the frontline worker and the customer.

■ For employees and managers alike, fighting the impersonal "they" (every bureaucratic institution) is almost always justified on ethical grounds.

■ While one can point to ethically superior (and profitable) firms, such as Herman Miller, most of us work in less-principled organizations. Dealing with "office politics" is a perpetual ethical morass. A "pure" ethical stance will lead you out the door in short order. The line between high ethical standards and a holier-than-thou stance is a fine one.

■ Though I sing the praises of an "action bias," ethical behavior demands that we tread softly in all of our affairs. Unintended consequences and the secondary effects of most actions far outnumber intended and first-order effects.

■ The pursuit of high ethical standards might be served well by the elimination of many business schools. The implicit thrust of most MBA programs is that great systems and great techniques win out over great people.

■ Can we live up to the spirit of the Bill of Rights in our workplaces? Can ethics and profits coincide on a routine basis? One would hope that the answer is yes, although respect for the individual has hardly been the cornerstone of American industry.

■ Each of us is ultimately lonely. In the end, it's up to each of us alone to figure out who we are, who we are not, and to act more or less consistently with those conclusions.

In my view, anyone who is not very confused all the time about ethical issues is out of touch with the frightful (and joyous) richness of the world. But at least being confused means that we are considering our ethical stance and that of the institutions we associate with.

That's a good start.

62 Butt Out, Mate!

Q: What's your reaction to the widespread use of drug testing as a condition of employment and random drug testing as a condition of continued employment?

A: Utter, unadulterated rubbish! Am I for spaced-out (booze, drugs) employees disrupting others and creating safety hazards in the workplace? Don't be absurd. Of course I'm not. But that puts the cart way before the horse.

Put aside productivity problems and safety issues. Let's talk about what makes any business tick: Super folks who trust one another, care about one another, and are committed to working hard together to create great outcomes for each other — and their customers.

Trust. Respect. Commitment. Mutual support. Each is wholly at odds with intrusive, impersonal assessment measures. That is, drug tests. (And, to my mind, canned psychological-assessment tests; and secret snooping on telemarketers et al.; and, heaven knows, lie detector tests.)

Start at the beginning. Your recruiting process should say to the candidate, "How'd you like to be part of our community, do neat things together, grow individually and with your peers?" Hence recruiting becomes a painstaking, two-way courting ritual, complete with coffee dates, flirting, weekend strolls, dinner with the parents, proposals on bended knee, and an exchange of solemn vows of fidelity. That is, *lots* of folks, including would-be peers (a must!), should spend *lots* of time with janitorial and senior-engineering prospects alike — in a variety of settings over several days, or weeks. In the process, there is little doubt — based on my 30 years of experience and observation — that the habitual substance abusers, malcontents, deadbeats, and ne'er-do-wells will be rooted out.

Is my recruiting model expensive? Yep. But what's more important than recruiting? Recruiting *is* strategy — though all too few firms, large or small, play it that way.

What holds in hiring obviously holds 10 times over after arrival on the scene: "Welcome aboard. Let's work to create something special. To care for one another. To cuddle our customers. And, incidentally, be prepared, upon demand, to take a monitored whiz in a bottle, slimeball."

No, that doesn't cut it.

What *does* cut it, once Ms. or Mr. New is aboard, is delivering on your promise of a trusting and nurturing environment. *And* sky-high expectations about performance and accountability. In such settings, the best "enforcers" by far are demanding coach-mentor-peers. And such peers, in my experience, are merciless toward those who violate the trust. (They don't want others screwing up their good deal.)

The answer I've given so far is clinical. Let me be more personal:

❶ I'm a Bill of Rights freak — and a privacy freak. A line in the anti-Vietnam War musical *Hair* goes: "I'm not dyin' for no white man." My equivalent, in this case: "I'm not pissing in a bottle for no corporate cop." It's how I feel personally — and, by extension, as a business owner/leader.

❷ I run a company with about 25 employees. They are wonderful people. (That's why we hired them!) I would no more consider submitting them to drug tests as a condition of employment than I would try to fly to the moon without a rocket. I am disgusted by the very idea at "my place" — and *yours*.

"But your place isn't some fast-food franchise with a bunch of poorly raised kids as employees," you rejoin. Maybe not. I suppose we've got more degreed and multi-degreed folks than the average fast-food place. But what's that got to do with the price of fries? If I owned a fast-food franchise, I'd take the same approach I do now. I'd only want neat folks on board — age 17 or 67. And I'd be out to build an environment of trust and respect — as much as in my own professional-service company.

"But what if you owned *twenty* franchises?" So what? If I owned 200, my top priority would be the folks who manage them. I'd want all 200 to be nifty folks I'd get a kick out of being around. I'd get directly involved in their hiring; and I'd make damned sure my People Department (that's what Southwest Airlines calls its human-resources activity) got the point: Hire neat people you like, we can train the burgers part.

No, I'm not pissing in no bottle. And nobody who works for me is going to be forced to do so either. And if there were a law that required me to ask them to do it, I'd close my place down before I'd comply.

If you want an environment of trust, care, compassion — which is the only kind of environment that will lead to trust, care, and compassion for customers — then stay the hell out of people's personal lives!

63

"Reward people based on accomplishment, rather than on being a model employee. People . . . do some of their best work away from the desk. . . . Dullness is the just reward of people who work all day and never take serious breaks."

David Kelley
IDEO

64

Add 10 "differentiators" to every product or service every 60 days. Little improvements. Things the customer might not even notice. A more comfortable chair for your receptionist or seat for your bus driver. A little thank-you note that goes into every order you send out. A rewritten section in an instruc-tion manual. Details count! Does 10 every 60 days sound impossible? It isn't. Tough? It is. But what's the option? Your competitors aren't sitting still.

65

Never hire Mr. (or Ms.) Right! His résumé is impeccable. He strides into his interview brimming with confidence. He reels off all the right answers. He fits perfectly. But wait — this is a highly imperfect world. People who live by the book die by the book.

Look instead for Ms. Slightly-off-the-Wall. Someone who can respond to and thrive amid chaos, who can mutate to meet the demands of the hour (or minute). Look for the offbeat credential, the gap in the résumé for the two years she was off climbing mountains in Tibet or teaching kids to read in rural Texas.

Look for a mischievous glint in her eye. Consider what Carl Sewell, the brilliant and wildly successful car dealer, calls the "fidget factor." Carl says he only hires folks who fidget during their interview. He wants that kind of uncontainable energy coursing through his company's veins. And so do you!

66   100 Days a Year

The number one leadership skill is the ability to develop others. That's not a new idea. But, boss, check your calendar: How much time are you devoting *directly* to people-development? One colleague at Apple Computer formally dedicates 100 days a year to what, with a smile, he calls "performance reviews." Twenty-five people report to him, and twice a year they spend two days, one on one, reviewing where they've been together and where they're going next. Talk about putting your calendar where your mouth is!

67

I'm disposed to incrementalism: The 1,000-mile journey begins with a single step, and all that good (and usually true) stuff. But if you're a bloated behemoth struggling to catch up with sprinting hares, you simply don't have time to take things slowly. The world is running on HST — hare standard time.

Recent history suggests corporations must reorganize pretty much all at once. The times are revolutionary. Mincing steps forward dissipate energy and engender suspicion in the hearts and minds of thousands. (They: "This is absolutely, positively the very last layoff." We: "Until they announce the next one; this is the fifth 'absolutely, positively' . . .")

68 DIS-abled? Baloney!

It's all a matter of attitude. Ho hum, bet you've heard that one before.

But it is! One person's nightmare is another's golden opportunity. Take the spirit of the Americans with Disabilities Act. What if . . .

What if we saw hiring the disabled as a success secret? A way to bamboozle the competition? That's what unfolded at $2 million Carolina Fine Snacks when Phil Kosak first hired a disabled worker.

During the 1980s, Kosak and his partners, Ray Lander and Craig Bair, faced 80 percent employee turnover every six months. The company never exceeded $500,000 in annual revenues.

In 1989, Kosak was asked by the State Department of Rehabilitation to attend a job fair that placed handicapped adults in the workforce. There he met David Bruton, who suffers from a severe learning disability. "I was impressed by his jovial attitude," Kosak remembers. "David was honest, sincere, and really wanted to work."

Kosak hired Bruton on the spot as a packer and shipper. "Not only could David do his job, he blew circles around the other workers," Kosak claims.

Bruton has been promoted twice and currently works as production assistant in charge of shipping. "Being the first handicapped person was a great challenge to me — I have a lot of responsibility," he told us.

When we visited, eight out of 16 CFS employees were disabled. Their handicaps range from severe learning disabilities to cerebral palsy to deafness. Kosak hasn't had to make any physical changes in the plant; company insurance costs have remained the same; and all employees get the same benefits.

Janice Griffin-McKenzie is an able-bodied worker who witnessed the growth of the company's disabled workforce. A former packer who currently works as a machine operator, she helped new hires learn the business. Though some workers were reluctant at first to teach disabled workers, most were happy to give the handicapped a chance to succeed, she says.

"Now we all have a good relationship with each other," she reports. "We can always count on them — they're never late and always show up for work. Their jobs give them great self-esteem."

To reduce the stress that some disabled workers feel in unfamiliar surroundings, CFS holds weekly staff meetings that educate workers about different jobs at the plant. Employees also have direct contact with clients, who are brought to the plant for guided tours. The personnel manager even learned sign language to make things easier for the hearing impaired.

Overall production has increased to 95 percent of capacity from 60 percent in 1989. Employee turnover has shrunk to a mere 5 percent.

"These folks have changed everybody's life," Kosak says. "Everyone here works hard as part of a team. The twist of fate that led us to hiring David really helped us create an atmosphere of pride and excellence."

69

"To learn, fail. . . . If nothing ever breaks, you don't really know how strong it is. Strike out fear of failure. . . . Reward success and failure equally — punish inactivity."

David Kelley
IDEO

70

"Education, technology and entrepreneurship are the three great creators of wealth in the modern economy."

Brian Quinn
Tuck School, Dartmouth

71

Support your community colleges! They are the unsung, under-funded backbone of America's all-important lifelong-learning network.

PENS, TOILETS, AND BUSINESSES THAT DO IT DIFFERENTLY

72   The Pentels of London

Good design is an Armani suit, a Lexus, or the exotic items you find in a J. Peterman catalog. No doubt about it. And I, for one (among many), appreciate it.

But good design is at least as much — from a commercial and aesthetic point of view — about everyday items.

There's a whole corner (or at least a corner of a corner) of the Jay Baker True Value Hardware in Gualala, California, devoted to Rubbermaid items. They look great, work great — and a lot of them can be yours for less than $5.

Ever put a salad in the fridge, and when you try to eat it the next day find that it's hopelessly soggy? Well Rubbermaid can't change the laws of physics — or maybe it can. The circular storage bowl I purchased last week has a little disk, with 1/4-inch legs, that fits in the bottom. The dressing collects beneath the disk — and the salad is (almost) as good as new the next day.

I love it. An honest-to-gosh better mousetrap!

Incidentally, I was first attracted to Rubbermaid by the "trivial" fact that you could readily peel the labels off the outside of its bowls. (Haven't you seemingly — seemingly, hell! — spent hours of your life scraping labels off items you've just purchased? What a waste!)

Occasionally I'll tell my wife: "Time to make another trip to London. My last Pentel ran dry." I mean it as a joke, but not quite. I love the Ball Pentel Fine Point R50 pens (I'm writing this with one — yes, I still do first drafts longhand); I love (there's that word again) the look, feel, ink flow. And I buy mine at Rymans shops in London — can't find them in the U.S. for the life of me.

Design can transform (big word, trans-*form*) any item, 25 cents or $25,000 a copy. Sadly, few laundromat operators or pen manufacturers seem to understand that. If you think design is the province of Armani and Bang & Olufsen, you're blowing what may be the No 1 opportunity to differentiate your (mundane) product or service.

Sorry, got to run . . . hang a few pictures. Ah, the *feel* of my Stanley Contractor-Grade Graphite hammer!

73 Export Stars

Winners for tomorrow? Export stars? Biotech? Software? Financial services?

How about pallet-racking systems for warehouses?

Why not? says Spacerack Systems Pty. Ltd., a Brisbane-based enterprise. Four years ago the company broke out of the local market and boldly headed to Southeast Asia. Rapid growth has followed, including major projects in Singapore, Thailand, Malaysia, the Philippines, and Taiwan for companies such as Nippon Paints, Singapore Airways, Bayer Pharmaceuticals, and Coca-Cola.

Spacerack, thanks in part to a partnership with the Civil Engineering Testing Centre at Queensland (Australia) University of Technology, has become the storage industry's innovation-leader and standard-setter. It is now beefing up its local distributors by creating an on-the-ground Asian technical support office. All this is a long-winded way of saying that, with imagination, almost any product or service, from a company of any size, can become a star in even the toughest, most competitive corners of the global marketplace.

74

Your company is wobbly. Market research on a prospective product shows that 40 percent of those surveyed "actively dislike it." And 10 percent "fall in love with it."

Time to cut your losses and bail out? That's what nine out of 10 companies would conclude — and do. But with the strident urging of the design director, Renault decided to ignore the carping 40 percent and cater to the adoring 10 percent.

Almost overnight, the sagging automaker's new Twingo became France's second-bestselling car.

Today's market for damn near everything is filled with look-alike products and services. Winners, I'd judge, will gather their nerve and bet on neat stuff like the Twingo. Go ahead, surprise the customer. OK?

75 Safe Is Risky!

"Today, more stores have gotten safe. Although it sounds contradictory, in Pressman's philosophy, safe is risky. It's risky in that as stores get safer, as they are run purely on the basis of financial decisions as opposed to marketing decisions, they tend to buy the same merchandise, look the same, design the same, and act the same. . . . We must continue to be different."

Bob Pressman,
Co-CEO, Barneys

Mr. Pressman, could you please explain that to about 90 percent — make that 98 percent — of the retailers I talk to?

76 There Are Plumbers, and Then There's DeeeeMarvelous De-Mar

It isn't every plumbing, heating, and air-conditioning company that trains its workers three days a week, offers unlimited income based on commissions, puts them through Dale Carnegie courses, and has a profit-sharing plan — just for starters.

But De-Mar ($3.3 million in revenue, 40 employees) demands a lot in return. Workers, called Service Advisers, are required to conform to the company's grooming code — no long hair, long beards, or long sideburns. "I want them to think like business-people, to understand that their truck is their franchise," says Larry Harmon, president of the Clovis, California, company. "I can't have them go to a little old lady's house at 2 A.M. looking like a Hell's Angel."

■ Wednesday Morning Revival Hour

The 6 A.M. Wednesday training session starts with Harmon shouting, "Can I get an amen!" and the team responding as if at a revival. Indeed, crack-of-dawn Wednesday sessions are aimed at getting over that midweek hump with customers. Transcripts of good phone calls are read, points are awarded, speeches given, housekeeping chores discussed, and the upkeep of uniforms critiqued. Today Harmon shows a video on service and offers $500 or a trip to Las Vegas for the best idea on providing exceptional service.

"Price complaints are value complaints," he declares, explaining that to win with its premium prices, De-Mar must clobber competitors on service. The meeting ends with a worker leading a De-Mar cheer.

ARE YOU SURE THIS ISN'T NEIMAN MARCUS?

■ Tough but Fair

"There's so much peer pressure, there's no need for supervisors, just team leaders," says Randy Newman, a Service Adviser and leader for the heating and air-conditioning team. "One guy totally messed up and I called to straighten it out. I described what I found and everybody jumped on him. If you don't fit in, you're weeded out by everybody. We send people home [for the day] if their truck's not clean. . . . People bawl when we fire them."

In fact, about half of all 1991 hires were fired within the first year. "But we give guys a chance," Newman adds. "The team does counseling. If you have a grievance, you go to a team leader. People speak right up, and we work anything out. One guy broke a rule and we let him go. He came back to appeal and the group took a vote. He got back in."

■ Workers Monitor Themselves

At 8:43 A.M. Newman reaches Job 9, an estimate for a new heating unit. He radios in his arrival time, talks to the customer, climbs onto the rain-slick roof, and later returns to the truck to prepare the estimate. He presents the estimate (an "investment" in De-Mar speak, never a "price") to the customer, explaining the company's five-year guarantee for all parts and service on

NOT JUST ANOTHER PLUMBER

- Guaranteed same-day service
- One-year guarantee on all work
- Price guarantee (quote to the penny, De-Mar eats miscalculations)
- Twenty-four hours a day, seven days a week, 365 days a year (no extra charge during off hours — there are no "off" hours)
- Flat-rate pricing (price book covers 98 percent of work; workers quizzed on it weekly and must score at least 90 percent)
- Gift certificates
- Senior-citizen discounts
- Thank-you cards
- Follow-up phone surveys
- Strict dress codes
- Spotless De-Mar yellow trucks (a special, registered color created for De-Mar by DuPont)
- Two percent of gross revenue on training (including a $10,000 video- and audiotape library)

new units. Newman also leaves him a brochure and discount card (should he decide to have the work done) and heads off.

Meanwhile, in the plumbing unit, Service Adviser Art Fuentes has spent all morning clearing a shower stoppage, ordering a toilet, and installing it in a tight space. It's now 1:05 P.M. and Fuentes sniffles as he steps into the streaming downpour toward his truck. Having worked in the same small bathroom since 8:30 A.M., he still bids his customer a "DeeeMarvelous Day!"

The genuine good cheer derives from entrepreneurial ambitions. Each year all Service Advisers fill out a goal sheet, declaring how much money they want to make, some personal ambition such as buying a house, and 20 ways they plan to reach their financial target. This keeps people focused on the service and courtesy necessary to get repeat business.

"It's a busy life to be a service worker with guaranteed same-day service," Fuentes explains as he calls in the job's end and gets dispatched to another. Fuentes started six months ago, when the schedule was even more hectic. He had come from a top competitor's shop, and feels good about his contribution to De-Mar, which is now beating his old company on service. "When I came here, my sales just skyrocketed," Fuentes says, "because they know if you treat workers right, they'll treat customers right. We don't sell what people don't need."

■ A High-Performance Environment

What's the distinctive treatment Fuentes refers to? "At the other company it was strict and you didn't want to smile," he complains. "They found something to yell about every day. How can you go to your customer's house with a fake smile?" Worst of all, he adds, "The boss would always monitor the radio." At De-Mar, workers value the ability to joke with each other by radio and keep up a friendly banter. "It almost feels like you're not at work," he says. "My dad said he could see the difference in me since I came here. What's unique here is everybody's so open and willing to help you out."

■ The Nuts and Bolts

Service at De-Mar is measured in terms of customer perception — how many good or bad phone calls and letters each worker gets, how often a Service Adviser must redo a botched job or gets a second job because the first went well. Everyone is on a point system based on such criteria, and the three top point-earners reap a 50 percent higher sales commission for the month. The lowest scorers are retrained

SERVICE ADVISER (SA) POINT SYSTEM	
Good phone call about SA	+1,000
Bad phone call	-1,000
Good letter	+2,000
Bad letter	-2,000
Customer requests particular adviser	+1,000
Does not want SA back	-2,000

or let go. A huge chart, prominently posted in the training room, lets each worker see exactly how all the others are doing.

"Each serviceman *is* your company," says Harmon. "They sell, serve, solve problems, and make people feel good about spending $900 to do it. I get goose bumps talking about what we do." (He really does!)

But the focus is on the "feel good" and not the $900. "People don't last long if all they care about is commission," Harmon says.

■ The Glowing Bottom Line

The Service Advisers' dedication produces astounding results. According to market research De-Mar commissioned, 80 percent of Fresno-area residents in 1988 thought of the competition first when they needed plumbing. By 1993, De-Mar, which grew 15-fold in the interim, was the first choice of 84 percent of those asked. Says Harmon, "The key is showing your people they need long-term customers, not short-term dollars."

So do you still think a plumber is a plumber is . . . ? *And* if "it" can be done (differentiation à la Harmon) in plumbing, why not in your 6- or 66,000-person business?

77

Q. Can you comment on management directions for the small accountancy (one to two professionals)?

A. I get irritated when automakers or computer makers tell me how tough it is to compete. I get flat-out angry when any professional-service firm chief says the same thing. (OK, that's not exactly what you said; I've implied that you implied it.)

The idea of professional-service delivery becoming "commoditized" is ludicrous. That's as true for the two-person firm as for the Big Six accountancy. Professional services are inherently personal. They are commodities only if you are a commodity — that is, if you don't have anything special to offer, if you're just another accountant, engineer, trainer, or professional whatever.

Each of us thrives to the extent that we achieve some distinction — an approach to problems, excellence in client relations, tenacity in implementation, all of the above.

My answer has to be blunt: Ask yourself what, on your turf (local or global), is clearly unusual about the services you offer. If your answer — in 25 words or less — isn't convincing to a prospective or past client (or even youself, heaven forbid), you *do* have a problem. And you *don't* get any sympathy from me.

Just can't tell 'em apart (pens, cars, boom boxes, legal services, engineering services). Heard it a hundred times.

I always try to personalize: Can I imagine saying, "Opened a management book today. Couldn't be sure whether it was mine or Peter Drucker's"?

That's the way I hear the Commoditization Blues. And what holds for me *should* hold for McDonald's, Burger King, Wendy's, Sony, GE, and RCA. (Remember De-Mar!)

79 Surprise!

The best always surprises. A play, a software package, an especially courteous bank teller or zany waiter, a football team on a roll, Post-it notes, whatever.

If surprise = success, could we build a SURPRISE FACTORY — i.e., an organization that keeps producing surprises?

If we could, then, scientifically speaking, it would certainly honor the principles of randomness and chance variation. Surprise *is* unpredictability (even in its minor manifestations — e.g., the zany waiter). So to inculcate surprise is to inculcate unpredictability.

To inculcate unpredictability is to honor rule-breaking (all surprises, by definition, break the rules), humor, naps, curiosity, eccentricity. In little ways (frontline service provision) and big (investing in off-center research and development).

To a large extent (entirely?), surprise can't be organized or planned for. To steal a line from management expert Henry Mintzberg, it's about wildflowers growing in abandoned lots, not tightly controlled greenhouses.

(Wildflower fields, unlike greenhouses, mostly have weeds. If you can't tolerate weeds, then you can't be in the surprise business. And if you are a close observer, you also know that scrutinizing an apparently nondescript weed often leads to the discovery of something wonderful — a minuscule flower, a leaf with such delicacy it brings a tear to your eye.)

Think about it: WHAT HAVE YOU DONE IN THE LAST 24 HOURS TO ENCOURAGE THE PARTIAL ANARCHY NEEDED TO NURTURE A SURPRISE FACTORY?

80 Don't take Dweeb for an Answer

David Maister is perhaps the world's premiere student of professional-service firms. He recently surveyed several firms' partners, asking them to assign their clients to one of three categories: "I like these people and their industry interests me," "I can tolerate these people and their business is OK — neither fascinating nor boring," and "I'm professional enough that I would never say this to them, but the truth is they are not my kind of people and I have no interest in their industry."

Those surveyed put about 30 percent of their clients into the "like" category, 50 percent into "tolerate," and 20 percent into "don't care for them."

Maister was appalled. Why, he wondered, spend the majority of your time working with clients who don't do much for you? "I readily conclude that there is boring work for dull clients out there," he told one group," but the question is, why do *you* have to do it?" The common response at his seminars: "But do I have a choice?"

Maister bounced off the wall again. "Of course you do," he insists. In a nutshell, he says, don't let second-rate clients ruin your career and perhaps your life. Reject lousy business (*fire* rotten prospects and clients alike!), position yourself to pursue clients who can make work "fun" (a word Maister readily uses).

My experience leads me to chirp, "Right on" — and, yes, it can be done. So what clients do you plan to can this month?

81

Fire lousy clients. (No kidding.) Don't let them enervate your organization or abuse your employees. David Maister advises it (see above). Legendary adman David Ogilvy bragged of having fired many more clients (that were messing with the minds of his folks) than fired him. British marketing services whiz Gary Withers turns thumbs down on dull, unchallenging business.

There is such a thing as taking (or keeping) business that's not good for the psyche of your company.

82 It Ain't That Hard, Folks

On New Year's Day, 1994, I was staying at the Radisson Hotel in Burlington, Vermont, after attending a friend's 50th birthday party. Wanting to catch the last half of the Orange Bowl, I switched the cable TV in my room to the local NBC station. The reception was unwatchably fuzzy. I called the front desk, and the clerk said she'd send up an engineer.

None came.

Early the next afternoon, I wanted to watch another football game on NBC. Turned on the TV. Same trouble.

I called downstairs, and, after I explained the previous night's snafu and its continuation, the desk clerk apologized. Said she'd send an engineer "right up." By the time I checked out, two hours later, he hadn't made it to the sixth floor.

You've heard such tales before, from me and others. And your own are just as annoying and probably more gory.

So what's the problem? As the late Dr. Deming told us again and again, screwed-up management. And the answer?

"It ain't that hard, folks."

I think I'll throw up the next time I hear Ross Perot say that while he discusses (if that's the right word) an intractable national-policy issue. But he *does* have a point when it comes to managing the average enterprise.

INSTANT CURE

Just show one's face for 10 or 15 minutes . . . and the whole world would have started spinning in the opposite direction.

In fact, that Perotism came to mind while doing emergency Christmas Eve shopping at a Vermont supermarket. The store was jammed, and I quickly gathered my handful of forgotten items, then headed for the express checkouts.

What a mess! The two lines for the two lanes crossed each other at least once, then snaked down an aisle, making shopping all but impossible. People were cutting in front of each other. Tempers flared.

As I stood there, alternately moving toward and then retreating from my distant goal, I wondered, "Where in the hell is the store manager?"

No, it's *not* that hard. I'd *love* the job of managing that store. You could make it over in your own image — no matter what kind of ninnies ran the corporation.

Take my sorry experience. Any store manager with the imagination of a turnip could have turned chaos into carnival. She or he could have taken the floor to play traffic cop/entertainer/talk-show host. The manager could have sorted out the lines, greeted customers *by name* (this ain't Manhattan, after all), helped people in the jammed aisles find an item they're looking for, and perhaps given the cash-register clerks a hand (i.e., bagged for them for a moment or two — and thanked them for keeping their heads while the storm raged around them).

I don't wear rose-colored-glasses, but believe me, this was *not* a problem. It was a golden opportunity. A chance to show one's face — not for hours, but just 10 or 15 minutes, at a critical time, to set the tone for customers and employees alike. The whole world (the part that was in that store, at any rate) would have started spinning in the opposite direction.

(P.S., I related this story and suggestion at a seminar. One attendee suggested that the store manager also lead a Jingle Bells sing-along and pass out mints or candy canes to those in line. I like it, though in this instance I would have been satisfied with far less.)

83

Re-read the above. I repeat: Just a 10- or 15-minute — 900 ticks of the clock, max — effort would literally have launched the entire operation in a brand-new, refreshed direction.

84 Fun in Financial Services

Here's the take on life at New England Securities, where a new president has shaken things up. (Hey, he read a Dr. Seuss story, *Oh the Places You'll Go*, at his first employee meeting.) According to the firm's new written philosophy statement, employees (called associates) are encouraged to:

1. Take risks. Don't play it safe.

2. Make mistakes. Don't try to avoid them.

3. Take initiative. Don't wait for instructions.

4. Spend energy on solutions, not on emotions.

5. Shoot for total quality. Don't shave standards.

6. Break things. Welcome destruction. It's the first step in the creative process.

7. Focus on opportunities, not problems.

8. Experiment.

9. Take personal responsibility for fixing things. Don't blame others for what you don't like.

10. Try easier, not harder.

11. Stay calm!

12. Smile!

13. Have fun!

One employee, Kate Lorinczi, who passed the philosophy statement along, tells us the company is walking the talk. She was ready to quit. Now she's a happy camper. (For the cognescenti, Ms. Lorinczi was the pissed off, anonymous, "Determinedly Seeking the Perfect Job" in *The Tom Peters Seminar*, p. 215.)

Pay attention to the market. Listen to your customers. Spend megabucks collecting customer information, to the point that you can treat even mass-market customers as individual "market segments." Not only are these the trendy ideas of the past decade, but their proponents (myself among them) are getting louder and louder.

Why, then, was I so taken with — and so disturbed by — the story of Milanese clothing and accessories designer Miuccia Prada, profiled by Ingrid Sischy in *The New Yorker?*

There is a distinct difference between doing something "for" the market, and being part "of" the market.

Market research? Intensive data collection? Forget it. Prada climbed to the pinnacle of the fashion world by listening to her inner voice.

"The clothes seemed to have something extra to them — or, rather, *in* them," Sischy writes. "They suggested that someone, not something, had caused them to be." Sischy adds that Prada's "imagination is a huge part of who she is, of how she does her work. . . . Her clothes are driven by her own feelings and by her sharp sense of where we are in the world."

But even Prada has blown it from time to time. "She used conventional, Seventh Avenue solutions," Sischy concludes of Prada's dubious 1989 collection. "The clothes were overdesigned, and it seemed that commercial considerations and self-consciousness, not the usual articulation of her unconscious, were leading her." Prada summed up the pratfall: "I hated all the people around me, and I told them it was the last time others would push me to do what I didn't want."

What does all this add up to? It's what I call the difference between doing something "for" the market, and being part "of" the market. "For" firms depend on data collection and manipulation, detached analysis, elaborate market plans, and planner-designer-marketers versed in the latest B-school techniques. "Of" firms seek out zany employees with out-of-the-ordinary views, nurture a spirit of adventure, cherish instinct and intuition, and dote on things that have never been tried before.

"Fors " doubtless embarass themselves far more often than "ofs." ("Safe is risky" — Bob Pressman, Barneys.) They are also responsible for close to 100 percent of all great leaps forward. So which are you?

86 The Rearview Mirror Faces the Rear

"European Union leaders should concentrate on leading, not on following every shift in public opinion."

Financial Times (June 15, 1994)

Amen. For European Union leaders and American presidents. And marketing executives at 20- and 200,000-person companies.

Would you agree that as market research becomes ever more prevalent, so do copycat products (and uninspiring leaders)?

Competitive businesses must *lead* their customers. The prospective buyer can't tell you what she likes until she has used it and lived with it. "The customer," says George Colony of Forrester Research, "is a rearview mirror, not a guide to the future."

Right on.

87 1,000 Little Things. . .

Design tip for hotels. A lot of your guests are over 45 (me, for one). Most people over 45 are far-sighted (me, for one). Many people, of any age, who wear glasses don't wear their glasses in the bathroom (me, for one). Most hotel shampoo containers have the word shampoo in fine print. *Some* hotel guests *regularly* attempt to shampoo their hair with bath salts, hair conditioner and other strange fluids offered gratis by the hotel (me, for one).

Advice: Use big print on shampoo bottles.

Bigger message: Little things like this add up . . . and up and up and up.

88

More on packaging! I nearly stopped and bought a can of maple syrup on Labor Day. The little roadside table, south of Stowe, Vermont, was so enticing.

How stupid! I own hundreds of acres of sugar bush in Southern Vermont, boil sap — and have cases of my own syrup in the basement.

Still, there was something about that little table-stand with checkered cloth, platoons of perfectly lined-up cans, a genuine Vermonter holding forth — and the jigsaw-puzzle clouds and mountains in the background, just as the leaves were starting to turn.

It got me thinking about the importance of context and thence packaging. J. Peterman certainly understands: His charming stories about how a catalog item was first used and subsequently discovered by him, along with whimsical graphics, have turned his firm into a phenomenon and high-growth superstar in an absurdly crowded market.

Likewise, giant, impersonal Safeway spent a ton a few years back to give its produce departments a bit of the flavor of outdoor fruit and veggie stands. Though the look hardly matches my Vermont farmstand, the investment paid off.

Even high-tech: A laser-parts company had been "packaging" sophisticated $500 items in nondescript plastic bags. Then, based on the advice of a frontline task force, it switched to a vacuum-sealed container, an ebony-colored mounting, and a gold-seal label. It's a safe bet that the engineers would never have thought up such stuff. The "new" product, offered at a substantial price premium, took off — so much for cold, rational decision-making by technical product buyers. (The same engineers who could never imagine the value of such packaging are nonetheless swayed by it as buyers — maybe they *are* human.)

In short, damn few of us (save for the Japanese, who are fanatics on the topic) take packaging anywhere nearly as seriously as we should. It's a lost opportunity — a big one, in fact.

While on a recent business trip, my wife called me out of a meeting in a panic. B-I-G paper jam in our new Canon NP2120 copier — and she was in a rush to send out manuscripts to readers. (Kate runs a small publishing company, among many other things.)

It's not that she's mechanically inept. (Well, she mostly is — and I'm *much* worse.) It's just that I'd not put the manual in an obvious place. (OK, it wasn't even in an unobvious place.)

I helped her find the manual and promptly hung up. She called back in about 10 minutes, blown away. She'd readily fixed the problem — and the manual had been a charm. Clear, easy to follow, helpful graphics, etc.

Bravo Canon! And, sadly, welcome to a very exclusive club: those who take instruction manual development *very* seriously — and do it *very* well. (Wish I could say the same thing about the guide to my otherwise superb Hewlett-Packard FAX-900, which lives next to the Canon copier in the little office on my farm in Vermont.)

90 You'll Catch the Death of Cold, Mr. Benetton

Anita Roddick (The Body Shop) and Richard Branson (Virgin Group). Rupert Murdoch (The News Group), Ted Turner (Turner Broadcasting), John Malone (Telecommunications Inc.), Wayne Huizenga (Blockbuster Video — and before that, Waste Management), Al Neuharth (USA Today/Gannett), Bill Paley (CBS), Barry Diller (QVC), and Samuel Goldwyn (MGM).

Roger Milliken (Milliken & Co.) and Michael Milken (Drexel Burnham). Steve Jobs (Apple, NeXt), Stan Shih (Acer), Rod Canion (Compaq), Andy Grove (Intel), Mitch Kapor (Lotus Development), and Edson de Castro (Data General). Herb Kelleher (Southwest Airlines), Bob Crandall (American Airlines), Don Burr (People Express), Fred Smith (Federal Express), and Jan Carlzon (SAS).

John McCoy and John Fischer (both Banc One), Walter

Wriston (CitiCorp), and Carl Schmitt (University Bank and Trust).

Soichiro Honda (Honda), Masuru Ibuka and Akio Morita (both Sony), and Hiroshi Yamauchi (Nintendo).

Les Wexner (The Limited), Don Fischer (The Gap), and Luciano Benetton (Benetton).

Some wore dark suits (Wriston the banker). Some wore nothing at all (Luciano Benetton in a famous/infamous — aren't they all — Benetton ad). All were mad as hatters. And they — rogues, scallawags, and dreamers — are the color-by-Kodacolor, Dolby Sound businesspeople I love. They *are* business to me.

They are creators. They are the larger than life, folks who make business and economics an adventure. They are the "animal spirits" John Maynard Keynes referred to — the sine qua non of economic growth.

So . . .

Mad Luciano (Benetton) shows up stark naked for a job interview at your company; or profane Anita Roddick arrives for the same purpose, in dungarees that are more than slightly worn and with a Latin American or African villager or two in tow.

Two questions:

■ **Would you hire them?**
■ **Would they come to work for you if you did offer them a job?**

I think you know the answers to both questions. And I think, in these madcap times, you'd better think about what you could do to change them.

91

In the little story above, I'm not sure I was clear enough. You know some *really* neat people, right? (We all do.) Stop reading. Conjure a list of five of them in your mind's eye. How many of them would want to work for your company?

Is that a little clearer?

Q: How would you restructure a church for the '90s?

A: It's obvious that, even with the same community demo-
graphics, some churches become magnets, some wither (and
even close their doors). While church dogma is more or less a
given for any sect, the energy and vision of the parish priest,
rabbi, or imam obviously make an enormous difference.

The effective clerical leader is especially well attuned to his or
her flock — but not a slave to market research, any more than is
the wise packaged-goods marketer or restaurateur. That is, the
cleric does not, in the name of close-to-the-customer, mindlessly
kowtow to community needs. (Close-to-the-customer dots the
theological management literature these days; oh God, what did
Bob Waterman and I start — and can You forgive us?) Rather he
or she *leads* parishioners, bringing old dogma to life in a relevant
and yeasty fashion while taking community needs into account
in the process.

Typically dull white folks (of any denomination) could learn
a lot from the best inner-city African-American churches, starting with Reverend Cecil Williams's inspiring, energetic Glide
Memorial Church in San Francisco. (**Hint**, for starters: Glide
doesn't have "services," it has "celebrations.")

93

Want your employees to pay more attention to diversity issues?
Easy: *You* start paying more attention to diversity issues. It's
about that simple.

Or, as Ann Herbert, Margaret M. Pavel, and Mayumi Oda
put it in *Random Kindness & Senseless Acts of Beauty*:

> *Anything we do randomly and frequently*
> *starts to make its own sense*
> *and changes the world into itself.*
> *Anything you want there to be more of,*
> *do it randomly.*
> *Don't wait for reasons.*

THE REV. CECIL WILLIAMS AND HIS HIGH-ENERGY FLOCK

I recently had dinner at a new Italian restaurant near my home. I'll go back. The staff was cheerful, instructive, and professional. The food was well prepared. The owner-chef had spent about six years, off and on, visiting relatives in several northern Italian cities. He's worked up a unique menu. In fact, the experience brings alive a bit of Italian history and culture, along with good food.

Did my town really need another Italian restaurant? If you'd asked me last week, I'd have said no. Now my reply is an emphatic yes.

The majority of new businesses quickly go bust. And, though the owners have probably mortgaged their home to the hilt, most that fail deserve their sad fate. But some start-ups do thrive. What distinguishes them from losers?

Distinction. Question No. 1 for the prospective business owner: In 25 words or less (15 is even better), how is my concept for a plumbing company, software house, whatever, notably different from that of others? If you can't succinctly explain how you're special to "the man or woman on the street," you're headed for trouble before you start.

Soul. The enterprise should make your prospective customers say, "Wow," "Neat," "Holy smokes." That is, it should be memorable — for example, featuring a special guarantee, remarkable service, or even extraordinary vehicles. If, say, you start a new cab company in a northern city, soul may be a commitment to spotless cabs (inside and out), despite winter slush that makes competitors' hacks look like motorized mud balls.

Passion. The life of an entrepreneur is occasionally exhilarating, and almost always exhausting. Only unbridled passion for the concept is likely to see you through the 17-hour days (month after month) and the painful mistakes that are part and parcel of the start-up process.

Details. While the overall scheme must be an attention-getter, only superb execution will win the day. At the restaurant I visited, the menu gives the genealogy of every dish; the furniture comes from the region of northern Italy that inspired the restaurant; guests are invited to tour the kitchen and chat with the chef; recipes are available upon request (with no missing ingredients); and the rest rooms live up to the rest of the experience!

Culture. "Corporate culture" sounds like the province of Bank of America and Federal Express. Guess again. Culture counts even for the one-principal consultancy that's supported by a part-time administrative assistant. The spirit, energy, and professionalism of that part-timer sets the tone for your service offering. Companies with 1.25 employees have as much "culture" and distinctive spirit (for good or ill) as their huge brethren.

The upshot: Most things the "big folks" do apply to you. Recruiting is, of couse, all important. Then spend time sharing your vision with that lonely part-time assistant, so that she or he gets it — and transmits it to customers and vendors in a host of tiny ways. Consider profit-sharing today, not tomorrow. A biweekly "What's up?" lunch is a must if you have two or more employees.

Community. A friend started a real estate brokerage a few years ago. By the time she'd added her second employee, she was a pillar of her 35,000-person community. No rule says that only the local banker or car dealer can organize the program to raise supplemental funds for the public library or send the high school band on a well-earned special trip. Participating in community affairs, with time more than dollars, is good business from day one. It gets your name around, adds to your distinctiveness, and, best of all, makes you an attractive employer (which is *the* key to sustained success).

Good Books. A good accounting scheme is not complex. To the contrary, a ninth-grader should be able to understand your books. But those books must paint an accurate, timely, and clear picture of how your business is working. Better yet, your bookkeeper-financial adviser should understand your vision — and be buddies with the local banker. His or her credibility, more than yours, will get you the $7,500 line of credit that you can bet will be necessary sometime (e.g., after the ice storm knocks out power for six days, and $4,000 worth of perishable inventory rots before your eyes).

A Pal. Whether a business partner or fellow start-up boss, you desperately need someone to counsel with — someone whom you trust but is not a flatterer.

Perseverance. For Sam Walton (Wal-Mart) and Anita Roddick (The Body Shop), the path to success was marked by early fiascoes. There are a million things — literally, I think — to learn about running a new business. No matter how many good books you read (start with *Running a One-Person Business* by Claude Whitmyer, Salli Rasberry, and Michael Phillips) or how many colleagues you consult, you'll do most of your learning the hard way. The key work in any business, of course, is *learning*. Walton and Roddick learned from their early pratfalls, small and large, and made adjustment after adjustment after adjustment . . .

A Taste for Reinvention. Perversely, small businesses, though the opposite should be true, are less innovative than large ones. If they are successful, they tend to get stuck in a rut — pounding yesterday's idea into the ground.

If any business is successful, it will be copied. That means the current owners need an appetite for revolution and reinvention, not just buffing and polishing. Unfortunately, that's far easier said than done. The passionate attachment to the idea that made them successful (see above) is millstone No. 1 when it comes to serious change.

95 Think Special! (Redux)

Thank you, Stephen and Paul Paliska, for putting me on the mailing list for your newsletter "Passion for Parking."

Ten years ago, the Paliska brothers founded Professional Parking Services Inc., a valet-parking and hotel "front" services

If any business is successful, it will be copie

company headquartered in Southern California. (I gushed about them in *Liberation Management* and *The Tom Peters Seminar*.) The newsletter, mainly aimed at customers, reports on current happenings — new programs like "aggressive hospitality," a completely rewritten training manual, new clients, etc. Mostly, it reminds me — again! — that *anything* can be damned special. If they can create valet parking that sparkles (and stands out from a mile away), why not you and your . . .?

96

"This is a business where a loose, creative, non-linear atmosphere in the halls translates into better ratings and a better work experience. . . . Part of what makes [broadcasting] a thrill is that you never have to grow up."

Randy Michaels
president, Jacor Communications (radio)
Cincinnati

And it ain't just broadcasting, my friends.

97

It's simple, says one exec: You get no character without characters.

Want zip? Zest? Energy? Then hire and promote zip, zest, energy — i.e., characters. The slightly cockeyed. The somewhat offbeat. (And, occasionally, the more-than-somewhat offbeat.)

So tell me, if **Innovation Я and Must Be Us**, what's the alternative? And if you agree there's none, what are you doing about it? (Review your last six hires, including in accounting — how do you do on the offbeat/more-than-somewhat offbeat metric?)

1. 200,000 different things to 200,000 different people

2. the precisely correct placement of an airbill on a package being shipped to a finicky Japanese (tautology time) customer

3. a nest in straw for each of six cans of Campbell's tomato soup displayed in a lovely wooden box in the window of a shop on Tokyo's Ginza

4. the fact that Lee Iacocca (ex-Chrysler) and Sonny Mehta (Alfred A. Knopf) are often on "best-dressed" lists — and that their cars and books respectively are daringly designed

5. an easy-to-use FedEx airbill

6. a ridiculously easy-to-assemble cardboard storage box by Fellowes Mfg.

7. the formal position of the chief designer on the corporate organization chart

8. the informal "cultural" power of the top designer and her/his mates in the corporate pecking order

9. the number of top designers the CEO calls good friends (e.g., knows their phone numbers by heart, has eaten social meals with in the last 45 days)

10. the number of times the CEO calls the chief designer in the course of the average week or the number of times the CEO stops by the chief designer's office (not vice-versa) in the course of the average week (and the proximity of their two offices)

11. numbers 9 and 10 above — please re-read

12. the ingenious gearing in my Le Creuset wine opener that makes it possible to extract a cork using my little finger (literally)

13. the recentness of the last corporate strategy session that was devoted *exclusively* to design issues

14. a visceral understanding that design is a/*the* primary way to differentiate a product or service

15. the garnish that makes a plate of meat and potatoes an elegant dish

16. a waiter who serves a Caesar salad at your table the way Placido Domingo sings the part of Rodolfo in *La Bohème*

17. the clever molded-plastic clasp (integral to the one-piece box) on my $2.99 Rubbermaid Keepers Snap Case

18. as important (or more so) in a 29-cent item as in a $29 or $29,000 item

19. mirrored in signage, forms, and office space as much as in the product or service per se

20. the official London subway map — which has a wonderful history, and has now become a global franchise in its own right

21. an attitude about life

22. an understanding that all the senses were created equal

23. part of the everyday vocabulary throughout the organization, in the training department as well as in engineering and research

24. parsimony in everything

25. cluttered spaces and places that are comfy

26. a 20-year-old sweatshirt that you love

27. the Lexus you bought yesterday

28. the smell of a new baseball

29. the feel of my Platypus Dave Brown match cricket ball (made in Australia, sitting on my desk, and lovingly fingered as I write this)

30. the fact that you sometimes buy books for the cover and wine for the label

31. found equally on farms and in high-fashion dress shops

32. as important to laundromat owners as hand-tool producers

33. things you can sense but not see

34. anything that literally takes your breath away

35. anything, like certain pens and hammers and bull-dozers, that are still taking your breath away 10 years after you first discovered them

36. recruiting for "design sense" in *every* position in the firm

37. outrageously pretty things that don't work worth a damn

38. unspeakably ugly things that work beautifully

39. equations like e=mc^2

40. words that invite (the "Please enjoy by . . ." message on Odwalla juice containers — see item No. 9)

41. usable instruction manuals

42. usable instruction manuals

43. um, usable instruction manuals

44. the care with which winery logos are reproduced on wine-bottle corks

45. stuff you can't explain but know is there

46. total consistency (a design sense that pervades every single thing a corporation does)

47. at least as important for corporations grossing $250,000 a year as for those grossing $25 billion a year

48. a methodology for insuring that design gets considered in every decision

49. the product of an organization that deeply honors playfulness and creativity

50. considering design at the outset of a product- or service-development project, not "later on" or "as appropriate"

51. populist, not elitist

52. teachable (or at least awareness thereof)

53. not expensive

54. holistic (to use an overused term that nonetheless belongs here)

55. heightened by diversity (race, national origin, sex, age)

56. something that old folks appreciate

57. . . . and crusty John Wayne-style men

58. . . . and wee kids

59. . . . and the handicapped

60. great packaging in 19-cent and $9,000 items

61. the product of constant, playful experimentation (nobody ever "got it right the first time" . . . or the 101st)

62. PASSION

63. METICULOUS ENGINEERING

64. stitching and buttonholes

65. more important in sweatshirts (I *love* great sweatshirts) than in a car (I couldn't care less about cars)

66. the opposite of number 65 above for you, perhaps

67. logos

68. business calling cards

69. who the hell you *are*

70. who the hell your company *is*

71. discernible in a flash

72. durable

73. the essential personality of a product or service (or company)

74. the degree to which you believe in the idea of "personality of a product," "personality of a service"

75. EVERYTHING

76. how fat a pen is (depending upon whether I'm having a fat-pen day or a skinny-pen day)

77. color, colorfulness

78. color, colorfulness in hydraulic valves

79. the binder you use in your introductory training course

80. annual reports

81. a pleasant surprise

82. worth a tremendous amount of time, psychic energy, and physical energy

83. worth a fortune

84. people leading companies who are thoroughly pissed off at the absence of great design in any nook and cranny of their company (or anyone else's)

85. the guts to lead

86. the guts to change

87. the guts to throw out today's winning product when you get a better idea

88. huzzahs for fabulous failures

89. recruiting adventurous souls

90. keen observation of the way people (prospective customers, for example) go about doing things

91. living (literally) with customers

92. how you use something more than how it looks

93. why I *fall* in love with things

94. why I *stay* in love with things

95. why I *hate* things

96. why I'm never *neutral* about things

97. the sound of a Mercedes door closing
    (yeah, I know that's not original)

98. J. Peterman catalogs

99. great brochures

100. everything that Richard Branson, Anita
    Roddick, and Luciano Benetton do

101. great tractor seats

102. brilliant control panels

103. artful (efficient, effective,
    ingenious, neat) wiring
    schemes beneath the hood of
    a car or inside a food processor

104. about the car dealer as much
    as the car

105. about the parking lot as
    much as the restaurant

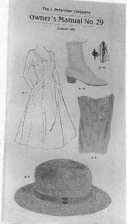

106. GREAT REST ROOMS (also see item No. 107)

107. the containers in which your hotel laundry is returned
    (whether at a $59- or $590-a-room hotel)

108. consistency (looks familiar — and good)

109. inconsistency (startles — and breaks with the past)

110. a warm and friendly feeling

111. a jolting surprise

112. eternal

113. never stays still

114. what you most remember about what you've produced

115. poetry

116. mechanics

117. art

118. small-minded perfectionism

119. wondering how I lived before Dennison Hi-Liters, Ziplocs, Saran Wrap, Velcro, Post-its — which are truly better mousetraps

120. understanding that the more apparently mundane-humdrum the product (or service), the better the chance that DESIGN MINDFULNESS can revolutionize it (BECAUSE MOST IDIOTS DON'T GET IT)

121. the ironclad requirement, at an Australian home-security systems company, that installers always wear slippers inside clients' homes

122. the ability to discard received wisdom about the way things work (and are used)

123. the frequent absence of cars in the showroom at Sewell Village Cadillac in Dallas, Texas (but the floral displays are *always* great)

124. Apple Computer's little bitten apple logo

125. the plain (The Body Shop containers) as much as/more than the fancy

126. the absence of overdesign (which is as bad as design mindlessness — or maybe the *ultimate* design mindlessness)

127. harmony (the fact that my Minolta 9xi feels as if it is an extension of my body)

128. a dozen modest changes (total cost = $25,000) that completely change the character — look, feel, livability — of a $530,000 house

129. the nifty engineering that went into effective fresh-fruit labeling

130. the pleasure the CEO takes in demo-ing his/her products

131. the extent to which a company's products are lying about throughout all of its workspaces

132. the passion with which the chief *financial* officer talks about the company's product (service) offerings

133. whether (or not) design is directly or indirectly mentioned in the corporate philosophy statement

134. a truck stop where you feel at home

135. the completeness and convenience of a jam-packed galley on a 34-foot inboard powerboat

136. grace

137. about LOVE and HATE, not like and dislike (research shows that long-term consumer attachment is tied to an emotional reaction to a product or service — "like" does not a long-term relationship cement)

138. about *relationships* (i.e., with a product or service)

139. like life. Marry for sex, stay married for hugs in the middle of long and lonely nights. Design is about orgiastic sex *and* nurturing (user-friendliness? ugh!) that last a lifetime

140. likely to be emphasized in a firm where the CEO plays a musical instrument, ties flies, is a gourmet cook, does fine cabinetry, spends hours a week in a greenhouse, watches birds, or has some other craft that links her or him closely to the tangible world

141. a scrawled handwritten note from the president (as opposed to a machine-signed letter)

142. in the age of phones, faxes, and e-mail, a scrawled personal note from *anyone*

99

What are you gonna do about the list above ? Today?

100

Q. Is it possible to reconcile the idea of your "crazy times call for crazy organizations" with the McDonald's "franchise model," where systematization is the key?

A. Oh, get off it. You're not trying to tell me that Mc-Donald's is still special!? Sure, I still stop at the local McOrdinary's for fabulous french fries from time to time.

Z-Z-Z-Z-

McDONALD'S OR McORDINARY

But the quality (Q), service (S), cleanliness (C), and value (V) on which founder Ray Kroc launched the firm are decidedly indistinct these days — outside of Moscow and Beijing, at any rate.

In today's world the premium belongs on *un*systematization: i.e., providing a special face to *every* customer, even if you are lucky enough to have millions of them.

Getting organized (systematization) is a must, don't get me wrong. But you can carry it far too far. And when blah becomes your signature in a crowded market, watch out.

101 No Electron Microscopes: Or take Your Software and . . .

I flipped out. I admit it.

I was getting ready to speak to an audience of professional-services folks from the architectural, engineering, and construction fields. Topping my conference information packet was an ad for software to help produce responses to RFPs (Requests for Proposal).

I'm sure it's thoughtful. I'm sure it's good. I'm sure it's flexible. I'm sure responding to RFPs, especially from government agencies, is tedious. (*I* wouldn't want to do it.) But . . .

I am so sick and tired of tools that foster cookie-cutter responses. I'm sick and tired of letters that all look alike. I'm sick and tired of business plans that all look alike. I'm sick and tired of presentations that all look alike. I said to the assembled group, "Give me a break! If you come to me complaining about 'the commoditization of engineering services' [they did, that's why I was there], then don't tell me the solution is to produce proposals that look like everyone else's proposals! It's bad enough if we're talking soap or soup, but 'me too' professional-services? It makes me want to barf. . . ."

It just poured out. (And I was surprised and pleased that heavy-duty applause followed. Maybe I *was* onto something.) So what was *my* answer?

I'm no expert, but I suggest that proposals ought to pass what I call the NO ELECTRON MICROSCOPE TEST. That is, take a look at, say, 10 proposals. Do any stand out in a flash? Or do you need an electron microscope to tell them apart?

(I remember an ad for a new automobile — actually a relaunch of an old favorite; it had arrows all over it pointing to the new features. If you need arrows . . . you get my point, eh?)

You don't need an electron microscope to know you're at Disney World, that you're flying on Southwest, or using America Online. In days gone by, you didn't need an electron microscope to know you were eating at McDonald's (see above) or driving a Ford Taurus.

And, Lord knows, your clients shouldn't need an electron microscope to figure out what's special about your professional-service offering — painter, gardener, photographer, accountant, or architect.

So, how about it, can you pass my NO ELECTRON MICRO-

SCOPE test? Do your business cards and stationery stand out? Your proposals (if you're in professional services)? If you give the "wrong" answers to such queries then don't dare complain to me about the fact that your service (or product) is "becoming a commodity."

Wake up!

102

Q. You talk a lot about listening to the customer. But what if you hear suggestions on which you can't deliver?

A. The premise of the question turns out to be a self-fulfilling prophecy. If customers offer outrageous suggestions, it invariably means you haven't been listening to their more modest requests on a regular basis. If you're out there listening (and asking) each and every day, you'll develop an ongoing dialogue that will allow you to nip problems in the bud and nurture improvements to their fullest bloom.

Monster caveat: The customer's "outrageous" idea, taken seriously, just might be your next breakthrough product — or your competition's. Also, see item No.103 below.

103 Picture Imperfect Quality

Want to get your message about quality problems or customer service snafus through thick, recalcitrant top-management skulls? Forget the 15-page memo, the well-reasoned 100-transparency presentation. Instead, take a $599 Sony CCD FX 230 video recorder on the road for a few days and interview five to 15 irritated customers. (In my experience, they're almost always willing to make time for you.) Then edit the tape down to 30 to 45 minutes (the CCD FX 230 includes editing capabilities); then show it to your colleagues, your boss, the divisional management team.

In my experience, these clumsy home videos (maybe, in part, because they *are* clumsy) never fail to start a *big* discussion in a way all those tidy charts, graphs, and "hard" data could never do.

If you are in a 15-person Mom-and-Pop operation, this applies, too. Borrow a buddy's video recorder (if you don't own one) and do a dozen, two-minute interviews with patrons as they leave your restaurant, copy shop, construction-equipment rental yard, whatever. Then show the tape, unedited, at your morning meeting next Wednesday. With or without accompanying popcorn, I bet you get the audience's rapt attention!

104

John Martin, CEO of PepsiCo's $4 billion Taco Bell, told *Forbes ASAP* he likes to "spend a lot of time wandering around. Not just in my own stores. I go to grocery stores. I go anyplace where people are eating to try to figure what it is that they are doing."

What kind of entourage accompanies this very big wheel? "[It's] just me," Martin says. "I go on road trips by myself. I just get in the car and drive for seven days and nobody even knows where I am."

How lovely to read those words, especially in the frenzied, hyper-hooked, give-me-another-200-pages-of-market-analysis mid-1990s. Gentlewomen, unplug your modems and start your cars!

105 Attaboy, John!

New York Times reviewer Michiko Kakutani calls John Updike's *Brazil* an "ugly, repellent novel." While I haven't read the book, Kakutani's criticism boosted my admiration for Updike. At age 62, after 16 novels and global literary renown, he's still reinventing himself. Kakutani admits as much, acknowledging that Updike has taken a "leap of imagination" and managed to "stretch the bounds of his fictional territory."

Maybe Updike stumbled this time, but courage like his is exceptional among the supersuccessful — individuals and companies. Bravo!

106

Q: You blithely badmouth human resource departments for being uninspiring, bureaucratic, and preoccupied with the minutiae of personnel policies. What would your ideal HR department be?

A: Here it is:

(1) Almost nobody is at home. All staffers are out — literally — working with customers (e.g., divisions, operations centers) on pioneering people projects. Some won't be "home" for months (maybe years!).

(2) If I (Tom Peters) sit down to talk with an HR vice president, here's the only request I'll make, "Tell me what you are doing that's neat." The star HR chief will excitedly respond with a WOW List (I *do* like that word) of a half-dozen projects in support of line operations — and I'd know in a flash that I'd want to write up at least two or three of them for our newsletter (*On Achieving Excellence*) or my next book.

Incidentally, these are exactly the same criteria I'd apply to a purchasing, accounting, or information-systems department. In these pages I've said in a dozen dozen ways that we ought to be pursuing products and services that are memorable. The "memorable"/"no electron microscope" tests clearly apply to staff-service departments as much as to line operations.

How about it, got that list of eye-popping projects to share?

107 It's the Loo, Dummy!

At my local Chevron station, the owner puts new flowers in the men's and women's rest rooms each morning. And it's almost no exaggeration to say you could, yes, eat off the rest room floors.

At Northshire Bookstore in Manchester, Vermont, the spotless unisex bathroom has attractive wallpaper, fresh flowers, and posters that capture your attention as you go about your business. Car dealer Carl Sewell spent $250 a roll on wallpaper for the bathroom at his Cadillac-Lexus dealership; he also saw fit to include an entire chapter on bathrooms in his superb book, *Customers for Life* (co-authored with Paul Brown).

Sewell has the right idea. It's the absolute truth that few things set you apart as much as scintillating rest rooms. Sure, that looks odd at first reading. But give it a second's thought. Now, don't you agree?

Incidentally, what's good for the goose is good for the gander. Employee rest rooms vary as much as customer pit stops. Some are clean and inviting. Many are foul and repellent. Some have showers and lockers. Most don't. Etc.

Yes, I'm actually suggesting that you vault rest rooms to the top of your next business-strategy session. They're a dead giveaways about how much you actually care about your oft-proclaimed "most important assets" — your customers and your workforce. As Walt Disney, who had an equal mania for film animation and parking-lot-attendant demeanor, might have said in his prime, "No one ever paid too much attention to the toilets!"

108

"For years companies have been trying to sell new products with new techno-this, or new techno-that. People take technology for granted these days. What they want are warm, friendly products — something to seduce them."

Philippe Starck
designer, Thomson Consumer Electronics

109

I *love* business. I admit it. I hate "suits." And pretentious bastards. But they're irrelevant. Business, to me, is about life in full flower.

Thank God I'm not quite alone. Ludwig von Mises, de facto founder of the Austrian school of economics, the *Financial Times* declared, saw business as "a creative activity involving inspired hunches and leaps of faith."

Let us all L E A P !

We went in search
of bathrooms in
ordinary places . . .

. . . and we found

The Good . . .

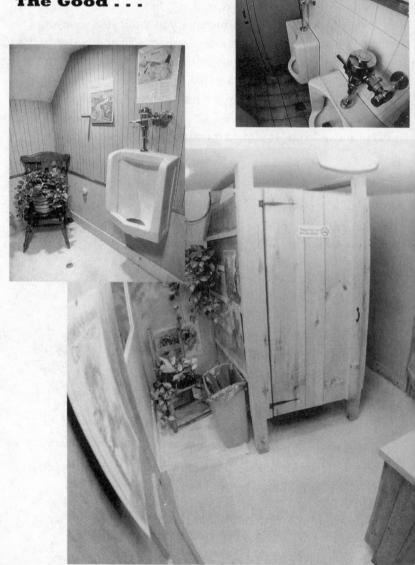

ALL IT TAKES IS A LITTLE TOUCH OR TWO . . .

The Great . . .

. . . OR A BIG TOUCH

The Ugly . . .

JUST SAY NO TO COMMODITIES

(And Yes to Free Spirits)

110 The Obsession Business

I was recently able to bring together eight talented senior managers to talk about, well, anything and everything. I just wanted to toss out the ball, watch it dip and slide, and then see where it landed.

First, why don't we all introduce ourselves:

My name is David Friend. I'm chairman and founder of Pilot Software. About 10 years ago we invented something called an executive information system, which is a point-and-click information-access tool used mostly by big companies. We have about 400 employees.

I'm Tania Zouikin, CEO of Batterymarch Financial Management. We manage over $6 billion in investments, mostly for pension funds. We now have 70 percent of our assets invested globally, which is a lot for a business like ours.

I'm Stephanie Sonnabend, executive vice president of Sonesta International Hotels. Sonesta is a small chain with 15 hotels in the United States, the Caribbean, and Egypt.

I'm David Hirshberg, CEO of Germaine Lawrence, a human-services agency in Arlington, Massachusetts. We provide residential services to adolescent girls who have suffered abuse. We have a $7 million budget, about two hundred employees. We've been around since 1979.

I'm Peter Duncan, and I'm with the Center for Simplified Strategic Planning. We're a very small consulting firm, five professionals and two support people. We specialize in strategic planning for small to midsize companies.

I'm Sheila Schofield, and I'm director of communications for Doubletree Hotel Corporation, which was created by the recent merger of Doubletree Hotels and Guest Quarters Suite Hotels. We've gone from 40 hotels to 100. Right now we're merging the two cultures, and moving from Boston to Phoenix.

My name is Ira Jackson, and I'm senior vice president, Bank of Boston, which has $85 billion in assets.

I'm Ben Cole, and I'm an entrepreneur to the bone and a banking consultant. My company, Cole Financial, Inc., maintains offices in Boston, Hong Kong, and St. Petersburg, Russia.

TP: Welcome. I'm obsessed.

STEPHANIE SONNABEND: Well, that's always a good sign.

TP: I feel like I'm drowning in boring products. Companies have reengineered, they've flattened, quality and service are up, product development time is down — now why isn't anyone doing anything exciting?

DAVID FRIEND: That's a big one.

PETER DUNCAN: It's *the* big one.

TP: I was called out to Steelcase. Ten years ago they, along with Herman Miller and a couple others, revolutionized office design. After looking at their analysis of why they had margin problems, I looked at their catalog. Great stuff, super quality, big investments in innovation, but it's just not very interesting.

Inevitable Commoditization?

SHEILA SCHOFIELD: The hotel industry — like all of the service sector — has become a commodity business. We're just like cars. It's become very hard for us to differentiate ourselves.

STEPHANIE SONNABEND: But people are looking for something unique — they don't want a cookie-cutter experience.

DAVID FRIEND: When something becomes a commodity, its value goes down and the differentiation becomes who can deliver it at the lowest cost.

PETER DUNCAN: Part of the problem is that customers have access to a lot of pricing information these days. And they're using it.

STEPHANIE SONNABEND: What I see in the hotel industry is "Let's Make a Deal." No one pays the going rate anymore, they're shopping around, negotiating with their travel agent, with reservation services. People walk up to the front desk and negotiate. It makes it very hard to make a profit.

TP: That's the fascinating — and terrifying — message coming out of the airline industry. Max Hooper, the information-systems guru at American Airlines, summed it up: Once you get the kind of transparent, real-time pricing information systems and open electronic market that we have in the airline industry, welcome to the world of losing billions of dollars a year.

TANYA ZOUIKIN: There are on-line services where you can find whatever you want — information or product — anywhere in the United States in a nanosecond or two.

TP: Barry Diller is saying why in the hell should people want to go into retail outlets at all. I think it'll be 25 years before that nirvana — or nightmare — comes to pass. But the old idea of "perfect information" that the economists talked about ain't a fantasy anymore.

DAVID FRIEND: The information glut is part of the problem. The challenge is to stand out in some way that goes beyond price.

TANIA ZOUIKIN: Which an awful lot of companies have trouble doing.

Making the Case for Innovation

DAVID FRIEND: Every year I lecture at MIT's Sloan School of Management. Innovation is a very tough thing for them to get their minds around because you can't see a definite return on investment. People are much more comfortable with things they can quantify.

Some crazy guy walks into your office and says, "Hey, I've got a great idea, we could sell a jillion." That's not a situation conventionally-trained businesspeople are equipped to deal with.

PETER DUNCAN: How do you train people to deal with spontaneity?

TP: That's the $64 billion question.

DAVID FRIEND: We have to find ways to evaluate — and value — innovation.

SHEILA SCHOFIELD: The suite hotel is an idea that's changed the hotel industry. People came in with that idea year after year and got rejected; finally somebody said, "Let's try it and see what happens," and it was a hit.

DAVID FRIEND: Companies have to try the crazy ideas. Try 10 of them, throw them against the wall. Some will work, some won't.

PETER DUNCAN: Look at the business of selecting colors for cars. You end up with the lowest common denominator all the time — "Let's find the least offensive color" — instead of finding one that's going to jump off the floor. It might flop, but then again it might hit.

DAVID FRIEND: When you see pictures in *Forbes* of the color gurus for GM and Ford sitting around in gray suits, you understand why their color choices are so drab.

What makes Boston and Silicon Valley interesting is that you see companies that do value new ideas. Making innovation a rock-bottom tenet of company culture is the key.

STEPHANIE SONNABEND: The only people financing hotels these days are in Japan and Hong Kong. U.S. venture capital has dried up.

TP: The problem is, venture capital tends to be run more and more by MBAs and not the great folks of the past, like General Doriot of Harvard Business School/Route 128 fame. He used to invest in the people he found kinky and interesting.

PETER DUNCAN: One of the ironies of innovation is that the crazy dreamers often lack organizational skills, so they have a hard time getting backing.

DAVID FRIEND: Digital Equipment was started with something like $50,000. Today, venture-capital firms laugh at the idea of considering anything thats needs less than half a million dollars.

TP: What's interesting is the goings on one level down from the formal capital market. When *Inc.* did its 500 fastest-growing companies list a couple of years ago, it asked how many bucks people had used to start their companies, and 75 percent had spent less than $100,000. Some insanely high number, like 35 percent, had spent less than $10,000.

Attracting Firebrands

DAVID FRIEND: I'm especially concerned about the big companies. What can they do to encourage nerve and spunk? One of my customers is a leading global office-products company. It's dull and boring, not the kind of place somebody with a lot of moxie is going to want to work.

PETER DUNCAN: It's a little bit of a Catch-22: How do you ignite your company when you can't attract the firebrands?

DAVID FRIEND: I've got the problem in my own company. The president is a business school type, and he rewards engineers by looking at the salary range for engineers with comparable experience. How do you reward someone who comes up with an idea that makes you $10 million? Do you say, "I'm sorry, you only have six years of experience, so your salary is going to be X." That's stupid. He's going to pack up and go.

TANIA ZOUIKIN: Managers have to understand that inspiration is a valuable commodity.

DAVID FRIEND: Exactly. You have to get them to understand that there is a management track and there is an individual contributor track. Most companies don't adequately reward the innovation track. Some, like Xerox and Hewlett-Packard, have made a big effort, but most companies give it lip service. They usually have one or two figurehead scientists who do what they want and get paid a reasonable salary.

PETER DUNCAN

TP: Let people do what they do best. If you've got somebody who loves to run a hotel, why in the hell make them a regional vice president?

STEPHANIE SONNABEND: But pay them as much as the regional vice president.

TP: Pay them more! Did Moses have a secret Eleventh Commandment that said that bosses have to be paid more than the people that report to them?

PETER DUNCAN: It's very hard for managers to grasp the concept of someone ostensibly under them making more money.

DAVID FRIEND

TANIA ZOUIKIN: A lot of it comes down to culture, tradition. Sports has a culture based on stars. American business has a long tradition of being very conservative, a culture based on conformity. To suddenly say to a manager, "Find your stars and pay them twice what you make" — well, sounds like a Maalox Moment.

TP: American business needs lots more Maalox Moments. We can't keep suffocating the risk-takers.

Crackle in the Air

DAVID FRIEND: It drives me nuts when I deal with senior managers in big companies. They all have their screwball inventor types off in some lab, and they talk about them in very patronizing terms. Anytime I see that, I know it's not a company likely to produce any exciting new products.

TP: Look at Banc One. Twenty years ago, John McCoy had the foresight to invest in John Fisher, who became banking's top information-systems wacko. They barely made a penny from Fisher's stuff until they became a huge institution. Then — pow! — they made a fortune from the pioneering technology infrastructure he'd put in place.

Old man McCoy was conservative in his lending practices; nonetheless, he had the guts to invest big in something that had the possibility of transforming the institution. And it did.

PETER DUNCAN: He was the boss. He had no one to answer to.

DAVID FRIEND: No senior manager ever got fired for seeing 10 to 15 percent growth. It's admired, but you don't get there by taking risks.

STEPHANIE SONNABEND: If the boss isn't taking risks, it becomes that much harder for anybody else to.

TP: You walk into some companies and you can feel the energy. Then I also see even software companies that would pick the same drab colors as the boys at General Motors.

TANIA ZOUIKIN: It really is an intangible, isn't it? That spirit you feel at some companies?

DAVID HIRSHBERG: Being a nonprofit, we have very little money to put into innovation, or anything else for that matter. Our commodity is beds, and we can't raise our prices because the current state administration is slashing the human services budget. So we work very hard to create a spirit of adaptability, of creativity. We want to keep morale high and encourage active, innovative mutation. It's working. And it's not about how much money we're spending.

TP: A lot of companies are spending jillions on innovation but all they're producing is the 64th variety of spaghetti sauce.

I don't think you get innovation free. But a lot of it has to do with the spirit of the enterprise. Microsoft invests heavily, but I don't think it's the dollar amount so much as the fanaticism, the technicolor life they lead.

DAVID HIRSHBERG: You can almost smell a company that's alive, there's something crackling in the air.

DAVID FRIEND: Guy Kawasaki, one of the original Apple Macintosh gang, had this motto: "Never buy a computer from a company where the president can't do the demo." Simply throwing money at innovation without involvement at the top is useless.

STEPHANIE SONNABEND: You can say, "We're gonna have real fun at this company," but if the environment and culture aren't there, then it's not going to happen.

SHEILA SCHOFIELD: Some suit can come in after having read a book the night before and say, "By God, what we need in this office is to have more fun, so let's start." Good luck.

TP: There's a lot of that going around!

DAVID FRIEND: Like the mandatory beer and pizza parties after work.

SHEILA SCHOFIELD: Exactly.

PETER DUNCAN: You ask the top people and they say they're having fun, they're energized. I bet if we took a poll in this room, we'd find that everyone likes going to work. But how far down does that spirit go?

Managers should ask themselves: "Why do I like my job?" And then: "Do the people who report to me like theirs?" And carry that question all the way down.

IRA JACKSON: It's very hard, if not impossible, to get a solid barometric pressure reading of a company like ours with 19,000 employees in over 20 countries and 500 communities. Whether people are having fun today in cash management as opposed to trade services in Asia, I don't know. The chairman's having fun, he's opening up a new office in Shanghai, and I'm having fun here because I'm not in the office.

PETER DUNCAN: Then the challenge becomes pushing the fun down and out, until it permeates the whole organization.

Fun = Autonomy

IRA JACKSON: Five years ago you would have characterized retail banking at the Bank of Boston as third-class citizenship, low on prestige, compensation, and fun. The lowest tier was the inner city in Roxbury — that was Siberia.

But we woke up one day and realized we had to do more in the inner city — not in the pursuit of fun but as a business opportunity/obligation. We rediscovered our roots — our old branch in Roxbury. We decided the only way we could do good and do well simultaneously was not through the large, monolithic culture that we had, but by giving autonomy to somebody to run our inner-city branches as a stand-alone business.

We found a very talented African-American woman who grew up in the neighborhood, and she started First Community Bank within Bank of Boston. From third-class citizenship in Siberia, today that's the most energized and successful start-up business we have. And we have lots of successful startups. They're visited by scores of businesses every year, mostly other banks, to see how we do it.

Is innovation possible? Yes! And it had nothing to do with R&D in a conventional sense, but with purpose. And commitment.

DAVID HIRSHBERG: When something like that happens it gives a lot of people

IRA JACKSON

license to start innovating.

TP: I have a good buddy who owns 22 Burger Kings down in Florida. Years ago, when they started their "Sometimes You Gotta Break the Rules" campaign, he hung every one of his Burger King signs upside down. He caught a lot of flack from headquarters, but he turned on 22 branches worth of employees.

INNER CITY WINNER

PETER DUNCAN: Ira's Roxbury story is a perfect example of how to turn people on: You give them control and pride of ownership and say, "You're special, you matter. Go to it and have fun." Usually it's: "Go to it and have fun until you run up against a rule or a boundary or a procedure manual."

STEPHANIE SONNABEND: Employees have to be have real power to help the customer. Having that responsibility can be scary, but even that fear gets the blood pumping.

The Murky Middle

TP: Here we bump up against a certain irony. Eighty-five percent of so-called empowerment programs are providing the front line more opportunity to step out, but when you look at the vice presidents and middle managers you see a sea of similarity.

I went to a company "retreat" with a couple hundred top managers — their resort clothes all looked like they were bought at the same store. And this was a so-called empowered company!

IRA JACKSON: Our problem with empowerment is definitely at the middle level. If the top level walks the talk it helps a lot. A couple of years ago we decided to cancel our executive golf tournament and do community service for a day instead. Eighty of us tried to rebuild a camp. We had to go back twice to undo the damage we'd done the first time. But we demonstrated to ourselves, and symbolically to the troops, that it's a very different corporate culture. We replaced comfort with caring.

The top folks are looking for innovation, and the bottom feels as if they're empowered. It's the middle level that is petrified. They see change coming at them from both directions. It's a very uncomfortable feeling because they're not the enemy, they're *us*. But they seem to have a psychological predicament — they know they're the most threatened.

SHEILA SCHOFIELD

SHEILA SCHOFIELD: The middle layer *is* most at risk, which has certainly been demonstrated in the last few years. They're evaporating.

How Many Mavericks?

PETER DUNCAN: While stars are vital, there are some people who just aren't cut out to light the skies. They have to be respected.

TP: I think most people have more fireworks in them than they're given credit for.

DAVID FRIEND: Your middle managers have to be shown the value of innovation. The first thing I see when I go into a company is the balance sheet. These numbers are the results of something that was done right — or wrong — way back in the food chain. I ask, "Well, what caused those results? Let's measure that." If the numbers are good and you keep working backward, you wind up looking at somebody's terrific idea. That really demonstrates the importance of innovation. Most people don't ever try to work through that process.

IRA JACKSON: Look at the success of Bank of Boston. We reshaped our image, and it turned out well-to-do yuppies like to leave their deposits at a bank with a social conscience. So that little experiment in Roxbury had an enormous ripple effect. Business schools train people to measure profits and losses and balance sheets and cash flows — not how happy your customers are or where the spark was that started the explosion that netted you $100 million.

TP: Let's get back to this notion that there's a large share of humanity that wants to come into work and face a predictable environment. I don't buy it. Look at Nordstrom with its many thousands of employees. What's special about that company is the ordinary people who seem to behave in extraordinary ways.

DAVID FRIEND: They're probably getting rewarded for it.

TP: They are in dollar terms [commission sales], but mostly they're given inordinate leeway, by retail's pathetic standards, to do whatever it takes to thrill — their kind of word — the customer.

TANIA ZOUIKIN AND
STEPHANIE SONNABEND

Mission > Money

IRA JACKSON: I think it has more to do with mission than money. When I was Massachusetts tax commissioner, taxpayer assistance at the Department of Revenue was like retail at the Bank of Boston: It was Siberia. We decided to allow those 150 employees to innovate. Did they ever!

They kept the office open until midnight on April 15 and paid for coffee and cookies themselves. They pledged to get taxpayers refunds within 10 days; it used to take four months. They did all of these things on salaries averaging $20,000, with no bonuses except having a purpose and helping their friends and neighbors. They took this dog patch and turned it into the most highly esteemed, pumped organization in state government.

DAVID FRIEND: How did it happen?

IRA JACKSON: They were finally paid attention to. And respected. They were getting more phone calls than the rest of state government combined, but they didn't have the technology to process them. Thirty-eight percent of the callers hung up, and there was a long wait for those who didn't. So we gave them technology and a physical environment that didn't treat them as if they were dumb public servants — ergonomically designed chairs and nice high-tech headsets and water coolers and refrigerators.

This is pretty pedestrian stuff in a high-tech company, but in state government it was unprecedented. They also set up taxpayer assistance tables at malls and rented a tax mobile to visit senior centers and public housing projects. They had a mission: To help honest taxpayers comply with their tax burden. And they just felt great.

DAVID HIRSHBERG: There's nothing more powerful than providing people with a mission.

Going Global

TP: Can we talk about the rest of the world?

TANIA ZOUIKIN: A lot of moderate-size companies have trouble reinventing themselves as global concerns.

PETER DUNCAN: I'd argue that's something that can't be done overnight. The mechanism can be put in place, but the results depend on developing relationships with people who probably have a very different way of doing business. That can't be hurried or it can backfire.

TANIA ZOUIKIN: I'd add to that: Hire local people. There's no substitute for someone who knows her way around a place inside out, as opposed to sending someone green who has to fumble his way around.

BEN COLE: I think you need both. We were the first American company allowed to do a study of a Russian state bank. Here's my card — it's in Russian. We've determined that you can't work in Russia solely with Russians — you need people who can translate our culture to them. I think this is probably true everywhere.

IRA JACKSON: We use Argentina and Brazil as sites for innovation. We just started the first bank-owned pension fund in Latin America,

IRA JACKSON

and our mutual funds, which Brazil innovated without our mucking it up, are among the best performing in South America.

When our Brazilian manager comes to meetings, the chief measure of success he uses is customer satisfaction. It wasn't even on our list of key measures! But it's how he *begins*: not assets, not profitability, but customer satisfaction.

PETER DUNCAN: I've seen an awful lot of small companies — in the $20 million to $30 million range — get involved in global activities. And I'm not just talking about having a sales rep in France, I'm talking about putting up plants in Europe, in China, looking into South America.

DAVID FRIEND: My company is relatively small, and we have 60 percent of our sales and 55 percent of our employees outside the United States.

IRA JACKSON: An increasing number of companies these days are born global. It's their focus from day one, if the will is there.

PETER DUNCAN: We traditionally track U.S. economic statistics for our small and midsize clients. Now they're all asking for global statistics. That's where their customers are, that's what they want to stay on top of. It's not a size thing.

DAVID FRIEND: But if you're selling a bank a computer system that's going to get used worldwide, they want to know, "What are we going to do when it breaks down in Cairo?" If the answer is "You call some guy in Boston," that doesn't cut it.

TP: McKinsey & Co. did phenomenally well going overseas. They sent their superstars at the outset. They went in with the best and established a toehold; now, 40 years later, virtually all their overseas managers are foreign nationals; and their new manging director is Indian born.

BEN COLE: The excitement, the adventure, is out there. All over the world. But cultural differences are challenging.

SHEILA SCHOFIELD: But those challenges are part of the excitement.

TP: *Inc.* magazine did a story about a year ago on how to go global. To summarize: "You gotta wanna." If you gotta wanna bad enough, then you'll figure out how to do it.

. . . And Passion/Moxie (Again)

BEN COLE: Because it's totally irrational. The risks are far greater, the chances of success are almost nil. So you need real passion. It's the essential entrepreneurial drive!

DAVID FRIEND: I look at some of my college friends who went to work for Procter&Gamble and General Mills and I'd say that the risk in going that route has turned out to be greater than the risk for my entrepreneur friends.

PETER DUNCAN: It's one more irony. People went to work for these big companies because they offered job security.

TP: Job security is an oxymoron.

STEPHANIE SONNABEND: It's a hard concept for people to let go of.

DAVID FRIEND: We all have to let go of a lot of preconceptions.

SHEILA SCHOFIELD: Things that shouldn't work, do. And vice versa.

DAVID FRIEND: That's the lesson big companies have to learn. If you take the crazy idea that's never going to work and put the right people on it, it could soar. It comes back to your original point, Tom, about how a company differentiates itself. Part of it is recognizing that people make the impossible happen all the time.

TP: But you've got to have the nerve to trust that person, who may not come with the best credentials, but is blazing with drive and commitment.

DAVID FRIEND

DAVID FRIEND: I'm convinced that moxie, that mind-set can be taught. There are a flurry of new courses over at the Harvard Business School — they're trying to figure out how to embrace the entrepreneurial spirit. They're starting to look for successful mavericks.

TP: I mostly agree it can be taught, and, among the sizable firms, few do it better than a Hewlett-Packard. You probably own a little bit of a project at HP within six weeks of hiring on. Independence is inculcated from the get-go.

It's critical for big firms to start learning how to hold on to folks who are off the beam — folks who stand a chance of launching them into something exciting.

PETER DUNCAN: There's a deeply ingrained bias that business is not the place for crazies.

But Passion Needs a Pal

DAVID FRIEND: Around my company I have the reputation as being the wild and crazy inventor. I wouldn't want to run my company on a day-to-day basis — that would make a lot of people uncomfortable. They like the fact that I'm out there coming up with ideas, but they also like the fact that there's an older, experienced professional manager running things. I think that combination works well.

PETER DUNCAN: We spend a lot of time teaching people to put their team together. If you've got all the same kind of thinkers in there, you're not going to get much creative spark. You want a give and take. You see wonderful things come out of the dialogue between the wild-eyed and the button-down. It's that tension that's the wellspring for vibrant ideas.

DAVID HIRSHBERG: You know what surprises me about this conversation? That there's this emphasis on recognizing the mad genius, and much less on nurturing people in general. Maybe it's because I've got a handful of 23-year-olds who aren't geniuses most of the time, but we have to develop their talent. The metaphor we use is the old Boston Celtics. What [Coach] Red Auerbach did was bring in a lot of outcasts, figure out what their strengths were, develop those strengths, and then combine them to form a team that would win championships. All the players complemented each other — the whole was more than the sum of its parts.

TP: Which brings us, among other things, to recruiting processes. It's all credentials. Dive into that hole in the résumé, you might find something interesting down there. Ask them about the lemonade stand they set up at age six. (Or didn't.) The art contest they won in high school. Does the room brighten when they walk in? If it does, hire them, even though their résumé looks like a piece of Swiss cheese.

When Nordstrom was getting ready to open its Stanford Shopping Center store, they put a help-wanted ad in the *Palo Alto Times Tribune* that was pure poetry. "We're looking for Neat People" was the banner, more or less. It went on: "We're in the business of entertaining people, we want to create an exciting environment, and if you think you're an entertaining, exciting person, come apply."

SHEILA SCHOFIELD: That's terrific. There's a small hotel in San Francisco, Campton Place, that ran a help-wanted ad in the *Wall Street Journal* for a softball team — catcher, pitcher, infielder, etc. They were literally putting together a softball team to compete in the San Francisco hotel league. What a great metaphor, great campaign.

TP: Sensational!

BEN COLE: I just spent several weeks with a terrific bank. The cooperation I saw was remarkable. There was virtually no hierarchy. They had performance incentives for everybody. Everybody. Suddenly people who didn't care before had a stake in how much profit they were making. I was at a meeting and the head of the mortgage division saw a form he thought could have looked better. One of the women piped up, "Would you like us to throw out four boxes or should we use them up and save the $36?" She had a stake in that $36.

IRA JACKSON: Sounds like our Roxbury branch.

PETER DUNCAN: That dynamic of change infects and infuses the entire organization. And defines it as innovative.

SHEILA SCHOFIELD: Just the way Campton Place's softball team approach helped to define it as a place that stressed creativity and teamwork.

TP: There are no cars in recent Ford ads. It's all about the people who build them. It's a super motivator for the people on the staff.

IRA JACKSON: Years ago they had the guy in the first "Quality Is Job One" ad, and he was back 10 or 12 years later, saying basically, "It worked, didn't it, and we're still committed." That's a long time for a company to stay committed, not just the slogan and the advertising, but the entire orientation on quality — from a company that was dying from its lack of quality.

TP: We've come full circle. Back to this great irony that we've reached a plateau where excellence, by yesterday's standard, is a given but everything looks the same.

SHEILA SCHOFIELD: Any answers?

TP: No.

SHEILA SCHOFIELD: Suggestions, then?

TP: How about destroying and reinventing your company in pursuit of a *new* passion?

IRA JACKSON: So you're saying sow the seeds of your own destruction?

TP: Precisely. Have enough crazy hothouses going so that one of them will drive you out of business before a competitor does.

STEPHANIE SONNABEND: It's a lot to think about.

TP: As long as we keep thinking, we're a step ahead of the game. Thank you all for coming. Stay obsessed.

111   Three MORE Cheers for Business's Wild Bunches

"A tale that once got out: Mercedes engineers, lobbying for zippier engines, 'disappeared' a Benz sedan for a few days. It returned with its hood chained shut, belly pan below, and its engine sounding stout. A few corporate fat cats raced it up autobahn and Alps, and then rushed back to see what great advance was in there. The engineers unshackled the hood to reveal a BMW engine. Mercedes revamped its motors."

Car and Driver
December 1993

■ Hey, bosses, would your engineers (designers, etc.) have the nerve to do that? Yes, you say. Are you sure?

■ Hey, engineers, got the guts to do that? No? Why not — think you can keep your head down and hang onto your cozy position for life? Guess again.

BREAKING THE MOLD

112 The 2760 Octavia Street Phenomenon

With an hour to kill before my next San Francisco appointment, I parked my car on Green Street, then headed down Octavia toward Union. The shop at 2760 Octavia attracted my attention — Khuri's Deli Cafe. I popped in.

A good move.

San Francisco (nay, the world) is loaded with delis. But, as with dry cleaners, travel agencies, banks, computer-makers, and steel companies, a few stand out. Khuri's is one. Its miniature space sparkled. And the food was fabulous. I asked for a simple tabbouleh, but the ebullient owner practically forced me to sample many of the rest of his offerings — an incredible German potato salad, a fabulous babaghanouj, hummus to die for, etc.

His enthusiasm filled the store. I got the history (going back centuries) of a couple of the dishes, how he prepared them, how his mother had taught him, differences in his and his mom's cooking style.

He also explained his catering service and tossed in a lecturette on nutritional value. Body Shop boss Anita Roddick couldn't have done better.

But we did cross swords. I told him he was a "fantastic salesman." He bridled at the billing, claiming he was no salesman at all, just an announcer for this marvelous food that he loved so much.

KHURI, MOM, AND FANTASTIC FARE

In sum, quality was tops, service was scintillating, and the impression was one of pure theater. While I enjoyed the food, the experience mostly got me thinking about . . . excellence — how a few "common" product or service providers stick out, how most don't, and how it only takes you about 60 seconds, literally, to tell the difference. And that's true whether the company is a steelmaker or a deli.

If you're ever in San Francisco, don't fail to stop at Khuri's for lesson No. 1 on how the potentially mundane need not be so. And if you want to conduct a fabulous seminar at your construction company, municipal zoo, or copy shop, have each employee identify the two or three little shops in your town that they love (not like). The Khuri's of the world probably have more to teach us about winning business performance at home and abroad than the Generals Electric, Mills, and Motors.

(Incidentally, this was not a one-shot phenomenon. A few weeks after I drafted the above, my wife, Kate, was intrigued enough by my Khuri's riff to stop in. She got the same treatment and then some — from the mom.)

113

In the 1930s, GM's legendary chairman Alfred Sloan observed, "In practically all our activities we seem to suffer from the inertia resulting from our great size. . . . There are so many people involved and it requires such a tremendous effort to put something new into effect, that a new idea is likely to be considered insignificant in comparison with the effort that it takes to put it across. Sometimes I am almost forced to the conclusion that General Motors is so large and its inertia so great that it is impossible for us to be leaders."

> **A new idea is likely to be considered insignificant in comparison with the effort that it takes to put it across.**

Talk about foresight!

114 An Ordinary Company (or Two)

The head of Toyota Australia admitted to me that, when he's out for a drive, he often can't tell his company's cars from others'! The same bug has bitten once oh-so-proud Sony. A top manager acknowledges the firm has become an "ordinary company." Sony's Handycam Comix 8mm video camera, *Tokyo Business* reported in its August 1994 issue, is "a blatant imitation of Sharp's LCD Viewcam, and looks identical to Fuji's vertical-design Simple-Hi8. Today's Sony has changed from launching breakthrough products to launching price offensives on `me-too' goods."

At precisely the wrong moment, a lot of businesses lost their nerve. When Sony was at its peak, it made products that turned *it* on, says *Tokyo Business*. Now it's seemingly become just another gutless, soulless corporation. How sad!

115

A very wise and very successful (financially and artistically) friend gave me his 30-second diagnosis of what ails most businesses, especially sizable ones: "I end up getting roped into social dinners with [executives] every couple of weeks. I usually come home in a stupor, and it's not the Pinot Noir. It's just that . . . well . . . they don't love the products they make. You never 'hear' that passion. I don't get it. Their language is so chilly, so abstract. . . . You know what I mean, don't you, Tom?"

Yes I do. . . . And then there's Herb Kelleher.

116 Service with Soul

"There are 50 ways to leave your lover, but only six exits from this airplane. . . ."

Start of safety announcement
Southwest Airlines

"Better quality + lesser price = value + spiritual attitude of our employees = unbeatable"

Herb Kelleher
on Southwest Airlines'
success formula

Southwest Airlines is so far ahead of the competition it hardly seems fair. Its costs are much lower. So is airport turnaround time. Its youthful aircraft fleet logs many more flights than other carriers'. Wages are high, but productivity is even higher. That's why the airline, now serving 41 cities, is so consistently profitable in an industry stuck in intensive care. Southwest also tops customer-service polls — and, according to one prestigious survey, was rated safest airline over the last 20 years.

What's the secret? The grand scheme is simple, even elegant. (Short hauls only, no baggage transfer, no seat assignment, no food, one type of aircraft, etc.) But there's more: Southwest has soul. Or, as the airline's larger-than-life CEO, Herb Kelleher, puts it, "We defined a personality as well as a market niche. [We seek to] amuse, surprise, entertain."

Kelleher is as shrewd a businessman as I've met. But it's his humanness that's so exceptional. He easily peppers his remarks with "love" (the airline's stock symbol is LUV), "fun," and "spirituality." He rips CEOs who sit on numerous outside boards and hang out mostly with one another. Kelleher insists he gets his kicks being around Southwest's people. "They are restorative and rejuvenating to me," he told me. "Ponce de Leon was looking in the wrong place when he sought the fountain of youth in Florida. The people of Southwest *are* the fountain of youth." (And the funny thing is, when you've been around Kelleher for a while, you're damn sure he means it.)

While Kelleher gives his customers a great deal and a great time, he's clear that the people of Southwest come first — even if it means dismissing customers! Are customers always right? "No they are *not*," Kelleher snaps. "And I think that's one of the biggest betrayals of your people you can possibly commit. The customer is frequently wrong. We don't carry those sorts of customers. We write them and say, 'Fly somebody else. Don't abuse our people.'"

Such beliefs — and actions — make Southwest one of the 10 best places to work in America, according to the authors of *The 100 Best Companies to Work for in America*.

HELL YES, WE HAVE FRILLS SAYS HERB

To be allowed to join Southwest's game, you undergo an intense hiring process that includes at least a half-dozen interviews. But you won't be subjected to psychological tests. "What we are looking for first and foremost is a sense of humor," Kelleher told *Fortune*. "Then we are looking for people who have to excel to satisfy themselves and who work well in a collegial environment. We don't care that much about education and experience, because we can train people to do whatever they have to do. We hire attitudes." Colleen Barrett is executive vice president for customers. (It's a revealing title; she began at Southwest as a secretary in 1971.) Barrett told us that the airline looks for "listening, caring, smiling, saying 'thank-you,' and being warm" — in the people it hires for accounting as much as in reservation agents and flight attendants.

The spirited, yeasty workforce is also flexible. Though unionized to the hilt, anyone will help anyone else in a pinch. "Our people are results-oriented, not process-oriented," Kelleher says. "They're not form-oriented, they don't focus on the organization hierarchy or position or title."

So this, then, is a profitable, no-frills airline? Whoops! Don't you dare use "no frills" anywhere near Barrett, who responded to such a claim, "Ohh. No. No. Not 'no frills.' A frill is something extra-special. And we offer something extra-special *every day*." Cheap means "more for less, not less for less," said another Southwest exec.

Kelleher's magic — matchless business acumen and over-sized heart — has led the way to 21 straight years of black ink in a viper pit of an industry. In the early days, Braniff (which, with the help of a few friends, blocked Kelleher's efforts to take off for almost five years) undercut Southwest's bargain-basement $26 fares. Kelleher's response to Braniff's $13 ticket price was to give *his* passengers an only-on-Southwest choice: $13 to match Braniff — or the regular $26 fare *plus* a bottle of premium liquor. (Southwest ended up distributing a lot of booze.)

Two decades later, *Fortune* wondered, on its cover, if Kelleher is the best CEO in America. He may well be. He's arguably created air travel's Greatest Show on Earth — plus you get where you're going on time, with your bags, and with your wallet intact; and *without* heartburn from typical airline food.

Not bad. And one more inspiring case of major-league service differentiation — against all odds.

117 Strategic Planning, R.I.P.

Southwest's Herb Kelleher, trained as a lawyer, can dissect a balance sheet with the best of them. But he understands that sustaining advantage comes from a relentless focus on the intangibles. McGill University professor Henry Mintzberg understands, too. That's why he worked so hard to undermine traditional strategic planning in his magesterial *The Rise and Fall of*

Strategic Planning.

To be sure, our mindless love affair with planning that bloomed in the 1960s effectively ended a dozen years ago (when then-neophyte GE chairman Jack Welch zapped his corporation's hyper-formalized planning system, and most of the headquarters planners along with it). Still, this academic yet sprightly text is, well, so encyclopedic, so damning . . . and so final. It puts the last nails in a coffin long in need of burial. As I see it the book decisively closes a major chapter of the American management saga. This dead horse need not be beaten again.

My own reading of *The Rise and Fall* consumed (correct word) a plane trip to London, a full night in New Delhi, then two more dusk-to-dawn stints in Dubai. The catharsis was profound. From time to time I'd even find myself sweating, despite an air-conditioned chill that kept me under blankets.

> **"A good deal of corporate planning is like a ritual rain dance."**
> **Brian Quinn**

"So far so bad," proclaimed the renowned political scientist Aaron Wildavsky, in 1973, of the elaborate planning processes introduced into the public sector by Robert (Body-count Bob) McNamara when he was U.S. secretary of defense. Others went farther. "A good deal of corporate planning . . . is like a ritual rain dance," wrote Dartmouth's Brian Quinn. "It has no effect on the weather that follows, but those who engage in it think it does. . . . Moreover, much of the advice related to corporate planning is directed at improving the dancing, not the weather." Columbia's Len Sayles chimed in, "Apparently our society, not unlike the Greeks with their Delphic oracles, takes great comfort in believing that very talented 'seers' removed from the hurly-burly world of reality can foretell coming events."

Mintzberg hardly limits himself to such gratuitous, if deadly accurate, barbs. In chapter after chapter, he meticulously builds his case, citing not just his own extensive research evidence, but that of other scholars. For instance, there's the French academic who, after a thorough consideration of planning effectiveness in 1978, succinctly concludes: "Those who say they make plans and that these work are liars. The term planning is imbecilic; everything can change tomorrow."

HENRY MINTZBERG

But Russell Ackoff was not so easily deterred. The oft-quoted grand champion of planning in the 1960s (and producer of some of the most elaborate — and ludicrous, in hindsight — planning schemes of all time) apparently destroys his own position. "Recently I asked three corporate executives," he wrote in 1970, "what decisions they had made in the last year that would not have been made were it not for their corporate plans. All had difficulty identifying one such decision. Since all of the plans are marked 'secret' or 'confidential,' I asked them how their competitors might benefit from possession of their plans. Each answered with embarrassment that their competitors would not benefit." Undeterred by the facts, Ackoff used the exec's critique as a spur to creating even more elaborate planning schemes.

But, Mintzberg observes, it's not just that planning doesn't work. It's downright dangerous. One hundred years ago an early champion of planning, Henri Fayol, admitted as much. Planning schemes, he said, not only don't encourage flexibility (the only sane response to changing times), but actually suppress it. Dartmouth's Quinn observed, decades later, that the annual planning process was rarely — never, in his research — "the source of radical . . . departures into entirely different product/market realms." The button-down nature of the procedure per se, he added, "essentially forecloses radical innovation."

A Termite-Infested Foundation

The meat of Mintzberg's thorough review is a brick-by-brick

analysis of planning's problems. Consider just three:

■ **Process kills.** Process was king for the champions of strategic planning. They exhibit a "passionate attachment to dispassion," said one wry commentator. They are "more set on deciding rightly than upon right decisions," another chimed in. Mintzberg reports with amusement: "'By the middle of June,' wrote [professors] Lorange and Vancil of planning in a large diversified multinational, 'top management has prepared an explicit statement of corporate strategy and goals.' One can almost see the executives sitting around the table at 11 P.M. on the 14th of June, working frantically to complete their strategy."

Mintzberg saves many of his best shots for Mariann Jelinek, who in the late 1970s gushed about Texas Instruments' rococo Objectives, Tactics and Strategies system, a scheme that one TI exec later described as "a paperwork mill that makes it absolutely impossible to respond to anything that moves quickly." (TI, like GE under Welch, trashed its system after a long string of marketplace blunders.) Mintzberg views Jelinek's belief in the possibility of "institutionalizing innovation" as the final performance of a long-running play. "The revolution that [time and motion study pioneer Frederick] Taylor initiated in the factory was being repeated at the apex of the hierarchy, and it would be fundamentally no different." The reduction of strategy-making to a mechanical act capable of being perfected — like Taylor's pursuit of the ideal way to shovel coal — was fundamentally wrong, and in attempting it, planners sowed the seeds of their own destruction. The "obsession for control" mirrored in planning schemes, wrote James Worthy, "springs from the failure to recognize or appreciate the value of spontaneity."

■ **Hard data aren't.** Not surprisingly, fanatics for process are also gaga for hard data. Yet Mintzberg thoroughly exposes the "soft underbelly of hard data," what he calls strategic planning's near fatal "assumption of quantification."

Planning's emphasis on "hard data" and "facts" leads to the fallacy of "measuring what's measurable." The results are limiting at best. For example, Mintzberg finds that planners show a pronounced tendency to favor "cost leadership strategies" (which emphasize internal operating efficiencies, which are generally measurable) over "product leadership strategies" (emphasizing innovative design or high quality, which are less measurable).

> **"Hard information is often limited in scope, lacking richness, and often fails to encompass important non-economic and non-quantitative factors."**

More generally, Mintzberg claims, an abiding emphasis on the measurable dismisses as irrelevant the "random noise, gossip, and impressions" that are vital to adapting in a turbulent environment. He approvingly quotes Harvard scholar Richard Neustadt, adviser to several presidents. "It is not information of a general sort that helps a President . . . not surveys, not the bland amalgams," Neustadt wrote. "Rather . . . it is the odds and ends of tangible detail that pieced together . . . illuminate the underside of issues."

Mintzberg concludes:

1. "Hard information is often limited in scope, lacking richness and often fails to encompass important non-economic and non-quantitative factors. . . .

2. "Much hard information is too aggregated for effective use in strategy making. . . .

3. "Much hard information arrives too late to be of use in strategy making. . . .

4. "Finally, a surprising amount of hard information is unreliable [which mocks our tendency] to assume that anything expressed in figures must necessarily be precise."

Overall, Mintzberg opines, "While hard data may inform the

intellect, it is largely soft data that generate wisdom."

■ **Woe betide the separation of thought and action.** Mintzberg next pounces on the "assumption of detachment," quantification's close kin. " If the system does the thinking," he adduces, "thought must be detached from the action, strategy from operations, and thinkers from doers."

Ah, those heady days when planning ruled the roost! Mintzberg, with near disbelief and undisguised contempt, cites an "astonishing" statement by a British planning manager: "Through the [planning] process we can stop managers falling in love with their businesses." Such was the unabashed goal, as another British executive reports with alarm: "The chief executive of a world-famous group of management consultants tried hard to convince me that it is ideal that top management . . . should have as little knowledge as possible relative to the product."

Of course Mintzberg hardly dismisses the value of some detachment (seeing forests as well as trees, and all that). Effective strategists, he wrote in summary, "are not people who abstract themselves from the daily details but quite the opposite: They are the ones who immerse themselves in it, while being able to extract the strategic messages from it." He gives his stamp of approval to a successful Canadian retail firm's top managers, who readily "invest themselves in a question about the quality of a shipment of strawberries with the same passion and commitment as in a question about opening a chain of restaurants." It is such "intimate knowledge," he adds, "that informed their more global vision."

Analysis Does Not Produce Synthesis

To expose the problems of planning schemes still misses the point. It implies that a fix is possible. But suppose, Wildavsky mused, that "the failures of planning are not peripheral or accidental but integral to its very nature." That's Mintzberg's contention, too. What I have reprised of his case to this point, in fact, is mere prelude to his clinching argument:

The fundamental assumption underlying strategic planning,

says its executioner, is that "analysis will produce synthesis, that decomposition of the process of strategy making into a series of articulated steps . . . will produce integrated strategies." Rubbish, Mintzberg snorts, and lights off a final, massive display of intellectual pyrotechnics that draws upon everything from economic to physiological (right brain/left brain) research.

"Planning by its very nature," he claims, "defines and preserves categories. Creativity, by its very nature, creates categories, or rearranges established ones. This is why formal planning can neither provide creativity nor deal with it when it emerges by other means." Strategies that are "novel and compelling," he adds, "seem to be the product of single, creative brains . . . capable of synthesizing a vision. The key to this is integration rather than decomposition, based on holistic images rather than linear words."

Head for the Weed Patch

Having scuttled strategic planning, Mintzberg proceeds to throw a life ring to planners, who, he admits can range from the "obsessively Cartesian to the playfully intuitive." Strategies that break the mold, he says, "grow initially like weeds in a garden, they are not cultivated like tomatoes in a hot house. . . . [They] can take root in all kinds of places." To effectively "manage" the strategy-making process, then, is "not to preconceive strategies but to recognize their emergence and intervene when appropriate." Thence Mintzberg's primary role for modern, artful planners: To be finders rather than designers of strategies. They'll best serve their firms by discovering "fledgling strategies in unexpected pockets of the organization so that consideration can be given to [expanding] them."

Mintzberg observes, ironically, that our passion for planning has mostly flourished during stable times (e.g., the 1960s). When faced with discontinuities of the sort that have become routine today, planners have been caught wearing concrete boots and looking back over their shoulders; not surprisingly, they have been routed. The importance of greeting discontinuities with bold strategies is more significant than ever. Just don't expect fast footwork and zany departures from green-eyeshade analysts promoting just-the-hard-facts-ma'am, systematic strategic planning schemes.

So now will you reconsider hiring Luciano Benetton when he shows up in the raw at your recruiting-office door?

118

"Sometime during the two-year curriculum, every MBA student ought to hear it clearly stated that numbers, techniques, and analysis are all side matters. What is central to business is the joy of creating."

> Peter Robinson
> *The Red Herring*
> (Robinson wrote the acclaimed *Snapshots from Hell: The Making of an MBA*, a recounting of the author's first year at the Stanford business school)

119

Lots of trees have been felled to produce articles and books about the cost of capital. The topic is surely important to finance ministers the world over. But my view, perhaps in the distinct minority, is that cost of capital is largely irrelevant to the individual business.

That is, if a project's success hinges on whether it costs you 9 percent or 14 percent to get your hands on the necessary funds, you're barking up the wrong tree. You should be looking at projects that promise to transform a corner of your industry. (Or at least transform your block — assuming you're opening a 15-table restaurant.) That is, the prospective returns (which, to be sure, will not always be realized) should be so high over the medium to long haul that even usurious lending rates would make little difference in your decision to attempt to climb the mountain.

"Once we have appointed our managers, we let them reinvent the wheel. . . . The world is changing so fast you'll always be needing different wheels for changing terrain."

Paul van Vlissingen
chairman, SHV
($10 billion revenue,
Dutch-based retailer)

Van Vlissingen says that integrity in all business dealings is a must. Other than that, the idea of a common corporate culture is wrongheaded. Keep finding and developing great people, he says, then let 'em do it their way.

I agree.

121 On Your Mark, Get Set, Get Slim . . .

. . . Then What?

Our giant firms (and their middle-size kin, if we're being honest) became phenomenally bloated. Then came the technology revolution and the demise of traditional hierarchies; no matter how you parse it, the massive white-collar cutting of the last decade has been justified. There's *much* more of it still to come.

But when "lean and mean" becomes gospel, then your church steeple is about to come tumbling down. The object of business is not to be lean and mean, not to reorganize and then reengineer.

The object of business is to invent, to grow — and *add* to employment over time. The trouble is, it's a lot easier to slash, burn, fire, and create new process-wiring diagrams than to leap tall buildings with a single bound and create.

Some research by Mercer consultants on "good guys" — firms with above-average profits in their industry segment — sheds light on this issue. The study's winners got to above-average profits via below-average costs (along with average revenues) or above-average revenues (with average costs).

In short, Mercer found creating beats cutting: Stock market valuation grew twice as fast for companies that got to above-average profits logging above-average revenue growth than for those who got unusually high returns courtesy of unusually low costs.

It's not quite "Q.E.D.," but you get the drift. Don't you?

122

George Roberts, of the investment bankers Kolberg Kravis Roberts & Co., says the CEO should have a substantial stake in his company — investing at least $300,000 to $400,000 of a $2 million to $3 million salary in his company's shares.

Makes all sorts of sense to me.

123   The Relentless Pursuit of Inconsistency

The 8 A.M. request seemed simple enough. I was arriving at the Washington, D.C., hotel at 1 P.M., and needed a room for the night.

Night? Try night*mare*. The reservation person said my "early" arrival (4 P.M. is standard check-in time) meant I needed a "day room," then a regular room for the night.

"Same room, though?" I asked.

"Probably. First you'll need to check with the front desk on the day room."

"You can't do that for me?" I asked.

"No, you need to set up the day room first, then get transferred back to me."

"Seems strange," I said.

"Well," she almost huffed, "it's two departments." (As if I gave a tinker's damn about the hotel's org chart!) "But," she added, sensing my frustration, "you *could* ask the front desk for the 'day room,' then after you check in, call down and extend it for the night."

"But I wouldn't be assured of a place to sleep tonight that way, would I?"

want that hotel reservation person to quit.......

"No, but the chances are good."

It was tourist season *and* World Cup 1994 time in D.C., and I wasn't sure my chances were that good. So, confused and defeated, I finally asked to talk to a manager. He was able to work things out for me and apologized for the two-department bit (though he took no apparent note of my pro bono suggestion that the current procedure was stupid).

All this brought to mind an exchange at a seminar in Edinburgh, Scotland, the week before. I'd been ranting and raving about the importance of giving frontline employees lots of authority to sort things out for customers. One participant came back at me: "But how do you insure *consistency* from frontline employees in these highly decentralized organizations?"

"Ah-ha," I almost shouted. "You don't! We're trying to nurture *in*consistency, the kind of personalized response you'd get from a Mom-and-Pop shop."

Look, I read the late Dr. Deming, too. I understand process variation, and the need for pilots and hotel housekeepers to carefully follow checklists. But I'm afraid our TQM fanatics go too far. Our heart's desire should be the pursuit, not the suppression, of variation.

To be specific, I want that hotel reservation person in D.C. to quit acting like a "reservation person." I want her to be Chairwoman, Founder, and CEO of Customer Care for anybody who calls. (Me, for instance.)

I know, as an experienced traveler, that when you call a hotel for a room that night, you usually get transferred to the front desk, which "controls" reservations for the current evening. But that's a convention for the hotel's convenience, not mine. When I phoned the hotel in D.C. (instead of the Four Seasons, where I normally stay), the staff was confronted with an opportunity: They had a chance to book a room for a day and a half (day room plus night room fees) *and* to make a friend, who just might be weaned from the Four Seasons long term. But, to do that, reservation clerks need an affinity for variation — i.e., for meet-

.........acting like a "reservation person," I want

ing my somewhat special (though hardly bizarre) needs.

Let's give my Edinburgh questioner his due, though. I'm not suggesting we just hire people and turn them loose. I would train the bejesus out of that clerk-reservationist-CEO of Customer Care. Next, the frontline employee should understand the economics of the business. Using the jargon of the day (the "open-book corporation"), she should have about as much information at her fingertips as the *real* CEO. (Ever wonder, Ms. Business Owner, why employees don't go through the same sort of decision-making process you do? Usually it's not a lack of motivation — it's a lack of information.)

Finally, our reservationist-turned-CEO should be part of a regular discussion group with peers and senior management that simply jaws about the hotel, its aims, problems, opportunities. The idea is not fact-stuffing (traditional training), but working together on the corporate ethos. It's what partners routinely do in a small business. And, hey, we're trying to get the "reservationist" to be just that — a *partner* in a business.

Business success at De-Mar (the plumbers!), Four Seasons, and cataloguer J. Peterman comes from making every customer, even when there are millions, feel human, unique, and the object of the frontline employee's total attention (for a minute or so). And, to belabor the oft-neglected obvious, that only comes from turning every frontline employee into a one-person entrepreneurial enterprise that happens to be embedded in a much larger corporate body.

Speaking of the power of inconsistency. . . .

124

Free speech — the right to say *whatever* we feel about our government, no matter how incendiary — is the bedrock of American democracy. This country wasn't founded during a polite roundtable discussion — it took a *revolution*. The constant hue and cry, the demonstrations, the political battles, keep us

her to be Chairwoman, Founder, and CEO of.......

honest as a nation — keep us fluid, adaptive, *changing*.

Unfortunately, many corporations haven't learned the lessons our Founding Fathers knew so well — and have suffered mightily by stifling dissent and encouraging blind (and bland) subservience.

The brilliant Supreme Court Justice Louis Brandeis said — in a statement every CEO should heed — "Those who won our independence . . . did not exalt order at the cost of liberty." Change that to ". . . did not exalt order at the cost of innovation" and you define the problem with order-loving, innovation-fearing, big corporate chieftains.

Brandeis didn't stop with order vs. liberty. "The greatest menace to freedom," he continued, "is an inert people." Again, his observation is uncannily relevant to a pillar of modern corporate malaise: inert workers, who aren't allowed to use their heads (and hearts and passions and *weirdness*) in service of their company.

Muted criticism has killed many a corporation. My experience with big-boardroom America is one of calm in the midst of the storm — scandalous denial of the maelstrom that surrounds them.

Free speech is a precious and precarious gift (a quick look at the evening news will prove that), one worth fighting for both in the body politic and corporate America. I've watched even young Silicon Valley companies ossify almost overnight because they've stifled the right to spunk, feistiness, and what Judge Learned Hand called "immodest and indecent invective" — i.e., rude disagreement with the chief.

Beware muted criticism and the absence of indecent invective! Beware an inert workforce! The very special bunch of people who got this country started 200 years ago have a lot to teach today's corporate honchos. Namely, open your ears (and hearts and minds) to raucous dissent and innovative disorder.

..........Customer Care for **anybody** who calls.

125

While speed-walking around the bottom of the South Lawn one late-August morning, I heard this phrase from a PA system speaker providing instructions to prospective White House visitors: " . . . the president and first lady are pleased to share it with you. . . ."

It dawned on me that, at age 51, I'd finally figured out the problem with government.

The Clintons (though I suspect the taped announcement predates his presidency) have got it ass-backwards. It is WE, the citizens of the United States, who granted our government very limited powers in 1787. It is WE, the citizens of the United States, who are pleased to share the White House with the Clintons for a few years.

Number one: It's the truth.

Number two: My story won sustained applause, a few hours later, from 2,000 folks at a client-server computer conference I addressed.

Number three: It's about more than inside-the-Beltway arrogance. All employees, in effect, grant their collective bosses certain temporary, limited power, in hopes of accomplishing more as a group than they could individually — this is the essence of what some call "servant leadership," a wonderful term.

> **"How difficult it is to accept that behind the facade of our tidy narratives rages the aimless human circus."**
>
> **Jack Hitt**

126

Logic? Rationality? Cause and effect? Can't live without 'em. And I suppose you'll also tell me the naming of America was an appropriate honor for a great explorer.

Jack Hitt, writing in the *Washington Monthly* ("Original Spin: How Lurid Sex Fantasies Gave Us America"), claims that Amerigo Vespucci was "a dweeb"; his immortality stems from letters "laced with wild adventures, bizarre events and lewd encounters" sent home from a voyage to South America. One of the racy missives, which were widely circulated as pamphlets, made it to Martin Waldseemueller, a cartographer who was updating "the most respected [geography] text of the day." When the time came to name the area we call home, Vespucci's titillating reports happened to be close at hand. We know the rest of the story.

"How difficult it is to accept that behind the facade of our tidy narratives rages the aimless human circus," Hitt concludes. So the wobbly tale goes, from Vespucci's time to ours. But surely our miraculous new knowledge-processing tools will lead us, finally, out of the bramble of incomprehension? Dream on.

Take the Rodney King video, a product of the ubiquitous home video recorder. Truth incarnate? A prosecutor's dream come true? Hardly. (After all, it took two trials and a possible violation of the Constitution's double-jeopardy rule to get a conviction.) Writing in the *New York Times*, Patricia Greenfield and Paul Kibbey assess one reason for the differing interpretations of the video: "Slow motion minimizes the violence. In the real world, a faster blow is a harder blow; a slower blow is softer." In fact, the authors write, one observer viewing the tape in slow motion claimed, "It looks like a ballet."

Modern market analysis is fraught with similar contradictions. Now that we can instantly procure a ton of information on any topic, we're more at sea than ever. Juxtapose a few relational databases, and the U.S. population of 250 million explodes into 250 million distinct markets. Then what? Besides mind-numbing overload, of course.

Economist and Nobel laureate F. A. Hayek understood the

limits of rationality. Economic progress, he explained, is a game of chance discoveries, the byproduct of millions of unplanned trials and errors. The best hope of success lies in having numerous projects percolating at once; this ups the odds of one of them boiling over.

There are no better examples of Hayek's thesis than Hollywood and Silicon Valley, infernos of unbalanced zealots harboring irrational beliefs in untested ideas. The mess is the message!

Given the continuing triumph of absurdity, are there any "strategies" to help individuals or corporations?

■ **Ready—Fire—Aim.** Want a strategy? Throw enough spaghetti at the wall and some just might stick.

■ **Loose the crazies**. For sizable corporations, decentralization that mimics Johnson & Johnson's lightly linked structure is about the only answer. **Caution:** Liberated units must be captained by self-assured leaders who rejoice in thumbing their noses at their bosses.

■ **Embrace naiveté.** The late Richard Feynman mused about the inordinate contribution of young researchers to high-energy physics. "They don't know enough," he said, "because when you know enough, it's obvious that every idea that you have is no good."

■ **Read Chekhov.** "You ask me what life is?" Chekhov wrote to a friend. "It is like asking what a carrot is. A carrot is a carrot, and nothing more is known." The great novelists understand what management gurus dare not admit: There are no rules. (For what it's worth, the Chekhov quote hangs above my writing desk.)

A carrot is a carrot, a bawdy letter brought America its name, and the kooky human circus continues. If we could learn to appreciate and revel in its yeastiness, lighten our attachment to logic, and back off our obsession with control, then perhaps we could concoct moderately useful strategies for business and life. And if the strategies didn't work, at least we'd have more fun.

127

"With many companies we start, we don't even do the figures in advance. We just feel there's room in the market. . . . We try to make the figures work out after the event."

Richard Branson
Virgin Group

Branson gets it. (See item No. 126 above.)

128

Engines of progress: I'm struck that at first glance most economies look alike. Average American and Japanese and Indian workers do about the same things: drive cabs, write memos, fix things. Except the ingenious Indian mechanic works on the street patching 15-year-old bicycles, while his Japanese and American counterparts doctor Infinitis or Lincolns in air-conditioned service bays, using computerized diagnostic tools.

The differences, mostly, lie at the edge — sophisticated products and services on which the rest of us piggyback our way to relative success. Breakthrough products depend, in turn, on an astonishingly small number of people. Providing a climate that produces great microbiologists, aerospace engineers, and architects — and then offers an entrepreneurial infrastructure that turns their work into gold — is essential.

129

Jim Abegglen, as savvy an Asian observer as you'll come across, insists the center of the industrial world is *not* shifting to Asia. . . .

It has *already shifted* to Asia!

"Does your business strategy reflect that?" he asked 125 big-business execs, with a tight, slightly contemptuous smile. OK, more than slightly contemptuous.

130

"Are you regenerating? Are you dealing with new things?

When you find yourself in a new environment, do you come up with a fundamentally different approach? That's the test. When you flunk, you leave."

Jack Welch
CEO, GE, on Jack Welch

131 Mutant as Savior

Accidents happen. In fact, accidents are what life is about. Ten thousand unpredictable factors spawn a Wal-Mart or a Nike. Hold your applause for the planners: It simply turned out that the companies' schemes suited the market's unanticipated needs at that moment.

Suddenly, new firms rush to copy the Wal-Mart or Nike model — until a new, happy accident occurs. Yesterday's stars, slaves to the rituals that made them excellent originally, have little ability to change; many either die or become irrelevant.

Charles Darwin, of course, explained all this 135 years ago. His theory of natural selection is crystal clear: Until there's an accident (random mutation), no progress occurs. Most accidents/random mutations are useless (just as most start-ups fail); but a tiny handful succeed — and are responsible for all progress.

Physics provides managers' favored metaphors. For example, Newton's sun-and-planets atomic model is attractive and predictable. (Most of today's aging execs didn't study quantum mechanics, which strikes a fatal blow at Newton's determinism.) Unfortunately, business analysts rarely consider biological models.

For those not schooled in biology (e.g., me), Carl Sagan and Ann Druyan's book *Shadows of Forgotten Ancestors: A Search for Who We Are* is a superb primer. Consider these statements from their chapter on DNA, mutation, and progress:

"Active mutators in placid . . . times tend to die off. They are selected against. Reluctant mutators in quickly changing times are also selected against."

Business application: In a calm market, slow-moving, orderly, methodical firms will thrive; crazies will perish. If you can count on your next generation of cookies, sweaters, or software to last a dozen years, then you should patiently nurture it. Don't jeopardize a brand by introducing a flurry of line extensions, let alone new categories that might threaten today's winner.

Alternatively, in a turbulent market, "reluctant mutators" — those who are afraid to challenge their current cash cow with, say, an aggressively early release of an adventurous new product — are headed for trouble.

As I see it, business problem No. 1 is that too many still follow the reluctant mutator strategy — e.g., IBM's continuing and ultimately futile effort to keep an iron grip on its major customers in a computational world gone bonkers.

"Advantageous mutations occur so rarely that . . . it may be helpful to arrange for an increased mutation rate."

Business lesson: Pursue accidents! The trick for an IBM, Sears, or GM is to create a Dell, Gap, or Honda in its midst. (Or, more accurately, to create many would-be Dells, etc., one of which might launch the company into an entirely new trajectory.)

Body Shop boss Anita Roddick says she seeks out anarchists, another word for mutators. It's easier said than done. In-house renegades, following a lucky first success, typically get co-opted by the mainstream and suffocated by the company's time-honored practices.

"It's as if, for every million dyed-in-the-wool conservative organisms, there's one radical who's out to change things. . . . And only one in a million (of the radicals) knows what it's talking about — providing a significantly better survival plan than the one currently fashionable. And yet the evolution of life is determined by these revolutionaries."

Business translation: Life's a bitch and then you (usually) die. That is, we depend entirely upon radicals to pull our chestnuts out of the fire. But most radicals are flakes who don't even know where the fireplace is. To "nurture the crazies" (my constant refrain) is to invite discord — and, usually, failure. But not to nurture the crazies is to flatly guarantee failure.

"We understand enough about biology . . . to recognize a powerful stochastic component."

Practical translation: Einstein's contrary assertion notwithstanding, God probably did roll dice in creating the universe. You'd better do the same. That is, chance determines success, and there's only one way to beat the odds: Lots of statistically independent tries unconstrained by "the way we do things around here."

"Natural selection . . . draws forth a complex set of molecular responses that may superficially look like . . . a Master Molecular Biologist tinkering with the genes; but, in fact, all that is happening is mutation . . . interacting with a changing external environment."

My advice: Commit this last statement to memory — and if you're the boss, pin it over your planner's desk. In retrospect, a 3M (among the best at spawning mutants) looks logical: Families of products fit rather neatly under certain headings — e.g., 3M's relatively recent, multi-billion-dollar success in medical products. But the truth is, 3M grew like Topsy, was pockmarked by failures, and was wise enough to capitalize quickly on the successful accidents — which whetted rather than diminished its appetite for unsettling mutants.

The 3M story is not tidy. But, then, neither is life — despite large corporations' continued efforts, futile in general and deadly these days, to try to make it so.

132 Think Disruption!

Amos Tuck School of Business professor Richard D'Aveni knows exactly what Sagan and Druyan are trying to tell you and me. He coined the term hypercompetition, claiming that today's outrageous pace of change calls for upside-down business approaches. "Chivalry is dead," D'Aveni writes in *Hypercompetition: Managing the Dynamics of Strategic Maneuvering*. "The new code of conduct is an active strategy of disrupting the status quo to create an unsustainable series of competitive advantages." (That's right, unsustainable — i.e., hunting for and quickly exploiting competitive edges, then abandoning them before the competition responds.)

"This is not an age of defensive castles, moats and armor," he continues. "It is rather an age of cunning, speed and surprise. It may be hard for some to hang up the chain mail of sustainable advantage after . . . so many battles. But hypercompetition, a state in which sustainable advantages are no longer possible, is now the only level of competition."

D'Aveni's favorite word is *disruption*. He offers a *vision* for disruption, *competences* for disruption, *tactics* for disruption.

Citing scores of compelling examples, from hot-sauce wars to computer skirmishes, D'Aveni's book makes clear there's no place to hide from this new world order. Hence his relentless attack on the *static* bias of most strategic thinking — e.g., McKinsey & Co.'s popular 7-S business model (strategy, structure, systems, etc. — I was its co-inventor back in 1978). McKinsey aimed to help clients fit together the pieces to create, for example, systems and a structure that frictionlessly support a strategy. Wrong, D'Aveni snorts: Purposeful *mis*fit is the point! He even gives us a new 7-S paradigm, including surprise, shifting rules of competition, and strategic soothsaying (looking for information in highly unconventional ways — perhaps Nancy Reagan's astrologer?).

The energetic, arm-waving (though academically sound) D'Aveni is a very fresh voice urging managers to "build" enterprises dedicated to perpetual revolution. Are we listening yet? Do we cheer (or do we grimace) when an idea is presented that threatens today's breadwinning service or product?

133 More Purposeful Disruption

Consider these words from Phil Twyman, chief operating officer of AMP Australia, that country's biggest insurance firm: "In the past, if a new business idea came along that threatened to cannibalize one of our existing businesses we would have stayed out

of it. . . . Our view now is that if any organization is going to cannibalize AMP, it should be the son of AMP. We have discrete
businesses for different market segments and we let them compete."

Twyman admits he's even willing to accept the occasional
confusion in the marketplace that internal competition gener-
ates. And perhaps a bit of customer confusion, too. (Who is
AMP? Which AMP?) Twyman's on the money as far as I'm concerned. Tidy times call for tidy strategic schemes. The times
aren't tidy, and so our strategic schemes shouldn't be, either.

I. e., disrupt yourself, stupid!

134

"Call it testimony to the total lack of imagination [on the part of
the two companies' leaders]."

> CEO, medium-size defense contractor,
> on the proposed Lockheed and Martin
> Marietta merger that would create $23
> billion Lockheed Martin

Do you believe in the tooth fairy? If you do, then pursue
"synergies" in your business strategy. It sounds great. But the
research evidence is clear: It rarely comes to pass.

135 Bombs Away!

"A pattern emphasized in the cases in this study is the degree to
which powerful competitors not only resist innovative threats,
but actually resist all efforts to understand them, preferring to
further entrench their positions in the older products. This
results in a surge of productivity and performance that may
take the old technology to unheard-of heights. But in most cases
this is a sign of impending death."

> Jim Utterback
> *Mastering the Dynamics of Innovation*

"Pattern" is a mellow term for the findings in Utterback's
(and others') research. Entrenched firms almost *invariably*

respond the wrong way to innovative competitors.

It works like this: A mature, slumbering industry (e.g., gas lighting) is attacked by a wild outsider (e.g., electric lighting). The Rip Van Winkles awake, shrug their immense shoulders — and get down to work. Soon productivity in gas lighting is surging (this actually happened) and the pipsqueak upstarts are on the run (many fold).

The battle is won but the war is already lost. In a few years the upstarts iron the kinks out of their early, awkward technology and yesterday's resurgent champs, having doggedly stuck to their old guns, will be overrun.

The story is mostly hopeless. (For the individual oldster firm, at any rate.) New technology incubators — skunk works, distant start-up divisions, hefty blue-sky R&D expenditures, alliances with innovative outsiders, etc. — seldom tip the scales for them. They generally fail (until it's too late) to alter the mind-set of the entrenched "culture" of marketing, technology, finance, whatever.

So what is "the answer"? You won't find it in Utterback's brilliant book. His final chapter on renewal offers no surefire ways out of the box, and not even much hope at the margin. (He's far too savvy to believe in pat answers.)

At least, books like his (there are far too few) should cause us to squarely confront the issue — which is as important for a 25-table Spanish restaurant as a jillion-buck technology firm. To own up to the near-hopelessness of the situation may make you slightly more willing to consider radical solutions. To wit:

■ Split the company into independent parts, with majority outside ownership of each. (Good advice for $10 billion *and* $10 million outfits.)

■ Take personal restoration seriously — e.g., six weeks off *every* year to retool and rejuvenate. (This one may be as wise for the 36-year-old staff professional as a 46-year-old business owner. See item No. 187.)

■ If you're founder-chief, step down sooner than planned and make sure your replacement (and much of her/his top team) comes from a very different environment.

Such ideas sound preposterous. But don't expect toothpicks to pry you out of steel traps. ☞█ **THINK ABOUT IT!**

136

These days we hear a lot about "relationship marketing" — the relentless pursuit of an almost familial bond between customer and product. General Motors' Saturn took this philosophy to its (current) limit in June 1994 when it threw a "homecoming hoe-down" for close to 30,000 of its "family" members at the Spring Hill, Tennessee, factory where the car is made.

Country music, factory tours, tents, food, drink, dancing, and, perhaps most important, the camaraderie of thousands of other Saturn owners was the lure that drew caravans of devoted Saturnites from all across the country.

How has Saturn created this almost cult-like devotion to a sturdy, well-designed, but hardly spectacular subcompact? By embracing the customer as a friend — an *intelligent* friend — from the moment the customer first steps into the showroom. With salaried salespeople, low-pressure tactics, superb listening skills, no-haggle pricing (the "no dicker sticker"), free car-care clinics, and "family" barbecues, Saturn dealers have created a welcoming atmosphere that has become the envy of the industry.

The customer tie is further strengthened by an advertising campaign that centers on the people who make the cars, and their direct connection to the people who buy them.

For a company in its industry — or in practically any industry, now that I think of it — Saturn practices unprecedented relationship marketing; and, here's the big idea, not just to a handful of customers, but to *hundreds of thousands*. How does it all add up on the bottom line? Well, Saturn's short history hasn't been problem-free. It went into the black for the first time last year and is not quite selling to capacity. But GM is in it for the long haul, and the long haul looks relatively rosy. GM has so

far demonstrated that it can change its stripes, and the car has succeeded in attracting younger, educated, and wealthy buyers and — most important — according to Saturn research, 60 percent of them intend to buy another Saturn!

As other car companies struggle to play catch-up (gone forever is the out-of-sight, out-of-mind mentality that clicked in when the customer drove the new car off the lot), Saturn has managed to stay one step ahead — by luring thousands of fervent followers down to Tennessee for some two-stepping.

Even the Japanese are watching! Very closely!

SATURN BUYERS, FUTURE SATURN BUYERS

137

Love to see those hungry folks from South Asia, East and Southeast Asia, Latin America, and the Caribbean surging toward our borders! Mind you, I've got no problem with Irish and Italian and German immigrants. (My paternal grandfather came to the United States from Germany.) But I was glad to read a recent statistical summary of immigration patterns that showed the European numbers dwindling, while the Asian and Latin American numbers were skyrocketing.

Immigrants are one of America's best-kept secrets (even from Americans, who bash them so routinely — and acidly). Their intense drive to succeed and willingness to work tirelessly is an inspiration to all of us who've been around a few generations and gotten a little too used to the good times (which we seem to think are our birthright). Their entrepreneurial energy is match-less and has been a significant element in Silicon Valley's success (immigrant engineers — many start-up CEOs among them — number in the tens of thousands there). Southern California, South Florida, and much of Texas also owe much of their vitality to immigrants.

I've often said in jest, I wish we could get all those electric folks from Hong Kong to move here in '97 when the British retreat from that island; we could turn the economy over to them, then the rest of us could take early retirement and clip coupons. Funny thing, I'm not entirely kidding.

138

Think Indonesia, says Asian expert Jim Abegglen. Indonesia today is where China will be in 10 years, Abegglen adds, *if* all goes well for China — a less than sure thing. Incidentally (that is, *not* so incidentally), Indonesia is the world's fourth most populous country.

Any plans to head for Indonesia any time soon? No? Why not?

139 Excellence in Concrete

The quality movement has been hijacked by bureaucrats. That's especially clear in Europe, where the ISO 9000 quality standard has become Holy Writ. Make that bureaucratic nonsense.

The problem? Richard Buetow, corporate quality director at Motorola, is clear: "With ISO 9000 you can still have terrible processes and products. You can certify a manufacturer that makes life jackets from concrete, as long as those jackets are made according to the documented procedures and the company provides the next of kin with instructions on how to complain about defects. That's absurd."

Indeed.

140

Terry Neill, head of Andersen Consulting's worldwide change-management practice, summarized in-house research that pinpoints "death by a thousand initiatives" as the chief reason corporate renewal efforts fail. Empowerment on Tuesday, TQM on Wednesday, reengineering on Thursday, a learning organization on Friday: All of these ideas are important, but when fired at employees like ping-pong serves, they overwhelm, confuse — and hopelessly diffuse organizational focus.

A better idea? An overriding, mobile, relatively loose picture of where the firm is heading; then spot these important notions (TQM, etc.) inside the frame.

141 Systems' Aesthetics

West Churchman, one of the fathers of operations research, claims there should be more to a good system than chilly efficiency criteria. The robust, renewing system also has ethics and aesthetics.

I like that. A lot. Sometimes I rail against "systems" — because I see so many people (employees, customers) ensnared by mindless, inflexible, demeaning, bureaucratic schemes. This even holds for *new* — reengineered — schemes, which are usually as soul-free as they are efficient.

And then you run across a De-Mar Plumbing (see item No. 76) or a Southwest Airlines (item No. 116). Systems? You bet they have systems! But their systems components (operating principles, rewards, hiring practices, measurements) focus with diamond-like clarity — elegance, integrity, aesthetics! — on "what's important around here." At De-Mar, it's "make a customer, not a sale" — i.e., focus on delighting the customer ("Have a DeeeeMarvelous day!"), keeping his business, and getting him to tout you to all his friends, far and wide. At Southwest, it's love, spirit — and an operating setup that is stunning in its simplicity (short hauls, one aircraft type , etc.).

I often advise businesspeople (and businesses) to describe how they are special in 25 words or less — what makes them stand out from the "me too" herd. If they can't do that, they ought to pack it up. We ought to apply this same test to our key business processes: Explain *their* aesthetics in 25 words or less. Which means that maybe you ought to have an artist or musician head your business process reengineering team, instead of an accountant or industrial engineer.

How about it?

> **"Effective pro-
> totyping may
> be the most
> valuable
> 'core compe-
> tence' an
> innovative
> organization
> can hope to
> have."**
>
> **Michael Schrage**

142 Leap, Then Look

"How do I know what I think until I see what I say?" I've heard that line attributed to several people, including W. H. Auden and E. M. Forster.

It's the most important line I've ever read.

Life is a series of approximations. (Science is about ongoing "conjectures and refutations," said the great philosopher of science Karl Popper.) This book is an approximation. It's what I want to say today. The final word? Don't be silly.

Innovation is *the* most important business topic in a crowded marketplace. And the number one key to innovation is, as I see it, "How do I know what I think . . ." or LEAP, THEN LOOK.

Innovation guru Michael Schrage put it a bit more prosaically, but profoundly and unequivocally, when he stated: "Effective prototyping may be the most valuable 'core competence' an innovative organization can hope to have." Little chance of misunderstanding that one!

There are two kinds of companies, Schrage goes on to say (and my observations support his): those that ponder and ponder, plan and then plan some more, and end up producing detailed specifications before they get around to building anything (Schrage calls these "spec-driven organizations"); and those that get a glimmer of an idea, cobble something together right away, and then quickly get on with the process of modification ("prototype-driven organizations," per Schrage).

The issue is anything but skin-deep. Schrage claims there is a wholesale "culture of prototyping" that pervades the leap-then-look gang at places like Hewlett-Packard and 3M. David Kelley, chief of product-design superstar IDEO, says, "Prototypes [and] an iterative culture . . . are a way of life" at some companies — and not at others.

Kelley's own firm is Exhibit A. Wander the hall of his Palo Alto-based playground for perpetually curious adults and you'll see (trip over is more likely) models of lamps and chairs and movie special-effects-devices and blood analyzers. Some are of the cardboard and popsicle-stick variety. Some are complex mechanical devices.

IDEO, like so many of the top innovators in services as well as manufacturing, literally THINKS VIA PROTOTYPES. In such outfits, prototypes become "the essential medium for information transmission, interaction, integration and collaboration," Schrage claims.

But maybe the feel of the playground or kindergarten classroom at Kelley's IDEO is part of the problem. It's not serious enough for the sober denizens of the average, dull (read noninnovative) business. "The idea that you can 'play' your way to a new product," says Carnegie-Mellon's Dan Droz, "is anathema to managers educated to believe that predictability and control are essential to new-product development."

Incidentally, the "sense" of prototyping's importance that Kelley, Schrage, Droz and I (among others) share was supported by some meticulous research conducted by Behnam Tabrizi and Kathleen Eisenhardt of Stanford's Department of Industrial Engineering and Engineering Management. Examining 72 product-development projects at 36 companies in Asia, Europe, and North America, the researchers discovered that the most effective performers iterate constantly; the least effective were the hyperorganized planners.

"Strong prototyping cultures produce strong products," Michael Schrage bluntly concludes. Or as Nike's Phil Knight might say, "Just do it."

So?

143

"Most people die of a sort of creeping common sense, and discover when it is too late that the only things one never regrets are one's mistakes."

Oscar Wilde

THE WACKY WORLD OR (MOSTLY), WHAT HAVE YOU DONE ABOUT ASIA TODAY?

144 Think A-S-I-A

We Americans can be a very provincial bunch. We still mostly (subconsciously) think the world begins and ends at our shores. We've been so rich for so long that we've grown complacent, a touch incestuous. While a great many foreign-made products will grab our attention (and dollars), most of the time the only culture we take much interest in is our own.

Well, if we're going to stay on top of the world economy, that it's-not-important-unless-it-happens-here attitude has to change.

Fast.

There is a giant stirring itself — and not far off, as the world is measured today. It's got unbelievable power and incredible wealth, and this particular waking/awoken giant is going to control the economic future of the world — a fact that we ignore at our peril.

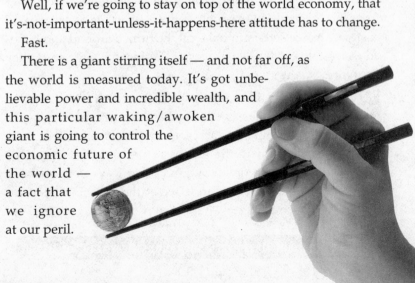

The giant is Asia.

Vast, teeming, and pulsing with raw entrepreneurial energy, Asia is, quite simply, where it's at.

A trip to two of its emerging powerhouses, Thailand and Malaysia, and then to its current if slightly graying champion, Japan, should serve to put us on notice.

First, a telling anecdote: I was booked on Northwest to Bangkok. Just as I was settling into my seat, the pilot announced: "Well folks, we're ready to go up here in the cock-pit, but there's a little engine problem." Unreal! The flight was canceled, costing me a full day — and a lot of hassle. And then a Northwest clerk chided me for (unquietly) questioning his explanation of the snafu. I guess he thought a major problem cropping up on a mostly empty flight — literally one minute after scheduled departure — was business as usual. For better or for worse, I remain skeptical. (Very frequent flyer=very sus-picious flyer=fact of life.)

Next day: Japan Airlines to Tokyo; Royal Thai to Bangkok. The service is so good, so attentive that it's spooky. Besides the fact that both flights left and arrived on time, you also got the feeling that baggage handlers, gate personnel, and flight atten-dants actually cared about what they were doing.

Once in Bangkok, more of the same. A white-liveried driver from the Oriental Hotel sought out Kate and me as we cleared customs. As we settled into the car, he turned around and hand-ed us ice-cold towels — this wasn't Presidential Suite stuff, they do it for *every* guest.

Tip: Take a vacation to Bangkok, but write it off — in good conscience — as business travel. That's legit if you stay at the Oriental; just watching its staff perform is an advanced course in service quality. To wit, the fellow at the 14th-floor concierge desk who pushes the down button as you leave your room so that you and the elevator car arrive at the 14th-floor elevator doors simultaneously!

(Very frequent flyer=very suspicious flyer=fact of life.)

Bangkok's heat is awful. Its smog is choking. The traffic makes Los Angeles gridlock look minor league. But what energy! A thick flock of construction cranes casts a permanent shadow as high-rise after high-rise races to the heavens. The people's faces seemed etched with purpose; everyone is in a hurry.

One morning, I stood on a wobbling dock waiting for a sooty old commuter "express" boat to arrive. Next to me was a crisply starched Thai businessman. (How they stay so well appointed in that wilting heat remains a mystery.) As he skillfully shifted his weight to keep his balance, he placed a string of calls on his portable cellular phone, talking excitedly. Wherever I went, I saw that kind of hustle, that kind of entrepreneurship, that kind of fervor.

PROBLEMS OF PRIVILEGE

Japan is experiencing a garage crisis because sport utility vehicles are currently all the rage and most garages were built to house small sedans.

You can actually *feel* the pulsating growth of Asia's sixth "tiger" — joining Hong Kong, Singapore, Taiwan, Korea, and Malaysia.

At times, I thought I was in a Japanese colony. Almost every car on the hypercrowded streets is Japanese. (I saw two American cars in eight days.) And my hotel was bursting at the seams with Japanese businessmen. Sure, they're closer to home than we are; but, frankly, it felt as if America has opted out of any effort to compete.

On to Malaysia. The skyline of the capital city, Kuala Lumpur, is also a blur of construction cranes; sounds of nonstop riveting, even through double-glazed hotel windows, make sleep almost impossible. Once again, I was swept up in a sense of excitement, of purpose. To the north of the capital, in Penang, Japanese and American electronics companies are going gangbusters. And it's sophisticated design work they're doing, not the rote assembly tasks that used to end up here.

And then Japan . . . Japan . . . By now the grand dowager of Asia, this powerhouse projects a pervasive, confident opulence that conjures up a giant Switzerland. Tokyo's Ginza district is closed to cars on Sundays and turns into a massive, upscale shopping mall. The story is echoed in the boondocks: In little Wajima, on the tip of Noto Peninsula, most garages sport two cars. In fact, Japan is experiencing a garage crisis (no kidding) because sport utiltiy vehicles are currently all the rage, and most garages were built to house small sedans. Talk about problems of privilege!

Walking these Asian streets, my spirits soared, my pulse quickened. I was seeing human enterprise flourishing, flowering all around me. There's nothing that can match the excitement, the sheer vitality of an economy that is racing to keep up with itself.

How did it happen?

A little history: After World War II, the Japanese had no military to support and a deeply wounded national pride to assuage; they poured their considerable energy and talent into manufacturing, and became world-class. Their economy took off. As wages and the yen soared, they started shipping low-value-added work to Korea, Taiwan, and Singapore. Next, Korea et al. raced up the value-added chain and began sending *their* lesser-value work to Malaysia and Thailand, who are themselves now shooting toward the high-end stratosphere — and in turn beginning to export their lower-wage tasks to places such as Indonesia. And newly rich Chinese coastal provinces are shifting mundane activities to less-progressive inland provinces.

Dizzying.

Some hard numbers: China's economy, recently classified as the **THINK ABOUT IT!** world's third largest, grew 14 percent in 1993; the growth numbers in giant and progressive Guangdong province hit 19 percent. Fixed-asset investment leaped 70 percent last year in "sleepy" state-run enterprises, 93 percent in locally run corporations. And, oh yes, citizens have been rioting to get share applications in the burgeoning Shanghai Exchange — 50,000 Chinese shareholders a week joined the capitalist rolls in 1992.

Staggering.

"Getting" Asia is daunting for Americans — physically, intellectually, and, especially, emotionally. But, if we want to remain on top of the ever-shifting hill that is the new world economy, we must understand that the luxury of having the world "come to us" is gone forever. The sobering fact: *We need them more than they need us*!

If I were a 25-year-old starting out, or a 35-year-old (even in a plum, fast-track job), I'd think hard about chucking it all for a couple of years and heading across the Pacific. Not to do business necessarily, but just to hang out and soak it up. I'm certain I'd come back a different — and, crassly speaking, more valuable — person. If you're serious, understand that nothing short of total immersion will do.

Asia is the 21st century's raw, voluptuous economic frontier. Period. How we respond to this challenge, this opportunity, will determine our own future. Period.

But there's more. . .

145 ... And, Now, India

On February 24, 1994, I awoke in New Delhi to these local newspaper headlines: "Kleenex-Huggies Set to Enter India," "India to Play Key Role in GE Growth," "Spanish Trade Delegation to Visit India." In my room at the Maurya Sheraton Hotel & Towers, the whole world was no more than 30 seconds away — via AT&T's Definity Voice-Data System 75. Downstairs, a group of 100 very senior seminar participants were gathering and raring to go; my experience two days before in Bombay suggested they'd be perkier than the 600 U.S. execs I'd addressed in Orlando the week before.

But what about the roadblocks on the drive from the Bombay airport, a response to terrorist bombings a few months before? And what about my walk last night? Out of the Sheraton, then, one block later, down a dirt lane. Half-clothed children, squatting, defecating. A line of men standing along a wall, urinating. The smell? Use your imagination.

Such blatant contradictions notwithstanding, it's no wonder India is a priority for Kimberly-Clark, GE, and the Spanish. The 250 million or so Indians in the middle and upper classes (about 40 million of whom make more than $40,000 a year) add up to a well-off population equal in size to the United States; moreover, they "want quality and are ready to pay for it," according to the South Asia head of the ad agency Lintas.

> **So which India is it?**
>
> **The one that ranked 123 out of 160 Third World nations on the U.N.'s Human Development Index?** ←

What a reversal! In the summer of 1991 India almost defaulted on its international debt. To the world's surprise, the colorless prime minister, P. V. Narasimha Rao, responded with unexpected vigor, and began to rip open the doors to a closed economy.

Many called India's economy the "license Raj," a vestige of British colonialism. New Delhi told companies what, when, and how to produce; where to locate, what technologies to use, whom to partner with. India's state governments were worse. "Armies of inspectors," as one commentator put it, traversed the country making sure companies accurately attended to the elephantine load of paperwork, license renewals, and so forth required by other armies of underemployed, form-making bureaucrats.

Has it all gone away? Hardly. State governments still get in the way; duties are still high; the planned sale of flabby state enterprises is going slowly; and as of my visit, ABB Asea Brown Boveri, which has invested heavily in India, had been waiting for approval to produce a new high-tech locomotive since 1987. Nonetheless, most licenses at the federal level have been abolished, bank reform is progressing, the average tariff is heading down from almost 90 percent to 25 percent, access to technology is increasing, and foreign multinationals can set up R&D facilities in the country.

Or the India that GE, ABB, and Motorola are betting will become an economic power?

The proof, of course, is in the doing, of which there's plenty. GDP growth is up from about 1 percent in 1991 to 5 percent, inflation is down sharply, and foreign-exchange holdings have gone from pocket change to $11 billion.

Most important, foreign investment, a $200 million trickle in 1991, is now flooding in at the rate of more than $2 billion a year. Approvals for Indian businesses to collaborate with big foreign firms jumped from one in 1990 and five in 1991 to 49 in the first six months of 1993.

Trade with China doubled in 1993, and U.S. exports to India rose 37 percent. (Imports to the U.S. from India jumped 22 percent.) The government has recently issued licenses to Coca-Cola and McDonald's, and IBM, booted out of India by Indira Ghandi in the '70s, is back, along with Walt Disney, Raytheon, AT&T, Morgan Stanley, and Sara Lee.

In Bangalore, the heart of India's entrepreneurial south, Singapore's visiting prime minister, Goh Chok Tong, cut a ribbon in January 1994 for Information Technology Park, a wonderland that may soon employ 16,000 software and electronics engineers. Nearby, elite Motorola engineers are designing components for the handheld satellite phone system, Iridium; the company's head of Central and South Asia calls opportunities in India "without parallel."

The statistical litany is overwhelming. And I was overwhelmed by the enthusiasm and energy of all those I met, not to mention the spectacle of hundreds of Nike-shod, sari- and Nehru jacket-clad joggers I passed (or who passed me) on the seaside promenade in front of my Bombay hotel at 6:15 A.M.

Still, 30 percent of the world's poor live in India, and at times I felt the fingers of each one scratching, in hopes of a tiny handout, at the windows of the cabs I rode in. One hundred million Indians are unemployed, several times that are underemployed, and the population grows by about a Canada a year, or more than 20 million people.

So which India is it? The one that ranked 123 out of 160 Third World nations on the U.N.'s Human Development Index? Or the India that GE, ABB, and Motorola are betting will become an economic power?

I am excited, repelled, and confused in equal measures. And, I think, in the end, that's about the right take on this most extraordinary country.

146 He Wants Your Job!

"You really scared them. Most head family-run manufacturing businesses, and are pretty darn conservative." That was the feedback from a talk I gave in the spring of 1994.

Funny, I didn't think I'd said anything that dramatic. I'd just returned from India (see above), and *had* commented on that country's newfound strength in industries such as software. I added that every nation I've visited in 1994 — e.g., the Philippines, Ecuador, Argentina — is aiming to create "a value-added, knowledge-based, export-led economy."

"Look," I told the sea of graybeards, "the bottom line is that the world doesn't owe us a living. We'll have to hustle like hell to maintain anything like our current living standard."

Textbooks laden with mathematical notation not withstanding, international economics ain't that tough to fathom. *The Economist* summed it up brilliantly in an editorial aptly titled "He Wants Your Job":

> For as long as there have been rich countries and poor ones, the poor have tried to catch up and the rich have tried to stay ahead. . . . Poor countries can copy the methods and technologies of their rich-country counterparts at relatively low cost; to continue to grow, the rich countries need to devise new methods and technologies for themselves. So, other things being equal, you would expect the poor countries to catch up. For the [most developed countries], that is the same as "relative economic decline." [But] as the gap closes, the follower countries lose their advantage. . . . With greater wealth comes demands for longer holidays, better pensions and healthcare, cleaner streets and factories.

There's good news and bad news in those words. The good: Relative decline for the likes of "us" is normal, healthy, and perhaps not happening fast enough, as economist Donald McCloskey points out in *Second Thoughts: Myths and Morals of U.S. Economic History*:

> The tragedy of the past century is not the relatively minor jostling among . . . the lead pack of industrial nations. It is the appalling distance between the leaders at the front and the followers at the rear. . . . Economists appear to have mixed up the question of why Britain's income per head is now six times that of the Philippines and 13 times that of India with the much less important questions of why British income in 1987 was 3 percent less than the French or 5 per-

Everybody can . . .

cent more than the Belgian.

The bad news: We *do* need to sweat blood. While we should focus much more on the alarming gap between "us" and "them," we also must cope with a global economy where employment gravitates quickly to the most talented workforces. Within America, the distance between haves and have-nots is already a chasm; while we spawn a school of millionaires at Microsoft, most American workers feel like fish out of water these days.

Moreover, the nation that *perceives* itself to be in decline turns inward. Witness the increase in ugly, dangerous, and ultimately self-defeating protectionist blather and anti-immigrant legislation in the U.S. The surest way to decline is to leave the most fertile playing fields (e.g., red-hot Asia) to the likes of Japan and Korea. In fact, America's recent and almost unprecedented reversal of relative decline is a direct product of a lingering willingness to allow feisty upstarts onto our field. Not only has that pushed us toward what we're best equipped to do (create more high-value services), but we've also roared back in autos and semiconductors, thanks to our witting exposure at home to direct external pressure (Honda, Toyota, Toshiba, et al.).

In an *Industry Week* article, Ross Operating Valve Co. COO Henry Duignan dismisses reengineering and TQM as "akin to installing power steering on a Model A Ford." Instead, he says, we need "new forms of wealth creation." Ross Valve's answer to high-volume, good-quality, low-cost challengers from the likes of China is revolutionary approaches to applying workers' imaginations to customer problems — creating so much productivity improvement for customers, so fast, that even an $18 difference in hourly labor costs becomes immaterial.

Ross Operating Valve is a perfect illustration of *The Econo-*

mist's message: Everybody *can* win. Less-demanding customers with less-demanding requirements will settle for quality commodity goods (e.g. valves), and buy Chinese. More-demanding customers will buy "old-fashioned" valves (which needn't be old-fashioned — that's the point) from a revitalized Ross Operating Valve. The relatively high American tide continues to rise (Ross employees and its customers' employees get richer), though still not as rapidly as China's, where the extra nickel an hour in workers' pay that comes from selling a quality commodity product amounts to a great leap forward.

The time-tested magic of open markets aside, my seminar participants had reason to quiver. For companies or individuals not willing (or able) to engage in perpetual revolution in an increasingly connected world, absolute — not relative — decline is a distinct possibility. No, make that a near certainty.

Big word, certainty.

147 People Are Different

A Dutch doctor managing a company clinic has a "frank discussion" with a Chinese subordinate, who has some easily correctable shortcomings. The Chinese doctor, who sees his boss as a "father figure," takes the criticism as "a savage indictment" — and commits suicide. The problem, according to seasoned Dutch business consultant Fons Trompenaars: "American and Dutch managers . . . do not understand the principle of losing face."

Trompenaars's book, *Riding the Waves of Culture*, is a masterpiece. (MEMORIZE IT, THAT'S MY ADVICE. I'M TRYING TO.) Based on meticulous quantitative research, as well as some 900 seminars presented in 18 countries, it boldly proclaims that most American management theorizing, by the likes of Peter Drucker . . . and Tom Peters, is next to useless. Echoing Deborah Tannen's views on men vs.

women (*You Just Don't Understand*), Trompenaars begins, "It is my belief that you can never understand other cultures. . . .This is the context in which I started wondering if any of the American management techniques and philosophy I was brainwashed with in eight years of the best business education money could buy would apply in The Netherlands, where I came from, or indeed in the rest of the world."

If you can't ever hope to fully understand another culture, at least you can become sensitive to differences. And that, says Trompenaars, would be a hell of a step forward in a global business environment where "understanding culture still seems like a luxury item to most managers."

To Lie or No to Lie

The heart of *Riding the Waves of Culture* is seven readable, anecdote- and statistic-filled chapters dealing with fundamental assumptions that define a culture. Trompenaars begins with the "universalist" vs. the "particularist" schism. Universalists (e.g., at the extreme, Americans, Canadians, Australians, and the Swiss) believe in "one best way," an invariant set of rules that apply in any setting. Particularists (South Koreans, Chinese, and Malaysians, at the other extreme) focus on the peculiar nature of any given situation.

> "It is my belief that you can never understand other cultures."
>
> **Fons Trompenaars**

Suppose you're riding in a car with a close friend who has an accident in which a third party is injured. You're the only witness, and he asks you to testify falsely about his driving speed. Universalists by and large won't lie for him. Particularists will. The difference becomes even more profound if the injury is severe. That causes the universalist to take his belief in the rules even more seriously. But the more serious injury increases the particularist's sense of obligation to his buddy, and therefore his willingness to tell a whopper to the authorities.

(Trompenaars acknowledges that within a country the intensity of attachment to any given cultural trait varies widely. Nonetheless, the quantitative differences among nations are profound: In the case of the accident, for example, 74 percent of South Koreans would stick up for their pal and lie, compared to just 5 percent of Americans.)

At the end of each chapter, Trompenaars serves up a yeasty summary (worth the price of the book by itself). The first part is "Tips for Doing Business with": Universalists (us, remember) doing business with particularists should, for example, "be prepared for personal 'meandering' or 'irrelevancies' that do not seem to be going anywhere"; moreover, we should under no circumstances "take 'get to know you' chatter as small talk" — it's the main event to particularists! Particularists doing business with us universalists should "be prepared for 'rational' and 'professional' arguments and presentations" ad nauseum, and should "not take 'get down to business' attitudes as rude."

The second half of each summary covers "When managing and being managed." Universalists (us) managing particularists (them) should, for instance, emphasize "informal networks and private understandings" and "pull levers privately." Particularists managing universalists, on the other hand, should "strive for consistency and uniform procedures" and "signal changes publicly."

Next up, "collectivists" (group-oriented) vs. "individualists." The U.S. and Canada are again (as is the case in general) at one extreme — individualists, natch. The "other end" is populated by Kuwaitis, Egyptians, and the French. Cutting to the chase (typical American that I am), collectivists dealing with us individualists in, say, contract negotiations should be prepared "for quick decisions and sudden offers not referred to HQ," and a negotiator who can make commitments that he is then "reluctant to go back on." Individualists working with collectivists, however, should exhibit "patience for time taken to consent and

Peter Drucker + Tom Peters = next to useless.

**Are you a . . .
Universalist,
Particularist,
Collectivist,
Specific,
Diffuse?
Or are you an . . .
Emotional?**

consult," and be prepared for a negotiator who "can only agree tentatively and may withdraw an [offer] after consulting with superiors." Talk about a gulf!

Next, the difference between those who show their feelings (Italians — one extreme) and those who hide them (no surprise, the Japanese). Trompenaars's advice, in part, to the taciturn: "Do not be put off your stride when [the emotionals] create scenes and get histrionic; take time out for sober reflection." What else/fat chance/good idea.

The next major distinction is the chasm between the "specifics" (task freaks who make clear distinctions between, say, the individual at work and the whole personality) and the "diffuse" (where every aspect of the person is considered in all settings). When the diffuse deal with specifics, they must learn "to be quick, to the point and efficient"; while specifics dealing with the diffuse must learn "to take time to remember there are many roads to Rome."

Trompenaars offers the case of an American (specific-oriented) firm competing with Swedes (also specific-oriented) for Latin American (diffuse) business. The Americans had a superior product at a better price — which they decisively (to their narrow minds) demonstrated in a masterful, one-shot presentation. The Swedes, by contrast, spent a week getting to know the Latin customer, discussing "everything *except* the product" (which they didn't even introduce until the last day). Guess who got the order? **Hint:** It wasn't the Yanks.

"But When My Great-great-great-grandfather Ran the Company . . . "

The difference between status that is achieved (the United States and Denmark at one extreme) and that which is ascribed (based on family, seniority, etc. — the Thais and Indonesians are extreme here) is next on tap. Sending a whiz kid to deal with someone 10 to 20 years his senior in an "ascribed" culture is a no-no. Translation by their businesspersons: "Do these people think that they have reached our level of experience in half the time? That a 30-year-old American is good enough to negotiate with a 50-year-old Greek or Italian?"

Not surprisingly, orientation to time varies profoundly among cultures. In part, there's the difference between a future orientation (us) and culture that emphasizes history (e.g., the Mexicans); ignore historical context with the latter, and you're in deep yogurt.

Also under this heading: An orientation toward doing business "sequentially" (one thing at a time) and "synchronically" (lots going on at once). A South Korean returned from a business trip and went into his Dutch boss's office. The boss, on the phone, merely nodded at his subordinate and continued with the call — then greeted the subordinate effusively after putting down the phone. The Dutch boss, like us, does one thing at a time. The Korean underling was deeply offended and interpreted the subsequent hearty greeting as phony — if the boss felt positively toward him, he would have interrupted the call. (In "synchronous" cultures, having a dozen things going on at once is normal. Ever been in a Brazilian manager's office?)

Toward Beginner's Mind

At the end of this dense, 176-page treatise, the human reaction is to throw up your hands in despair at the hopelessness of it all. Trompenaars's solution: "We need a certain amount of humility and a sense of humor to discover cultures other than our own; a readiness to enter a room in the dark and stumble over unfamiliar furniture until the pain in our shins reminds us of where things are."

I think such a sense of playfulness is on target. My own experience, though I'm identified in print as the universalist enemy by Trompenaars, is that it's OK to make blunders, even big ones, in other cultures. What's not OK is cultural arrogance. If you come to another's turf with empathy, sensitivity, and open ears — what the Zen masters call "beginner's mind" — you're halfway home. Moreover, I think Trompenaars is correct when he says that we'll never master anybody else's culture (I certainly haven't mastered even the enormous *regional* differences in the United States in 51 years); which means that keeping that beginner's mind in perpetuity is a must for successful — not to mention less-stressful — dealings throughout the emergent global village. (Especially, hint, hint redux: Asia.)

148 Truth Is More Boring Than Fiction

Oh, those ugly Americans! Historical sense? As our guide Fons Trompenaars says (see above), it's about equal to that of a gnat. Our business folks? Driven by next quarter's earnings.

But, ah, then there are the Japanese. Always thinking of the long term. A 500-year plan at one company. (I read that somewhere.)

And then along comes David Montgomery, a quantitative nut and longtime marketing professor at Stanford. Yes, his recent research shows that the Japanese *do* look farther ahead, on average, than we do. More precisely: 8.6 years for "them," 7.2 years for "us." (For what it's worth, the Europeans have a 10-year time horizon.)

Though there *is* a difference, day and night it ain't. (And in a rapidly mutating world, is it all that clear that the longer view is the more valuable one?)

149 Mind Over Matter

"The biggest barrier you'll face [as a small company considering going global] is internal, not external: You have to decide you really *want* to sell to overseas markets. Once you've made that decision, everything else will fall into place. The reason I emphasize that psychological barrier is that it's very real. You have to overcome a fair amount of skepticism within your company and perhaps in your own gut as well."

Jeffrey J. Ake
vice president of sales and marketing,
Electronic Liquid Fillers

Now, let's really get down to the nitty-gritty. I travel to Europe, Latin America, and Asia a half-dozen times a year and have done so for about two decades. Here are a few things I've learned — invariably the hard way.

We've got to send ur wideouts deep

■ **Read in.** A couple of weeks before a trip, I start perusing appropriate newspapers, magazines, and miscellaneous background material I've been accumulating. Staples include *The Nikkei Weekly* and *Asiaweek* (for trips to Asia), *The Economist* and *Financial Times* (for trips to Europe).

■ **Mind your language.** Even in England, the language is *very* different. Over the years, I've learned to s-l-o-w d-o-w-n and consciously translate myself during seminars and business meetings. In particular, I'm careful to simplify my phrasing — and never, ever resort to baseball, football, or other peculiarly American metaphors. It's not just that other people won't understand; often they do. But talk of "a full court press," let alone "sending the wideouts deep," telegraphs cultural insensitivity. (I.e. that you're a ninny.)

■ **Watch your humor.** I rely on humor at home, because I believe there's no better way to establish rapport and move a discussion forward. (And besides, I can't help it.) But overseas, I rarely joke around (even after 20 years of visiting some locales). There's nothing more local than humor. The one-liner your friends back home roared at invariably leaves a perplexed look on the faces of your mates abroad — in Australia and Ireland let alone Japan and Dubai.

■ **Slow down redux.** Tuning in to body language and spoken language simply takes more time in another culture. We instantly "understand" thousands of subtle cues in our own environment, from physical trappings to the nuances of certain phrasing. But in foreign settings, getting even a hint of what's going on calls for intense concentration.

■ **Watch your schedule.** This holds for 25-year-olds and 60-year-olds alike. Don't overbook yourself! It takes a lot more emotional energy to do business and make personal connections when you're out of your element. (I routinely find myself literally sick with exhaustion at the end of a "routine" day of meetings in other countries.) Also, take it especially easy right after you arrive. At age 25, you think you're in fine fettle after a flight from San Francisco to Tokyo. Take it from me (who was once 25 and cocky), no matter how you *think* you feel, you're in rotten shape — and it shows. Schedule yourself accordingly. (And at 50, *do* give yourself the extra day, that all the guide books suggest, before even trying to get started on your professional agenda.)

■ **Make room for social interchange.** Learning about other cultures — and about your would-be business partners — comes mostly from schmoozing. The lengthy lunch, cocktails, and the five-hour dinner can be far more important than any formal presentation you'll make.

■ **Make friends.** There's little that's more important for doing business in another country than having two or three natives who can act as trustworthy sounding boards. It's probably best if they're not business associates. Then, among other things, they can freely laugh at you when you make a fool of yourself (as you inevitably do — regularly — in foreign settings).

■ **"Use" your weekends.** Not for more meetings, you nose-to-the-grindstone dullards (damned Americans!); but for hanging out, visiting pubs and museums — and joining newfound colleagues in recreational pursuits.

■ **Contribute.** If you open a one-person shop in another country, work from the start to become a member of the community. Make it clear you're there for the long haul by joining appropriate associations, contributing to fund-raising drives, and spending time on local issues.

■ **Learn the language.** Just mastering greetings, pleases, thank-yous, and a handful of useful phrases in someone else's tongue says that you care and are paying at least passing attention to the local culture. (Except in France, botching pronunciation is OK. It's the perceived effort that counts. And even the French aren't as bad as advertised — most of the time.)

■ **Walk the streets.** Nothing helps you soak up the culture more than a two-hour stroll through the streets of Frankfurt, Milan, or Kuala Lumpur. Look at the toys, the appliances, the foods, the posters in the travel shops, the houses, the people. Buy a few papers and magazines and thumb through them — you'll be surprised at how much you can "get," even though you probably can't understand more than a few words. Overall, work at tuning your senses to your surroundings; at the very least, the odds are you can use something you saw during that stroll in a conversation the next day.

> **Don't overbook yourself! It takes a lot more emotional energy to do business and make personal connections when you're out of your element.**

■ **Keep jogging (or whatever).** Foreign travel, even for the old hand, is disorienting. Stick to a few of your back-home habits. Exercising outdoors tops the list for me; it puts me in charge, and leaves me a little less at odds.

■ **Tomorrow is another day.** Be patient with others — and yourself.

151

The *"International" Herald Tribune* offers daily weather reports from 40 European cities, 10 Asian cities. Funny, I thought Asia, with several times Europe's population, had big cities , too.

152

Oh, grow up. W. Edwards Deming didn't sire Japan's quality consciousness. Tidiness, quality, and presentation are the flavor of the millennium, not the month, in Japan. In fact, Shinto, the Japanese state religion, deifies order, simplicity, and beauty.

Take the practice of flower arranging, or *ikebana*: Reverence for stark beauty is obvious. Moreover, the packaging of *everything* is a fetish in Japan. The bagging of a single postcard at a tiny retail shop is a wonderful production.

You'd also think jaywalking was a capital offense in Japan, even in the boondocks. And the families of people who jump in front of a Tokyo subway are fined for disrupting service — the penalty varies according to the number of passengers delayed by the suicide!

The Japanese have long been order freaks. No wonder emulating such obsessions is so difficult for Westerners. (Assuming that we should.)

153

Asia is on the move. Whoops, make that stuck. In the face of extraordinary economic growth, Bangkok traffic has reached the point that it's spawned a hot consumer product. The Comfort 100 is a "red plastic bottle," *The Economist* reports, "which is being sold as a portable urinal. The device — which comes with an optional cone-shaped funnel for the use of female motorists — is now widely available at petrol stations throughout the city."

Ah, prosperity!

154

Light

of

the

moon

moves

west,

flowers'

shadows

creep

eastward

Buson

SEARCHING FOR THE DIVERSITY ADVANTAGE

155

"Deborah Kent will become the first African-American woman to run an auto plant, as manger of Ford's Avon Lake, Ohio, assembly facility."

USA Today
September 16-18, 1994
page 1

A short stroll down the streets of any major American city is all it takes to realize that this country will never again be the lily-white land of *Father Knows Best*, picket fences and simple answers (no matter how hard Pat Buchanan and other small-minded, cold-hearted isolationists huff and puff). Personally, I find the polyglot parade of races and nationalities stimulating, fascinating, exciting. It's called diversity. It's a fact of life. Not only on our streets, but in our business-es. Large and small, hi-tech and low, the face of the American workforce is more varied than ever before in our history. This clash of cultures can cause conflict. But it can also lift a company to new heights. The trick is in creating a corporate ethos that brings out the diverse work-force's full potential.

In order to explore this critical issue, I recently went down to Memphis to talk to some folks at Federal Express, a company that is in the forefront of seeking competitive advantage through diversity.

TP: First of all, thank you all for coming. Would you please introduce yourself and tell us what your job is.

My name is Neal Johnson, I'm a senior manager, Publishing Services.

I'm Linda Edwards of our Leadership Institute.

My name is Rangi Ranganathan and I'm a managing director in Finance.

Thonda Barnes, specialist at the Leadership Institute.

I'm Sonja Whitemon and I'm a senior specialist, Media Relations.

My name is Lillie McGhee, I'm a senior manager of Hub Operations here in Memphis.

My name is Steve Nielsen and I'm the managing director of the Leadership Institute.

I'm Edith Kelly, vice president, Purchasing and Supply.

I'm Fred Daniels, senior manager of Operations, Miami.

I'm Patricia Steele and I'm a senior Service Agent. I am very impressed and very happy to be here.

My name is Pamela Buford. I work in the Hub as a checker/sorter for Chicago flights. One week out of the month I'm a tour guide.

I'm David Bickers. I am a dangerous-goods specialist and also a Hub tour guide.

My name is Todd Ondra. I'm a senior manager in Corporate Security.

I'm Dianne Stokely, a vice president in Ground Operations.

I'm Regina Taylor, a senior specialist in Community Relations.

My name is Glen Sessoms, vice president, Retail Marketing and Operations.

TP: Welcome. It has long been my belief that diversity is an awesome opportunity as opposed to a problem. At the same time, I find the issue completely and thoroughly confusing.

I'm a 51-year old white male who was born outside of Annapolis, Maryland. My mother insists we have blue blood in our veins, including some from George Washington. My father's father came over here from Germany around 1870. He was a wealthy contractor who almost lost everything in the Depression; my father seemed to attribute this in part to the fact that his second wife was a Catholic.

I remember the "colored" and "white" bathrooms on the ferries that crossed Chesapeake Bay when I was a boy. When I went off to Cornell, my parents were dumbfounded that I was assigned a Jewish roommate; they sent me to the preacher for counseling on how to survive this catastrophe. Later on at Cornell, I played lacrosse and on the road roomed with a guy who was an All-American, whose father was a leading physician at Johns Hopkins and who happened to be black. My father was none too happy. That is, it was a garden variety American life for a WASP born in 1942.

Things have changed. I hope. I'd like you to go wherever the hell you want with the issues of race, color, creed, gender. What does diversity mean? Why are you wrestling with it? Why does Federal Express have a course, and a long one at that, on the issue?

What We Don't Know Does Hurt

FRED DANIELS: The course is needed because

FRED DANIELS, SENIOR MANAGER OF OPERATIONS

communication is needed. I thought I was pretty well educated on the issue of race, but I quickly realized I had a lot to learn.

Being a black male, I understand black rage — but I was shocked to hear the rage white people feel towards blacks. To hear it freely expressed.

LINDA EDWARDS: One of the things we do in our week-long session is allow people to openly discuss their feelings in a comfortable setting. It takes a while for people to open up, to get past political correctness. Some never do. But when they do, really interesting things happen; people get inside each other's heads and develop a visceral understanding of others', and their own, beliefs.

FRED DANIELS: I work in South Florida where 75 percent of our workforce is Hispanic. After taking the course, my first goal was to learn as much Spanish as I could. I bought computer programs and got books and tapes, not only on the

NEAL JOHNSON, SENIOR MANAGER, PUBLISHING SERVICES, AND LINDA EDWARDS OF THE LEADERSHIP INSTITUTE.

language but on the culture as well. If I'm going to work with Hispanics, I need to understand them and they need to understand me — and we all need to feel comfortable.

Another thing that shocked me in the course was how naive and backward so many men are on women's issues. Men have got to treat women as equals, complete equals. Period. I went back and discussed all these issues with both my management team and my frontline folks.

I came away from the course inspired to get more involved in fighting racism, not just from the corporate standpoint, but from a personal standpoint.

NEAL JOHNSON: I came into the course a blue-eyed white male who had grown up in an environment where I was often the only white kid on the basketball court. I'd been around black people all my life, yet for the first time I realized we were strangers.

I went into this thing thinking: "Hey, it's not that big of a deal, I relate to everybody pretty well." Then I realized I was often insulting to my peers or subordinates, either overtly or subtly, without knowing it. Until you see yourself through that other person's eyes, you just don't get it.

One of the things that really jumped out at me was how I communicate with women. I have a real bad habit of interrupting. It's a male thing; I want to jump right in and solve the problem. I need to be more sensitive, I need to learn to listen. Women communicate differently than men.

DIANNE STOKELY: When I came out of the course, I needed to look in the mirror. Here I am, a senior female, and I didn't have any female directors. Do *I* have a problem with females working for me? Do *I* suffer from this queen bee syndrome where I want to be the only one?

We All Share the Same Air

LILLIE McGHEE: I grew up in the north Memphis ghetto. My mother was a maid. She worked for a wonderful Jewish family. She would take me to work with her from time to time. That family was very good to me, they gave me a lot of encouragement. They didn't care what color I was. They taught me a lot about bringing out the best in everybody, which is really what diversity is all about.

I think it's important to understand our own backgrounds and the way they shape us. Because mine was disadvantaged, I was probably more vulnerable and also more eager to please. I think when people with prejudices look at their upbringing,

PAMELA BUFORD, CHECKER/SORTER, AND
TOM PETERS

they'll often find parents with prejudices. That knowledge helps you work through the animosity. The course provides a forum for that kind of self-examination.

I was the first black to work in purchasing at Federal Express. When they hired me, they were making a statement: We want good people, no matter what color they are. At the time I was called a token. That's certainly been proved wrong.

DAVID BICKERS, DANGEROUS GOODS SPECIALIST,
AND PAMELA BUFORD

I've had my pros and cons here. It takes a strong person — black, white, whatever — to deal with hostility. Being a black female, I'm constantly reminded that I'm different. But if I understand the reaction I engender, the threat I pose to certain people, then I can deal with it.

PAMELA BUFORD: I started out a year ago unloading freight that couldn't be placed into the conveyor system, which is probably the second hardest job in the Hub. When I was hired there were two other females. We had to move all these motors that weighed more than we did. It would take two and sometimes three of us to unload them. But we did it. I may be weak physically, but I'm strong mentally. I kept saying to myself, "I'm not going to be doing this forever."

I've worked in places where I was the only female or the only person with dark skin. I am unique. You are unique. We can all get together and make something that is out of this world.

PAMELA BUFORD, DAVID BICKERS, AND TOM PETERS

Sometimes when I'm driving to work I ask myself if Fed-Ex will continue to grow. Times have changed since this company began on April 17, 1973. We have to move towards the future. We must continue to shed the old and try on the new, like our body creates new skin cells every day. That is how the company must be. That is how each individual in the company must be. As we inhale and exhale the air in this room, we are all sharing it. We're all in this together.

[**TP:** I'd guess this young woman is about 25 . I confidently predict she'll either be president of FedEx or the United States some day!]

DAVID BICKERS: When I do Hub tours, I talk about the reasons Fed-Ex is in Memphis. The irony is that this town is stalemated on race. There are men who make their living perpetuating [racial] myths, and that's true on both sides. There are white guys who have staked their entire careers on playing on people's fears. It's sickening. It's all about using fear to amass power. It erodes our humanity.

Corporations and companies have moral and ethical obligations. Companies that ignore these moral obligations find their bottom line suffers.

Let me give you an example. We have ramp agents who are responsible for loading the aircraft. They're the guys running the show, they're well trained in weights and balances. Under them are the folks who do the actual loading and unloading. Now a white ramp agent will often hesitate to ask a black worker to do something because the worker will complain he's being asked because he's black. He'll tell the ramp agent to pick on someone else, he's tired of being the only person asked. It happens all the time. You also have black ramp agents who find themselves in a state of limbo because they don't feel close to the other ramp agents, most of whom are white, and they find themselves cut off from their old frontline friends, who they've worked themselves up from.

That kind of race-based decision making affects us monetarily. It cuts productivity.

FRED DANIELS: I was the first black senior manager in South Florida. When I first got there, people talked to me using black slang. It was all "Hey, bro" and "Yo, man." I was appalled.

I explained to people that they didn't have to talk to me like that. We can be friends or not be friends, but don't patronize me. I just want to be treated like any other senior manager.

In the diversity course, a lot of people finally realize that. I had a gentleman sitting next to me and on the last day he said, "Just sitting next to Fred was an experience for me because I don't have any black friends. I understand now this man is no different than me and I hope we stay in touch." He went through a real evolution.

SONJA WHITEMON: I was introduced to the idea of diversity when I was asked to write an article about it for an employee publication. I took the course. It made a deep impression on me. People came in generalizing — black about white, white about black. I didn't think anyone was changing. Then at the end, when people made statements about what they'd gotten out of the class, I realized that people were talking about *individuals* as opposed to "you blacks." I could sense they were trying to understand. And that's a good beginning. You can't erase a lifetime of preconceptions in a week.

FRED DANIELS: I do think it's important that the course is a week long. A lot of growth happens after you go home at night and think about what you heard that day.

When I took the course, on the last day a woman stood up and told us she was a lesbian. She'd hadn't come into the course planning to do that, but hearing what she did all week, and thinking about it at night, gave her the courage by Friday to stand up and tell us. She grew comfortable enough to do that. I don't think that would have happened in two or three days.

TP: So on the last day everybody says the right things and it's all fabulous and then you go back to work. The question is: Does it translate to the real world?

The (Adulterated) View from on High

SONJA WHITEMON: I think it does. After finishing the course, I worked on publications designed to spread the message. Most of the people that I talked to had gone through the course and were making changes in the way they worked. I was impressed. But it's a very slow process. The cultural change is going to take years and years.

What I try to emphasize is that this is a *business* issue. It's not personal, an "I like you, you like me" kind of thing. Diversity is good for business.

TP: What about people who don't get it?

SONJA WHITEMON: I think they're going to fall by the wayside naturally. Their work is going to suffer, they're not going to be happy. The people who do get it are going to rise and the others are not.

EDITH KELLY: The unfortunate fact is that the further you are from the front lines, the more you think everything is OK. I felt a lot of people in my class didn't get it. The last day of the class one man said, "I can relate to this. When my wife goes shopping dressed in jeans and a t-shirt she gets treated differently." Well, all his wife has to do is go and change clothes and she'll get treated very well! I can't have a sex-change operation or polish myself white.

The officers in this company think everything is OK because they don't see the tensions on a day-to-day basis. They think, "What a great company. We're an equal opportunity employer."

> **The further you are from the front lines, the more you think everything is OK.**

THONDA BARNES: When people hear the term "managing diversity," they think it's about special interest groups. Actually managing diversity is about leadership. As a leader, I want to know about my people, what their potential abilities are and how as a group we can come together and create an environment where everyone can soar. If I only know how to manage people of my own sex and color, then I'm losing out on all that potential. For me, managing diversity means understanding the white male.

EDITH KELLY: And gays and handicapped people too. One of the things I got out of the course is that I have my own prejudices. I was frightened to death when we had a homosexual come to class.

NEAL JOHNSON: When you do get the message and start to spread it around, then suddenly you have to deal with the backlash, which can get a little scary. Here I am standing up in front of an audience talking about gay issues, gender issues, race issues. Afterwards, people I thought were my friends come up and say, "Do you really believe that crap?" They'll pull out the Bible or talk about the time their cousin was mugged. You have to point out that they're generalizing, and you have to stand firm.

Either you are going to own this issue and go out and do something with it, or you aren't. If you aren't then get the heck out of the way because we are going to take this journey and we are going to succeed.

In Publishing Services, we produced a document about diversity. The director turned it over to the individual managers and said, "Here is a snapshot of where we want to be going. Oh, by the way, I am expecting quarterly reports on this and it will be a part of the performance reviews." All of a sudden those managers are interested! You begin to force a certain level of ownership. If that's what it takes, fine, but it's not nearly as satisfying as seeing someone with a burning passion to make things better.

There is a price to be paid for being a zealot about this. You need to recognize that. That's true no matter what color you are, but I think even more so if you're white and blue-eyed.

STEVE NIELSEN: I disagree with Sonja about it not being personal. I think it has to get personal. The course deals with beliefs, with what is going on *inside*, where it came from. Until you make it personal, you can't own it, because no two people can own it in the same way. It all relates back to your childhood, your parents, your upbringing. Most of us don't even think about where our beliefs and prejudices come from. You've got to open up the wound and clean it out before the healing can start.

I'm the director of the Leadership Institute, home of the diversity course. I thought I was in pretty good shape on the issues. Then I sat in on a course with the intention of sitting in the back and taking notes. Suddenly I was asking myself how I'd feel if my son brought home an Asian fiancé. Or a black woman. Because of who I am and the way I was raised, I knew that it would bother me.

I will always be prejudiced. But if I am aware of that prejudice and make sure it doesn't have an adverse impact, and continue to deal with it, then I can still be an effective leader. And this company will make a larger profit because we are utilizing human beings better. Yes, it is about business, but to get there I had to go through the personal first.

By The Numbers

SONJA WHITEMON: Sometimes I think too much emphasis is put on numbers, on getting more women and black people into management.
Well, I'm not interested in being in management, but that doesn't mean I don't have any issues.

LILLIE McGHEE: The white male has one key concern: Meet the numbers! Don't get me wrong, affir-

STEVE NIELSEN, MANAGING DIRECTOR OF THE LEADERSHIP INSTITUTE, AND EDITH KELLY, VICE PRESIDENT, PURCHASING AND SUPPLY

mative action is very important. We haven't reached that stage yet where we don't need it. But numbers don't tell the whole story.

THONDA BARNES: Federal Express is a numbers company. You can't manage what you can't measure: How many blacks, how many women have I promoted or given special projects to? Really, the ultimate goal of managing diversity is one number: 100 percent customer satisfaction.

NEAL JOHNSON: Numbers traditionally are an external measure, be they affirmative action or courier stops per hour. Diversity training has to happen on the inside of each of us. You can't put a number on someone's sensitivity to other human beings. It's more subtle than that.

DAVID BICKERS: Diversity isn't about a fixed figure and when we reach that number, we can breath a sigh of relief and say: "Well, that's taken care of." Diversity is a concept and a commitment. It's dynamic. It's exciting. It's constantly in flux.

RANGI RANGANATHAN: The interesting thing in listening to this discussion is who was picked to be here. I don't see a white man who really disagrees with

what's being said. In any kind of sample there should be one dissenter, so why isn't there one here?

The white male is an endangered species today. Nobody wants him. In engineering and finance, everybody wants to hire women and minorities. But when we go looking for them the pickings are pretty slim. One of my managers has been trying for the last eighteen months to find qualified female applicants. Meanwhile, the qualified white male is shut out.

There are some highly qualified African-Americans that are coming up now through MBA programs. All the major companies fight to hire those few people. Same with the women. Where does that leave the white male?

The course I attended didn't devote a lot of time to trying to understand the white male viewpoint. They're being asked to give up something. If we don't grasp that and treat them with sensitivity, it's going to take longer to get this thing done.

TP: If you want to figure out why I've been successful, start with my being born in 1942, white, male, Protestant, in the United States, of relatively intelligent parents. I would have had to work to screw it up. Whenever I hear a successful white male say, "I'm here because I worked hard," I think, "Bullshit."

RANGI RANGANATHAN: Some of the people in my class said, "I'm sorry, I'm a white male, what can I do about it?" They were frustrated. The United States is where it is today because of what the white male has done. Many feel they have never personally discriminated against anyone. They feel they are paying the price so that other people can catch up. In the process, they're being made to look like the bad guy. Nobody wants to look like the bad guy.

Looking a Little Harder

TP: One of the things that bothers me most about the United States is that it's credential mad. There's a lot more to this country than what comes out of the Harvard Business School. I wonder whether we really look for talent in unlikely places, which is where we're likely to find it. It's the business school grads who've created the dinosaurs of corporate America.

RANGI RANGANATHAN: How do you tap into that pool that you know is out there? We encourage our people not to limit their recruiting to the big schools. We go to all the consortium schools. We go to minority job fairs and minority colleges. We have two senior vice presidents who only have high school educations.

EDITH KELLY: They're both white! We certainly wouldn't hire blacks who don't have degrees. I think the threshold is a little higher for minorities.

DIANNE STOKELY: It's very easy just hire someone who looks like you. It takes effort and commitment to move beyond that. Some people aren't as aggressive as others. That doesn't mean they're not as talented. You do have to look beyond the surface. You have to ask the right questions. You have to be aware.

SALLY DAVENPORT, SENIOR SPECIALIST, PUBLIC RELATIONS, AND RANGI RANGANATHAN, MANAGING DIRECTOR IN FINANCE

A white male may give a very different answer than a black female. The white male answer will probably tend to be more by the book. That doesn't make the black female wrong. In fact, she might bring a fresh perspective that could help the bottom line.

TODD ONDRA: The mix makes us stronger. When you hire a white male clone, you lose out on that creativity, all that wonderful input that comes from seeing things from a new angle, from a different cultural viewpoint. It's the coming wave and if we don't catch it, other companies will, and we'll be left behind.

In addition, having a mix makes for a livelier, more fun workplace. That leads to better productivity.

The course influenced my view of the hiring process. We were hiring several management people and before the course I wouldn't have been as open. I would have sat in the room with white males and not realized the huge pool of untapped talent that was out there.

DIANNE STOKELY: What you don't want to do is force someone to go out there and hire just to meet a quota. I happen to be a supporter of quotas because if we don't start somewhere we are never going to get anywhere. If it weren't for quotas some of us probably wouldn't be in this room right now. But you have to be careful, because some people will go out and hire their quota and then turn around and say, "By the way, the reason we aren't making our productivity goals is because I did what you told me to do."

EDITH KELLY: Even after getting hired, things are harder. You're not part of the network. My first job out of college was in an accounting firm. I was the first black they had ever hired. All of these white males had been fraternity brothers. They knew what jobs they would get assigned to. They met the partners. Then there's me. It took me a lot longer to move up because I had no "mentor" to give me inside tips.

I tell other blacks and women to talk to me after five o'clock; I'll try and give them some information on a project coming up, or advise them to take a computer class, get their name out there, increase their visibility.

TP: It's the toughest nut to crack. Because the truth of the matter is that organizational life is really about the informal network, the schmoozing, getting the right advice from the plugged-in person.

PATRICIA STEELE: I started working when I was 17 years old. First black in the office. Started as a file clerk.

DIANNE STOKELY, VICE PRESIDENT IN
GROUND OPERATIONS

Every time there was a meeting, I was the person asked to get the coffee, make the coffee, do whatever. There was a white salesman who was always trying to hit on me. I never told anybody because I was afraid I would lose my job. I dealt with it for five years, until I decided I was going to stop it. The next time he tried it, I gave him a kick. I didn't have any problems with him after that. Sometimes that's what it takes.

I worked my way up from file clerk to office manager. They would send me out of town on business. I remember going to Arkansas and being told the better restaurants didn't welcome blacks. I had white men come into the office and say, "I don't want your kind to wait on me." I said, "OK. I'll go get someone else." I never let myself get bitter; that's a luxury I couldn't afford. I had a job to do.

I love working at Federal Express. I love working with customers, I love working with people. Today if I feel someone is treating me unfairly, I speak up. I don't care who you are, what color you are, if you make $900,000 a year. You're no better than I am.

Spreading the Word

FRED DANIELS: I've had people walk by me like I'm the Invisible Man.

PATRICIA STEELE: Sometimes you just want to grab them and scream, "What's your problem?!" That's when I take a deep breath, count to 10, and say to myself, "Well, you know, this man needs praying for."

LINDA EDWARDS: Not all of our 3500 managers have taken the course. Some tell us they don't think they need it. Then we watch their behavior and they do need it. Some of them see [diversity] as one more stress in an already stressful job.

NEAL JOHNSON: I don't want to be sitting around waiting on some managing director to come down and wind me up. I want to take charge of the situation. I don't think we need to worry about how many of the 3500 managers have taken the course. I think we need to worry about our own turf, make it work there, lead by example.

STEVE NIELSEN: Each manager who puts this into action and makes it work is a brick. You don't build a house in one day. You just keep laying those bricks.

I think it is also important that we understand that this course isn't the be-all and end-all of life on this planet. It's an awareness tool. An evolving one at that. This course talks to the pocketbook, the heart, the head. It's about making people think and feel. It's about making Federal Express a better company.

It has a ripple effect. One person comes to the course, they change, they talk to other people, it spreads out in waves. We're very proud of this course, but with 3500 managers and limited resources, we know we're not going to get everybody. So we want the people who do come, who do get it, to take it and push it down, or up, or sideways. Those bricks will eventually support all 105,000 of our employees.

DAVID BICKERS: Every time a black man looks at a white man with compassion and understanding, every time a straight man looks at a lesbian and sees beyond his stereotype and his prejudice, that's real human progress. And at 3 A.M. out on that ramp, that straight man is going to realize that the woman working opposite him can love whoever she wants to, what matters is getting the job done and done well.

LILLIE McGHEE: In my area, we are going right to the courier, the handler, the hourly worker. We want *everybody* trained. Leaders get broader training, but everybody gets something. I'm a strong believer that one life affects another.

I like to view my hourly employees as people who may someday be my boss. We get back into our prejudices when we assume that because someone's salary is lower they may not have the intelligence to manage or lead. I'm throwing out the parent-child model, which is how I used to manage.

I don't care if you make $900,000 a year. You're no better than I am.

STEVE NIELSEN: This isn't something new at Federal Express. You go back to day one, and read the manager's guide on how you are supposed to treat people. It's in there.

LILLIE McGHEE: It all comes down to right and wrong.

PATRICIA STEELE: We have front-line managers who don't treat people well. A courier sees this

PATRICIA STEELE, SENIOR SERVICE AGENT.

and thinks, "When I get to be a manager I can do the same thing." That's bad.

LILLIE McGHEE: It takes a certain amount of courage to come forward and say, "I have observed So-and-So doing what I feel is the wrong thing." I speak up. I have to do that to live with myself. I may have to deal with retaliation or peer disapproval. So be it.

Girls and Boys

LINDA EDWARDS: I think we have plenty of work to do here at home. We're a long way from equality between the sexes.

TP: Maybe the perfect management style would be half male, half female. I frankly think there's less understanding between men and women than there is between races.

I read an article in *USA Today* about a former men's soccer coach who now coaches the University of North Carolina women's soccer team and has won twelve NCAA championships with them. He said when his men's teams were behind at half-time he would kick wastebaskets because men don't understand unless you get pissed. Now he hugs his players at halftime and tells them to support one another, because women aren't terribly turned on by wastebasket-kicking dumb jerk males.

LINDA EDWARDS: In the course the gender issue sometimes gets trivialized. A lot of men think they're experts. One said to me, "I have a wife, a daughter and a female dog. I understand." Most of us don't live with people of a different race, so that issue seems more mysterious and complex.

In my era women were raised not to make a big deal out of anything. You went along to get along. I don't think women have found their powerful voice yet.

TP: I remember meeting an AT&T sales manager at one of my seminars. He sold very sophisticated equipment and he had an astonishing record. He told us his secret was hiring all women to sell for him. He said when he had males selling, they'd walk into a [customer] company like John Wayne and announce they only wanted to speak to the CEO. Women, on the other hand, would invest mega-hours in penetrating the customer organization. They didn't give two hoots in hell whether they were talking to a frontline employee, a middle manager, or the CEO; they were interested in blanketing the place with relationships.

It gets to my theory about the raw commercial potential of harnessing diversity. Having sat in dull meetings with white males all my life, I can't imagine things wouldn't be more interesting with an Asian, an African-American, and some women thrown into the mix. It's all about turning diversity into a big, serious, bottom line win in the marketplace.

PAMELA BUFORD: Women do see things differently than men. As we continue to gain power in the world, it almost behooves a company to listen to us. A female — black, white or Asian — can come up with an idea and it may not be what you thought you were looking for but, hey, but it might work — and make a lot of money.

DIANNE STOKELY: My husband used to be a chauvinist. Now whenever we get annual reports, he comes and shows me the pictures, "Look at this, all white males." As bad as we are [at FedEx], and we certainly could be better, we're leaps and bounds ahead of most companies.

DAVID BICKERS: We have to be very proactive about it. We need to be putting people into place today so that five or ten years from now there's a diverse pool of qualified people in the company. When FedEx celebrates its fiftieth anniversary [in 2023], instead of having two or three minorities, women, or handicapped people to pick, we'll have 275.

Who Said "Handicapped"?

TP: As far as I can tell, companies like McDonald's who have been smart enough to hire the handicapped, for example, have had incredible results — like employees going years without a late day. The world is loaded with talented disabled people who tend to be radically underutilized.

GLEN SESSOMS: I think the challenge will be match the job with the person. And also to expand our definition of what the handicapped are capable of.

The Indianapolis Hub has hired a number of deaf people. They're running deaf cultural awareness classes for their managers and co-workers. What's our response going to be when they want to move up the ladder, to be managers, to fly planes? What accommodations do we have to make to allow them to do those jobs? Obviously someone in a wheelchair isn't going to be driving a vehicle that makes 28 stops an hour. There are specific limits. The real trick is not to start thinking limits from the start.

TP: We came across a fabulous plant that is mostly staffed by the handicapped. With a little Rube Goldberg-ing, not a jillion dollars per person, they retooled the production line. The productivity is bizarrely high. It works. The place makes a lot of money.

GLEN SESSOMS: It's important to expose yourself to other worlds. One of our [non-hearing impaired] managers in Indianapolis went to a disco for the deaf. They turn the sound way up and feel the vibrations. And they dance. Diversity is about that, about possibilities.

REGINA TAYLOR: We're sponsoring a deaf family picnic, because a lot of parents of deaf children don't believe those children can grow up and become highly functional in society. Personally, I'm getting a real education. I wondered if the deaf can drive. They can. And isn't our new, deaf Miss America terrific?

We have a hearing-impaired corporate neighbor team. One of the projects they are taking on is to adopt a hearing-impaired student. They want these kids to understand that they can be successful.

Beyond the Walls

LILLIE McGHEE: It's very important for me to give back. My most recent project is working with gangs in the school system, which has a lot of parallels to dealing with a diverse workforce. It's about power. One gang has to be superior. Versus the team approach, which is about loving one another and working together. That sounds corny, but it's real. I've seen it work here at FedEx. As individuals, as a company, as a nation, we'll never reach our full potential until we all work and live together.

GLEN SESSOMS: We have a responsibility to go into the community and show children what they can do with their lives. There are no role models out there. It's either Michael Jordan or nothing.

These kids need realistic, middle-class role models. They listen to a black FedEx manager and they start to see that there's a lot of opportunity out there. Because the message they get on the street is a no hope message.

We had a tour where children came to the office. One little girl asked, "Who works in this office?" And one of the managers answered, "My boss." And the girl asked, "Where is he?" And the manager answered, "*She* is not here." I wish everyone in the world could have seen that little girl's face. A light went on. It was the light of hope.

TOMORROW'S STRANGE ENTERPRISES

156 They Organize Themselves!

"Fluid, interdependent groups of problem solvers," say Texas Instruments' Steve Truett and EDS's Tom Barrett, will replace today's still-lumbering bureaucracies. "But how do I ORGANIZE these crazy, dispersed, far-flung networks?" one frustrated seminar participant almost shouted after I flashed the Truett and Barrett comment on a giant screen.

The answer: They organize themselves!

EDS is a monster firm, with over 70,000 employees. Moreover, it's known to this day for the paramilitary culture Ross Perot instilled at the start in 1962. Yet disciplined, enormous EDS is self-organizing.

More than that, self-organization is one of its vital secrets. The company has tried hard to develop orderly human resource-allocation schemes. But they have invariably failed. Busy people are smarter — and faster — than the most clever systems, explains EDS marketing head

Barry Sullivan.

It works this way: Nancy R., a respected account manager, calls you, Joe Bloggs, and says she heard from Dave G. about your sterling performance on the ABC Corp. project. She's got something similar, with a couple of neat twists, coming up for her client, XYZ Corp. How'd you like to be project manager? If so, when will you be free?

> **The definition of effective project management includes a finely honed skill at Rolodex development and exploitation.**

Suppose you sign up (you're finishing up your current project within the month) and agree to a starting date six weeks hence. The moment you get off the phone, you turn to your Rolodex (paper or electronic) and tag seven names (working on seven different projects in four countries on three continents), and start dialing. Or e-mailing: "Mary, just got through talking to Nancy R., who conned me into working on the XYZ account. Sounds fabulous. And it would allow you to learn a lot. I'm gonna try to nab Yoshi O. and Miguel L. as well. We start in about six weeks, though I could fudge a little on that. Up for it? Let me know. Cheers, Joe Bloggs."

In the next 72 hours, you successfully recruit the nucleus of the dozen-person team you'll need to get started. (You also talk a globally renowned professor-specialist from the London School of Economics into giving you six days of consulting time in the next four months.)

Sullivan told me, in effect, there are two kinds of project managers: Those who wait to have people assigned to their projects, and those who round up their own teams. Guess which go on to fame and fortune?

I smiled at Sullivan's recollections. Though EDS is a lot bigger than my former employer, McKinsey & Co., the tale he spun mimicked my experience. Without an order barked, the billion-dollar plus consultancy effectively reorganizes itself every day along the exact lines Sullivan sketched.

One moral of this story: There's nothing new under the sun.

Hollywood has always done it this way. So have construction companies. And McKinsey, EDS, and almost every other professional service firm. (The EDS example also suggests — no, proves — that there's no size limit associated with effective self-organization.)

Another moral, per Sullivan's observation: The definition of effective project management includes (at or near the top of the list) a finely honed skill at Rolodex development and exploitation.

A third moral: It ain't reengineering!

Margaret Wheatley, author of *Leadership and the New Science: Learning About Organizations from an Orderly Universe*, ripped reengineering in a recent *Industry Week* interview:

> Reengineering is the supernova of our old approaches to organizational change, the last gasp of efforts that have consistently failed. What is reengineering but another attempt, usually by people at the top, to impose new structures over old — to take one set of rigid rules and guidelines and impose them on the rest of the organization? It's a mechanical view of organizations and people — that you can "design" a perfect solution and then the machine will comply with this new set of instructions. . . .
>
> Reengineering doesn't change what needs to be changed most: the way people at all levels relate to the enterprise. We need to be asking: Has the organization's capacity to change increased and improved? . . . Or have we just created a new structure that will atrophy as the environment shifts?

What *is* new, according to Truett and Barrett, Wheatley, and me (among many others), is that the self-organizing phenomenon is becoming pervasive — i.e., the hallmark of *every* industry — in these times of constant flux.

And that leads to the bad news: While self-organizing is time-tested, it does require a culture (I think that's the right word) of self-motivation, self-responsibility, and personal accountability.

> **"Reengineering doesn't change what needs to be changed most: the way people at all levels relate to the enterprise."**
>
> **Margaret Wheatley**

At EDS and McKinsey (and Fluor, Bechtel et al. in the construction business) you learn approximately by midafternoon of your first day that you're on your own. It's up to you to make things happen. That message comes as a shock to many raised in companies with dependency cultures. Such people live and die by the nuances of their job descriptions and expect assignments to be just that — assigned.

Changing a culture of dependence to a culture of self-organizing independence is hard work. But at least what I'm reporting here suggests that it doesn't go against the human grain. Yes, Virginia, 71,000 people (EDS) jolly well can reinvent themselves every day without the hand of God (or Ross Perot) being laid upon their collective shoulders.

157

New York Times reviewer James Oestreich cheered conductor Robert Shaw's production of the Benjamin Britten chorale, *War Requiem,* at Carnegie Hall. After several days of drilling the chorus, and only two days before the performance, Shaw revealed that baritone star Benjamin Luxon had gone almost totally deaf in recent years, making coordination with the chorus exceptionally difficult. "[Shaw] put all his painstaking preparation at risk," Oestreich wrote, "because, he said, Mr. Luxon 'brings a human quality to this piece that I have never heard anywhere else.'"

Robert Shaw also has something important to teach us about virtual organizations. He brought his singers together for the first time on a Tuesday and produced a world-class product (performance) that Sunday. "This is an extraordinary chorus," he told the *Times'* Oestreich on Thursday. "I don't know its equal anywhere in the world, and it's two and a half days old now."

A stunning statement. True, many of the singers had worked with Shaw before. Nonetheless, the configuration was unique — and, furthermore, the nascent group quickly adapted to the mostly deaf Luxon. You see, you *can* create an effective virtual organization almost overnight. In fact, this "new" way of doing business is old hat in the arts.

158 Housepainters and Prozac

I have a friend who's a housepainter. He doesn't chug Mylanta; he doesn't pop Prozac; and he doesn't have a future, at least not by my dad's standards.

My dad worked for one outfit, Baltimore Gas & Electric Co., for 41 years. He was pretty sure, from one year to the next (from one *decade* to the next), what door on West Lexington Street he'd enter at 8:30 A.M. any given Monday through Friday. Despite the job security, the work gave him an occasional first-class bellyache. (And that was before the era of middle-management genocide.)

My housepainter friend has no idea what portal he'll traverse three Mondays from now. But he's comfortable that there *will* be a door to pass through, then paint.

Complacent? Never. Comfortable? Absolutely.

He shows up on time. Finishes the job on time. Returns phone calls promptly. Meets his budgets. He's careful. And he's a little offbeat, with a hint of the artist in him.

His clients recommend him to others. Top contractors (the sort that build million-dollar homes) like him to add the finishing touches to their gems. And he actually advises them and their interior designers on color schemes; he's developed a reputation for an unerring eye. Add it up, and my friend has what I'd call, well, *job security*.

He's got no home on any organization chart. No job description. (He does have great business cards and a snazzy truck.) He has no prestigious business address, though as a computer buff, he does have an e-mail address.

I thought about my pal after an acrimonious exchange with a journalist over my "crazy" view of the economy. I believe traditional job security is gone, and not just in my Silicon Valley environs. I believe, along with British management guru Charles Handy, that a "career" tomorrow will most likely consist of a dozen jobs, on and off payrolls of large and small firms, in two or three industries.

And I believe that people *can* cope with these changes. Millions upon millions, like my friend, already are. (Although not always with adequate health care: Got that, Senator Dole?) They're housepainters and gardeners. Accountants and software designers. Marketers and ad copywriters. Photographers and journalists and surgeons and TV camera operators. Even execs for rent.

I take all of this personally. At McKinsey & Co., I never knew what my next assignment would be. Or where. Or with whom I'd be working; in seven years I never worked even twice with the exact same team.

I did know that if I hustled and kept picking up new skills, some project manager somewhere would recruit me before my current assignment was over, that maybe a couple of high-profile project managers would actually fight to sign me up (see item No. 156 above).

To Dad, my life at McKinsey looked chaotic. To the entry-level employee of the 1950s, who went to work in the GM plant (or the purchasing department), it looked positively nutty: That new GM hire knew *exactly* what he'd be doing and where he'd be doing it for the next 30 years or so — barring war, a bad back, or a liver that revolted against ritual after-work pub stops.

To me, my glamorous life as a consultant (one McKinsey colleague called us "the movie stars of the business world") felt humdrum. Another damned 12-hour plane trip from San Francisco to London. Another client company in another industry to put under a microscope. Another three colleagues (from England, Germany, and Japan) to learn to work seamlessly with. And, in six short weeks, a progress report was due the client chairman. Blow it and you were on the carpet.

But, as I said, ho-hum.

No, I don't envy for a moment the laid-off, 52-year-old middle manager who's spent his entire career in the womb called IBM. My life, my housepainter friend's life, the life of any independent contractor looms as a frightening and unnerving prospect to him. As a nation, we ought to do a lot more to help that fellow and his several hundred thousand dislocated — discarded? — kin.

But that's not the same as saying, "C'mon, people can't cope with constant change. They need stability." Of course they need stability! But stability can come in many costumes. It need not be clothed as the same old corporate logo on a biweekly paycheck or as the same old door to enter for 220 workdays in each of 41 consecutive years.

Real stability is my housepainter friend's fabulous reputation. Truth is (I'm not kidding), I envy him. Not only does he get to work outdoors much of the time, but I think he's got a more secure future than I do: He seems able to keep on top of his game more readily than I can.

Want to avoid Mylanta and Prozac? Quit your job at General Electric and learn to paint houses in a way that delights two lifetimes' worth of prospective clients.

159   mgullixs@apr.com

Gentry magazine, June-July 1994. A multipage advertisement for Silicon Valley realtor Alain Pinel includes, yes, each agent's Internet address. For example, you can reach Mary S. Guillixson at mgullixs@apr.com. One friend, who works for the firm, tells me she arrives at work each morning to about 100 e-mail messages!

160

"The basis of competitive advantage in the 1990s is how well a company captures and deploys its knowledge assets."

Joe Carter
Andersen Consulting

Tired of reading mindless praise for the so-called networked (virtual) organization? I am. How about somebody who's actually living the image?

VeriFone, the $259 million Redwood City, California, company — which dominates the U.S. credit card-authorization market and is a growing force overseas — is wired from top to bottom. Employees get a laptop before they get a desk, internal paper mail is banned, and there is 24-hour-a-day, real-time computer networking. The dynamic CEO of this fast-growing company, Hatim Tyabji, works hard to create what he calls a "culture of urgency." Believe it or not, his paradigm for this 21st-century firm is the distinctly old-fashioned blueberry pancake. But let him tell us:

> VeriFone's organizational model is the blueberry pancake — independent units (blueberries) held together by a unifying medium (batter). We are completely decentralized and expect each blueberry to generate its own ideas, strategies, and tactics.
>
> All blueberries are created equal. There isn't one big, fat blueberry sitting in the middle of the pancake, calling itself headquarters and intimidating all the smaller blueberries. For purposes of our annual report, Redwood City is listed as company headquarters; but I consider VeriFone — and I mean this seriously — to be a company without a headquarters. Our board meetings rotate between offices in Atlanta, Dallas, Honolulu, and Redwood City. No one refers to Redwood City as headquarters. It isn't. It's just one of the company's offices.
>
> I tell all our people the same thing, "Folks, you have thoughts and ideas. You know where this com-

All blueberries are

pany is screwing up and where it is doing halfway decently. Talk to me. And don't expect wisdom to pour forth from headquarters. Because guess what, sports fans, there isn't one."

I translate those words into action by traveling 80 to 90 percent of the time but I'm not interested in having a lot of empty offices scattered around the country, just waiting for me to show up. When I arrive in San Antonio or Boston or wherever, and I need to sit down and do my e-mail, I just use any room that's available.

There Is No Paper

Our company runs 100 percent electronically. There is no paper. It's fun to watch people's reactions when they start here and realize that everything is on e-mail and there are no secretaries. They suffer some withdrawal symptoms. You get them over those, and then they say they don't know if they'll be able to keep up with 75 e-mails a day. My response is, "Bullshit."

Just as you get junk mail, you get junk e-mail. It's a matter of learning to separate the real from the junk, the important from the trivial.

We get a fair amount of resistance to the use of e-mail. The key is mind-set. I tell people I don't mind being overrun with e-mail. In fact, I personally respond to every piece of e-mail within 24 hours, unless I'm on vacation or somewhere like Tahiti where it's impossible.

It would be impossible for me to run a traditional company and also travel as much as I do. All those memos and papers and reports would pile up until I got back. Then I'd have to read them and respond. Then my secretary would have to make copies and

created equal. . . . . . .

send them out. Instead of all that, wherever I am in the world, I sit down at my laptop and instantly respond. Everything happens in real time. When I come back to my office, the only paper that is on my desk is "p-mail", or physical mail, usually magazines.

Psychology, the Critical 95 Percent

The technical details of this extreme decentralization are secondary to the psychological adjustment. It takes time for people to grasp, and when all is said and done, no matter how advanced the technology, a company is made up of human beings.

When I was at Sperry, I was the only corporate officer who wasn't based at headquarters. Some people felt that I needed to be there. My comment to my CEO was, "I'll be there when you need me, I guarantee the work won't suffer, and that I'll provide results."

I have brought this philosophy to VeriFone. Get away from the fixation that people have to be around you and that things have to be done a certain way! At Sperry, I'd joke and say that I have to pay homage to the Wise Men in the East. [Headquarters.] I don't want anyone in VeriFone to say that they have to pay homage to the boys in Redwood City.

Getting that message out isn't easy. The most difficult thing in life, personal or professional, is changing ingrained mind-sets. I have a poster in my office of twelve dogs in a row. The first eleven dogs are standing and "sit" is written under them. The twelfth is sitting and the caption reads: "Some messages have to be repeated a few times." I take that poster with me to every staff meeting and say, "Ladies and gentlemen, you are dealing with human beings, human psycholo-

.There isn't one big, fa

gy. Don't give me all this crap about technology."

Utilizing information technology is only 5 percent of our challenge. Our technology isn't superior. Some of it isn't even cutting-edge. But that's not the issue. The real issue is changing the way people work.

We have about 1,800 employees, and we're hiring all over the place. We have recruited from Sperry, IBM, and AT&T. We're all products of our environment, and these people carry a certain amount of baggage. We don't subject them to any psychological tests, which I think are demeaning and unreliable.

However, we do have a VeriFone culture that we reinforce at every opportunity. We have a company manifesto called Commitment to Excellence. It's made up of e-mails that I have written. That is our bible. It covers company philosophy, strategy, and tactics. Everyone has a copy.

E-mail is the lifeblood of this company. It's direct communication, totally unfiltered. People are resistant to this egalitarian way of doing things. We use technology to help us overcome that resistance, and to turn VeriFone into a stronger company at the same time.

Every October since 1988, we've laid out a corporate calendar. The first year everyone chuckled because they didn't think I'd stick to it. After five years, no one questions my discipline.

One of the key calendar elements is "MGT Week." Every six weeks, in a different location, my direct staff and I meet. There are about 11 of us. At some time during that week we also have an "all-hands meeting" for everyone there. I'll talk, my staff will talk, and then we throw it open for questions. Any

lueberry sitting . . . . .

question is fair game. It's a very good forum for reinforcing company culture.

But open meetings aren't limited to every six weeks. I'm on the road continuously and wherever I am, I have an "all-hands meeting." If I'm going to Atlanta to meet customers, I'll carve out at least half a day; there's no substitute for intensive contact.

It's a race with no finish line. When you're dealing with human beings, there are no simple answers. The blueberry pancake is always cooking, never done. We work very hard to keep VeriFone bubbling, a fun place to work; we want to create a sense of permanent anticipation, of looking forward to the next challenge.

Cracking the Protective Shell

Open communication is one of the foundations of this business. Anyone can talk to me. All they have to do is send an e-mail. There's no recrimination for telling me bad news. When new people come into the company, they're often skeptical, even cynical, about this openness. To free them from the inhibitions and fear they bring with them is a very difficult, painstaking, never-ending job. But once we do crack through that self-protective shell, the rewards can be enormous!

I remember introducing myself to a new employee at one of our Asian locations. He was surprised that I would talk to him — at his previous job he had never even *seen* the CEO. I encouraged him to send me e-mail and let me know what was happening. I left, figuring he agreed with me. Turned out he was just giving me lip service. About six months later, his superior told me he had developed an attitude problem. I decided to have a talk with him.

. in the middle of the

So next time I was in his region, I took him out to lunch, which blew him away. He couldn't believe the CEO would have the time, let alone the interest. I listened to his point of view and told him I was glad he was unhappy, because it meant that he cared. Then I asked how he expected to get anything changed if he kept his gripes to himself. I said, "You're creating a self-fulfilling prophecy. If you tell me your concerns and nothing gets done, then you have every reason to be pessimistic. If you choose not to say anything to anybody, then screw you. Nobody can help you."

He appreciated my honesty and understood exactly what I was saying. After our lunch, I had a changed person on my hands. But that's not the end of the story. During the course of lunch, he told me that we were fouling up. We were shipping products from our factory in Taiwan to other Asian factories, where we would modify them to fit each country's specific needs. We were then shipping the product to the customers. This was the wrong thing to do, he said, because there were strict quality controls in the Taiwan factory, and by opening the products up and modifying them on site we were potentially compromising that quality.

He went on to say that he had designed a process that would enable us to make the modifications — not just for those countries but for most of the world — right at the factory.

Well, I listened and I realized he was on to something. We implemented his plan, and it led to a profound change in the way we work. Our build-to-order time fell from three months to about 15 days!

ancake calling itself

In terms of competitive advantage, that is one heavy-duty win.

I'll be the first to tell you that I would never have come up with his idea; I'm not smart enough. The whole thing happened because we created — and kept working on — an environment that encouraged him to speak up. And then we listened.

The Network Reacts

We've used technology and our culture to score big-time. We were fighting tooth and nail to win an account down in Colombia. It was a major customer, and we were going to install systems with PIN pads for a debit network — I won't bore you with the technical details.

The day before the final presentation, our competition told the customer that VeriFone didn't know anything about debit and that they'd be fools to take a chance on us.

So, our people went into the meeting the next day and got hit between the eyes with a 2x4: The customer has been told that we don't have any debit installations. Understandably, they wanted to know why they should do business with us. The rep on the account had only been with us for three months. He didn't know whether we were big in debit or not. So he asked the customer for 12 hours.

Then he ran back to his hotel room. He put out an e-mail to our salespeople all over the world saying that he was in a knock-down, drag-out fight and it was a big order. He added that he needed specific ammunition. It was a call for help.

Within six hours, he had the specifics of 24 debit

. . .**headquarters.**

installations we'd done; in 10 of those cases, he had specific customer references. He went back to the prospective customer and just blew them away. We were dealing with hard facts, and we won the account.

This electronic communications web can work for any company, large or small, high tech or low, cosmetics, clothing, or cattle. It's a state of mind. It allows us to cover the globe, all working together as equals — it's that blueberry pancake.

This Is the Way It's Going to Be

The biggest hurdle to making the blueberry pancake work is convincing people that it's not just the strategy du jour, that you're serious and you're not going to revert back to a monolithic, hierarchical structure when the going gets tough.

There is only one way to address that skepticism — staying the course. Don't waste time making a lot of speeches. Lead by example. Once people realize how serious I am, they begin to change. It evolves. It's a slow process. Some people will come aboard faster than others.

Overreliance on all this technology is one big pitfall. People can forget they're dealing with other human beings. If you disagree with a colleague and call him up or meet for lunch, you can usually hash it out. Nobody wants bad blood face-to-face. But if you send an angry e-mail missive, you will exacerbate the problem. I think that it's crucial to realize that technology, like everything else in life, has its limits. I travel extensively. I am constantly meeting with people from all over the world. I personally have never come across a company that comes close to our mode of operation. I believe that in 10 to 15 years, with increased globalization, companies that don't work the way we do are going to be history. I characterize us as John the Baptist: The Messiah is coming, and we are there ahead of time.

The new corporate Messiah mixing blueberry pancake batter — quite the image, eh? But is Tyabji smoking funny stuff — and inhaling — when he says VeriFone's hot-wired culture will be the norm in a few years? There's a good chance he's right — good enough that if you aren't heading in his direction you should worry.

But as you do begin the trip, never lose sight of Tyabji's other message: New technologies are the peerless enablers of his bizarre organization — but dealing with the human factor is what makes it all work. It's 5 percent technology, 95 percent psychology — and that from an unabashed technologist.

> **It's a race with no finish line. The blueberry pancake is always cooking, never done.**

162 There Are Two Companies . . .

"Businesses that have pervasive use of electronic mail operate differently. It squeezes all the slack out of the system. It also gives you the opportunity to course correct more rapidly. . . . Companies that use e-mail are much faster, much less hierarchical.

"You can only use e-mail . . . if you do it yourself, if you're available to anybody and everybody. The elimination of the screening process in my e-mail . . . [leads to] a more democratic way of operating. . . .

"There are two companies — one that operates this way and

one that doesn't, competing with each other. How long will the one that doesn't . . . stick around? You're either going to do it or disappear."

Andy Grove
CEO, Intel

163 The 747 Factor

Electronic networks are making instant global communications and knowledge exchange a piece of cake.

Sorta.

The wisest, thoroughly modern companies understand that to exploit 21st-century electronic wizardry, you must match it with 1st-century face-to-face, belly-to-belly communication.

Thus VeriFone's Hatim Tyabji, as we heard, spends 90 percent of his time on the road — to keep the human juices flowing along with the electrons. And Pat McGovern, founder and boss of International Data Group (publisher of *Computerworld* in numerous languages, and about 220 information-industry magazines and newspapers in total), spends like a drunken sailor on travel; though he declares his company *is* an electronic network, he believes that constantly getting people together in person is essential to foster a culture of constant exchange.

Sun Microsystems CIO Bill Raduchel sums it up perfectly, "The indispensable complementary technology to the [electronic] net is the Boeing 747."

Think about it. (Long and hard — on your next flight.)

164

"The three Rs — reading, 'riting, and 'rithmetic — are no longer enough. We must add the three C's — computing, critical thinking, and capacity for change."

Fred Gluck
former managing director
McKinsey & Co.

A lot of computer software is a pain to use. A lot of software manuals have apparently been written by human beings with major neurological deficiencies.

But soon, say some (many?), all that will be cured. Using a computer will be a walk in the park. As easy as mastering that older, now ubiquitous technology, the automobile.

Rubbish.

To master anything is hard work. You've just forgotten how long it actually took to become an expert driver.

Cars: In a few minutes, you can learn to propel an auto forward. Computers: In a few minutes, you can get started with a computer (or a particular piece of software).

In a few days, you can "drive" a car reasonably smoothly. In a few days, you can do a few basics on your computer.

In a few months, you can refine your skill at dealing with city-freeway automotive operations. In a few months, you can turn the computer into your pal.

In a few years you can drive well, even wisely. (Hey, some do.) In a few years, you can be a computer ace.

Ever gotten behind a driver's school neophyte? Don't tell me that driving is like breathing! Getting good at any damn thing takes work; getting artful takes hard, continuous work. Bikes, skates, sailboats, gardening . . . and computers.

So don't wait for tomorrow, hoping that the arrival of the no-brainer computer will make you a facile member of the 21st-century technology club in the space of a few minutes.

166   **. . . and Looking the Fool**

"When we see that *to learn* we must be willing to look foolish, to let another teach us, learning doesn't always look so good anymore. . . . Only with the support, insight, and fellowship of a community can we face the dangers of learning meaningful things."

Peter Senge

167

"Distance learning." "Flexible delivery." Education *is* changing! Fort Collins-based National Technological University is a/the leader of educational satellite learning. In 1993, using the electronically linked-up services of faculty members from 45 leading engineering schools, NTU offered 528 graduate courses to more than 5,000 enrollees from 85 corporations who support 338 satellite-connected sites. (One-hundred eleven students earned master's degrees, via the network, from NTU in 1993.) Some 20 universities offered another 213 short courses by the NTU net; and 46 non-U.S., NTU-affiliated sites conduct videotape-based courses from NTU-net instructors.

Countering charges that such learning is dessicated, NTU points to an evaluation conducted by an outside consulting group:

■ The majority of students in 58 percent of NTU courses agree that their instructor was "among the best teachers they had ever had."

■ The majority of students in 53 percent of NTU courses agreed that the courses were among "the best they had ever taken."

Distance learning *is* the wave of the future. Are you riding it?

168

Consultants, investment bankers, and ad agencies typically have "account managers" — a lead person with overall responsibility for a particular client. Though there's lots of useful debate about how powerful such account managers ought to be (too powerful, stifle creativity; too weak, fail to present a unified front), there's general agreement that the time-proven concept is a good one.

So, Mr. Training Boss, Ms. Purchasing Chief, why not swipe a chapter from the book by professional-service firms?

Some have. Eli Lilly's information-systems department

recently gave several managers additional duty as account managers for specific line units in the corporation. I think the idea is wise — and generalizable across *all* internal service functions.

169

Make a list of your 100 top customers. Put it in your desk drawer. Every week call four of them, just to check in, listen, see if there's anything they want to talk about. Anything. When you get to the bottom of the list, start all over again from the top.

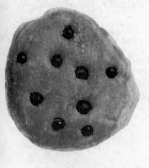

Entrepreneurs' Dreams

170 The Entrepreneur's (Strange) Lot

One recent Monday morning in Boston, I was able (through some scheduling miracle) to bring together 11 entrepreneurs for a free-for-all discussion on the perils and joys of starting your own business. A wildly eclectic group, they're making their mark in everything from French lace to damaged remainders, from croissants to yes, umbilical cord blood. Here's the gang:

I'm Frank von Holzhausen, owner of Group Four Design in Avon, Connecticut. We are a 50-person product- and package-design firm with about $7 million in annual sales. We've been in business about 22 years, seen three recessions come and go.

I'm Anthony Harnett, and I founded the Boston-area natural-food supermarket chain Bread and Circus, which I sold a year and half ago. I thought I'd retire. For about three days. I'm now starting a chain of alternative pharmacies called Harnett's — we've already opened our first two.

I'm Dick Friedman, president of Carpenter & Co., a real estate company. We developed and run the Charles Hotel and Charles Square shopping complex in Harvard Square. I'm also developing a new hotel at the airport, and am involved in a gaming venture.

I'm Cynthia Fisher and I founded Viacord, a biomedical company, about nine months ago. We'll be freezing and banking umbilical cord blood from newborns. Cord blood has been found to have a high concentration of stem cells, which are found in adult bone marrow and are responsible for manufacturing blood. It's an exciting new field.

I'm Jerry Ellis. I run a cultural institution called Building 19 that deals in merchandise of all descriptions — and some beyond description — salvaged from train wrecks and earthquakes and whatever. I've been in business 30 years. In my spare time I started Buck a Book, which is three years and 17 stores old.

My name is Pam Kelley, and my company is Rue de France, located in Newport, Rhode Island. I import lace and fabrics from France, make them into curtains, and sell them by catalog. I have a store in Newport, and 26 employees. On the side I maintain a small law practice.

I'm Steve Kapner, co-founder and an owner of MacTemps, a seven-year-old employment agency specializing in temporary and permanent computer personnel. We now have 25 offices across the U.S. and a token international office in London, our foray into globalization.

I'm Bill Davis, founder of a direct marketing and advertising agency, Holland, Mark, Martin, in Burlington, Massachusetts. We're eight years old and employ about 150 people. Recently I also created an offshoot called the Production Company.

I'm Louis Kane, co-chairman, co-CEO, co-founder, co- everything of Au Bon Pain, a chain of 225 French bakery/cafés based in Boston.

I'm Nancy Wilber, founder of Time Resources. We're a brand-new company. We introduced our first product last July. We've got 14 employees and growth has been rapid. We offer time-management training seminars and goal-planner products — books, tapes, and videos, as well as software and electronic organizers. [TP: Any of my stuff, Nancy?]

Hi, I'm Judy George, founder and CEO of Domain, a home furnishings company. It'll hopefully do between $40 and $50 million this year.

TP: So what's on anyone's mind?

Partners, Envelope Scrawls, Sluggers, and Single Hitters

JUDY GEORGE: I'm scared. I hope I've evolved from the typical entrepreneur into someone capable of managing a business. But

I still feel like I'm standing on the edge of an abyss. Any help as I take my business to the next level?

JUDY GEORGE

LOUIS KANE: I've been through a similar evolution several times. The first time was with Healthco, a health services company that grew from ground zero to $200 million in sales in two years. We acquired over 50 companies over those two years — nursing homes, hospitals, suppliers, laboratories. And, I made every mistake possible.

First, I didn't surround myself with the right people. I thought I could do it all. Big mistake. Second, I suddenly had to deal with a number of entrepreneurs who had started their own companies, but were now part of my larger company. They were chomping at the bit and I was pulling in the reins. I should have given them much more autonomy. Third, I made the critical mistake of not understanding the power of the computer. I felt it cost too much money — $100,000 to $200,000 — and we were doing $200 million. Talk about penny wise!

If I had to boil it down to one lesson — surround yourself with absolutely the best people possible!

NANCY WILBER: When I started my business, I sat down and took an inventory of what I was good at and what I wasn't good at. An honest inventory. Then I went out and found someone who was strong where I was weak. He's my second in command.

TP: I like that personal inventory idea. Recently, a pal and I ran down the companies in Silicon Valley that really hit it big. We found a lot of two-person teams at the top, where there was genuine equity of the partners — not the "Solid" No. 2 to the "Almighty" No. 1. Call it symbiosis. The classic case is Hewlett-Packard, where Bill Hewlett was the tinkerer-engineer and Dave Packard was the operations-money guy.

I also came across a fascinating story about one of the most successful real estate partnerships in California. The two founders have been in business together for over 25 years — and have never been in each other's homes! Their unshakable mutual professional respect is the glue that holds them together.

JUDY GEORGE: I like the idea of creating a two-person team, I'm just not sure that I know how to do it.

LOUIS KANE: My partner, Ron Shaich, and I each run a different part of Au Bon Pain. We come together on all major decisions, of course, but aside from that we pretty much leave each other alone.

Judy, I'd also advise you to stick to your basic concept. Our original Au Bon Pain game plan was written on the back of an envelope. Ron was a wonderful day-to-day operator, he knew how to bake and how to sell. These were things that were beyond me, but I had a whole set of skills Ron didn't — financial and real estate and growth skills.

On the back of that envelope we wrote down how we were going to conduct our business from day one, and 14 years later we're still doing it. We don't spend a load of time in each other's houses.

JUDY GEORGE: I'm very creative. I like hitting home runs. I'm trying to learn how to hit singles. It's kind of painful, the change — you use different muscles. But I still want to lead this business.

TP: All of us, from time to time, have got to learn some new wrinkles, but I do get nervous when I hear you talking about going from fence basher to bunter. It implies taming your dreams. Of course, I admit, long ball hitters are sometimes reckless; they do tend to strike out a lot.

JUDY GEORGE: It's the striking out that scares me.

TP: If you've got a great percentage hitter, a singles-genius with great financial skills who can wring every last percent of efficiency out of your company, it gives you more leeway to aim for the bleachers.

JUDY GEORGE: Good point.

Do What's Best . . . for You

BILL DAVIS: Let's slow down a bit. I don't think you should be desperately trying to find a partner because it's the latest rage. Everyone needs to find the way that works for them. Some people fly better solo — Judy, you may be one of them.

FRANK VON HOLZHAUSEN: Yes, but. . . . I have an equal partner — he sells and I handle the inside stuff — and the nicest part is that there are no hidden agendas. I know exactly where he stands. I started the business with three other people and they're all gone. My present partner came up through the ranks, became partial owner, and then a full partner, and then we divested of the other partners — it was a long process. I think it's a wonderful to have a partner, because it's lonely at the top.

ANTHONY HARNETT: But to Bill [Davis's] point, I don't really know of that many partnerships that work. I think the ideal is something you might pursue, but it's very hard to achieve. Maybe, Judy, you should be chairman of the board and have a hands-on president who takes care of the day-to-day operations, but reports to you.

JUDY GEORGE: I've been through two presidents, so I'm batting .000. I did hire someone four months ago as chief operating officer. I was very movie star driven before; I wanted to be the star of the show. I don't know if it's from maturity or falling on my ass so much, but now I'm a lot more open to sharing power. I think.

TP: It *is* lonely at the top. It's hard to find out what's really going on in the ranks, to get the straight skinny.

JUDY GEORGE: I hate being vulnerable in front of all of you, so you can imagine how I hate being vulnerable at my own company!

ANTHONY HARNETT: I think Tom is right. You must have people who can tell you when you're off base.

JUDY GEORGE: I have five or six people who can do that, who can sit me down. I don't like being at the top alone anymore. It's too lonely, it really is.

ANTHONY HARNETT: It's no fun.

JUDY GEORGE: Yeah, I haven't slept in eight years.

Using Advisers

CYNTHIA FISHER: I feel one of the smartest things I did when I started out was to reach out to other people. There's one person in particular, now retired and enjoying life, who is my adviser. I can pick up the phone and say, "Jim, tell me what I should be doing here." He comes in and shoots it straight to me. It's wonderful.

TP: One of the toughest autocrats I've ever worked with is Roger Milliken, who runs a textile company in South Carolina with his name on the door. He owns the joint, yet he does a better job than anyone I've ever met at really using an advisory group. He has the nerve to bring in people who are wiser than he is in certain areas. I've never met a better billionaire-listener in my life.

LOUIS KANE: One of the problems an entrepreneur has to face is not being in a position to pay someone. I had a lawyer friend who was a mentor, but his law firm was getting a lot of fees from my company. It's got to be a two-way thing. It's unfair — you're so excited about your business — you're calling everybody up and you expect that same excitement to come back, but people are busy, time is money. If you want to have a mentor, make sure that person is compensated.

STEVE KAPNER: Hey, there are people you already pay you can get good advice from — your employees! Probably because we were young and naive, we purposely avoided the outside mentor/adviser role. We had this crazy notion that we wanted to invent everything ourselves. It was highly inefficient, but it was a good learning experience.

Remarkably, it turned out all right, and we continued to grow in spite of ourselves. Now when we need advice, we go straight to the people who know the business best — our top managers.

Coping with Growth = Developing Managers

TP: Whether it's employees or outsiders, companies are absurdly parochial in the places they go to seek ideas. Regardless of your energy and enthusiasm and creativity, we all get stale. How do you completely reinvent MacTemps five years from now, Steve? Advisers tend to be a conservative lot, whether they're 63 or 33. How do you really stay infused with spark and spunk?

STEVE KAPNER: Reinvent your company by reinventing your people. We have employees whose skills and attitudes were right for us seven years. Now they're just not suited for the direction we're heading in. Because there was no better way, we're in the process of firing or demoting close to a quarter of our branch office managers. That's been very tough.

ANTHONY HARNETT: How do you demote someone and have them remain loyal to the company?

STEVE KAPNER: My experience says people know when they're out of their league — they may not admit it, but they know it. On the other hand, they still like the company, like the people they're working with, like the culture. We try not to frame it as a demotion, but that we're bringing in someone above them who has newly-needed skills.

We gave everyone a choice. Some just left the company. That was actually the easy part. The tough part is our senior management crew. If we wait too long the company will have grown so fast that we won't be able to say, "Just go to business school for two years," because by the time they come back, the company will be 10 years ahead of them.

BILL DAVIS: One thing I've seen — in my own business and elsewhere — is that we do a lousy job of letting people know up front that they're expected to keep up with rapid-fire change. If we did and they still can't keep up, at least they were warned.

LOUIS KANE: Shouldn't there be a training program in place that really moves people along — a program where people who have been with you for a while can learn the skills needed to keep pace with the company?

STEVE KAPNER

STEVE KAPNER: We tried to do that — to give people financial and business skills they might not have — but that's only part of it. You can't simply say to someone, "Now we're going to make you a manager." If someone is a star at their job it doesn't follow they'll be even better as a *manager* in that job. If there is a way to train people to do that, I'd love to know it.

LOUIS KANE: We make all our managers partners in the business. That person essentially has ownership in his million-dollar outlet. It's marvelous how fast a person learns — working 70, 80 hours a week — the skills he or she needs!

ANTHONY HARNETT: How's the turnover in that?

LOUIS KANE: Tiny, it's tiny.

TP: I've felt for a long time that — whether a company has six employees or 60,000 — we tend to do a rotten job of helping people make the transition to manager. It's not an overstatement to say the move is like getting married.

BILL DAVIS

BILL DAVIS: More like puberty.

TP: Pick your metaphor, it's a huge deal. So often folks are just appointed manager one day, whether it's of three people or 33, and told to have at it. Then we wonder why the hell they flounder.

JUDY GEORGE: How do you know if someone is managerial material?

ANTHONY HARNETT: Some of us use a test. Properly used, it gauges judgment and — with the résumé and experience factored in — there's a high probability you can predict a person's chance of success.

CYNTHIA FISHER: I use such a test.

LOUIS KANE

TP: I've got a strong, strong bias against those tests because they're usually applied in a way that's mechanical, with no room for give and take, for shades of gray. The only time I've seen them work is when the results are used solely as a communication vehicle, something to be shared with the employee so that the whole process becomes an open learning experience for everyone. Frankly, even then I'm skeptical — the test becomes a de facto "you've got it" or "you don't" red flag; it becomes a cop out ("Cynthia can't hack it — see her score"), a substitute for painstaking, time-consuming attention to human development.

Communication Never Ends

JUDY GEORGE: I got a big shock recently when I surveyed our 200 employees and asked for their perceptions of how the company was run. Believe me, the way the middle managers viewed the company was very different from the responses on the survey. That devastated me!

LOUIS KANE: Communication is essential to keep everyone on the same frequency. Our half-dozen senior managers meet every two weeks. The next 20 people, including those managers, meet every four weeks. These are four-hour meetings, where we go through what the company is doing and where it should be going. Every quarter we bring together staff and managers, and we sit down and really open ourselves up.

First, we have a full presentation on what's happening, and then my partner and I each speak for half an hour. We really tell the story all over again, the story that started 15 years ago. We have to keep inculcating people who come into the company with that original enthusiasm.

Then we get report cards from everyone who attended the meeting, with no names attached. People can say anything they want. It's really pretty amazing to sit there and read what your people are thinking about. We pay attention.

JUDY GEORGE: I remember one of the comments that came back from one of my managers, "Judy, we know how much you love the customer. Could you love us as much?" I heard that as, "We know that you love us, but would you show us?" It's not just money. They want attention; they want their voices heard.

LOUIS KANE: We make sure that everyone knows that what happens in our South Boston headquarters is unimportant. What's important is what's happening in that individual unit out there, and we are there to support those units. Otherwise we have no reason to exist.

BILL DAVIS: Communicating that origianl passion helps to renew it. Pass it on to your people. Any way you can. Then let them talk back.

TP: Hal Rosenbluth, who runs giant Rosenbluth Travel, is up-to-the-second technologically, but he also sends his folks crayons — crayons! — and has them draw pictures of what they think the company is all about. Talk about getting some strange responses! But it works because everybody knows Hal's gonna look at their pictures.

JUDY GEORGE: Getting those honest survey responses was the best thing that ever happened to me. The whole world changed — it's like night and day. It shifted my focus to the people instead from my own pain in trying to "make it." The company's emotional well-being has improved. My terror level has abated.

Complacency and Reinvention

FRANK VON HOLZHAUSEN: Isn't there a danger that losing that "terror level" can lead to complacency?

TP: Absolutely! The one thing I believe for sure is that success kills. It leads to conservatism and arrogance. You don't even have to get to arrogant; conservative is enough.

FRANK VON HOLZHAUSEN: And, what's worse, you don't even realize you've grown conservative.

TP: You have be willing to blow up your business.

NANCY WILBER: Sorry, I'm not willing to blow up my business. Aren't there alternatives?

TP: I don't think so.

FRANK VON HOLZHAUSEN: Tom, you've got a business. Are you willing to blow it up?

TP: Yes. But in a way, that's too easy an answer on my part. The hard question is — because my business includes writing — am

I willing to start writing books about, say, education, instead of business management? I'm not sure, but I know it would be a good idea, even if I eventually come back to business-management writing. It's tough. How do you give up your baby?

DICK FRIEDMAN: Easy. I have no interest in running things. I like the initial glory, then I get bored. I stay with something for a while, get it going — then I'm outta there. I'm so entrepreneurial I can't manage anything, including my own life. My secret is that I know it.

NANCY WILBER: I know we can't manage the future, but to what degree should we focus on it?

ANTHONY HARNETT: Staying focused on the customer is the key. Let the customer lead you into the future.

TP: But which customer or customers? Ed McCracken, CEO of Silicon Graphics, talks about "lighthouse customers" — people who tend to be five years ahead of things and drive him into the future. Listening to them keeps him in touch with the market — and ahead of it.

FRANK VON HOLZHAUSEN: We have 10 clients that represent about 70 percent of our business. We really have to be driven by them.

TP: Hold on. You can get too close to a big customer. The relationship becomes dull, neither one of you is fresh. By then, you're turning off your people and not doing the customer much good either. That's when it may be time to dump that key customer. As a consultant, I've done that more than once.

JUDY GEORGE: It takes guts.

TP: Yes and no. A stale person dealing with an undemanding client can kill you over time. It keeps you from reinventing. From breaking the mold.

Just look around, everyone is using the same computer-aided design program — my camera looks like my bathtub looks like my car. I'll often be driving behind a blue-chip vehicle, and it turns out to be some little $11,000 number that's used the right CAD program. One casualty of this sameness, no surprise, is brand loyalty.

New Bases for Brand Loyalty

BILL DAVIS: I don't think brand loyalty is dead, it's just being redefined. Consumers are beginning to define brand around themselves and their interests. They've developed a holistic view. Nobody knew who manufactured Charmin and it wasn't important. Now people increasingly want to know the company behind the product, what it stands for, how it treats its employees, how it treats the environment.

TP: The Nike, Body Shop, and Tom's of Maine phenomenon.

BILL DAVIS: Exactly! It's a feel-good thing, and that's the way the good companies are differentiating themselves, ignoring the traditional product-based brand.

ANTHONY HARNETT: I'd hate to be a manufacturer these days. I think retailing has almost total power to influence the customer — if the retailer has delivered a high level of service, has an unusual marketing thrust, and has built a reputation. I think that innovative retailing can take away from manufacturers any sense of customer loyalty.

TP: I agree that a superb retailer can convince you, as Nordstrom has done for years, that there's nothing worth having that isn't in its stores. But my rejoinder is that a manufacturer with nerve can also dazzle.

At a party for Cornell engineering alumni, I met the guy who invented the machinery that puts those brand-name labels on oranges and apples. It's a fabulously sophisticated technology, and he's been a raging success.

JUDY GEORGE: I don't think anything new has happened in the furniture industry in years. Everything creative comes from the retail end. I would love to have a manufacturer-partner who is looking at new ideas and development.

TP: Didn't the people at Bloomingdale's pull that off? They reinvented their store as a collection of shops and were able to develop superb relationships with very hot-shot designers. Barneys and a few others of the world have knocked that idea off, but Bloomingdale's had a pretty long run.

If it happened once, it can happen again.

JUDY GEORGE: I'm even thinking of sharing stock. Giving producers a little incentive to really go the extra mile.

TP: I'd wager the farm [not a metaphor, I have one] that your home runs, if any, will come from discovering a small, innovative supplier who's going to do something very special for you. The issue is, do you have the time and energy to ferret out the Thos. Moser-type [a Maine-based maker of fine furniture], who'll do a gorgeous table that's $750 or $2,000?

JUDY GEORGE: That's what I'm looking to do.

PAM KELLEY: Judy, do you know the story of Calyx and Corolla, the direct-mail firm that sells fresh flowers? I heard the founder speak, and she set up two partnerships, one with wholesale flower growers in her state, the other with Federal Express.

DICK FRIEDMAN: In my business I find it's very unproductive to give suppliers equity. If they're not entrepreneurs themselves, they don't think that way. I think it's actually counterproductive. The best thing you can do is be a good customer.

BILL DAVIS: I agree.

JUDY GEORGE: Then how do you get people excited?

DICK FRIEDMAN: I think you pay them well and treat them right, but I don't think you do something like give your supplier 1 percent of your business — it's tokenism and they see it as tokenism. I also try not to do business with people I don't like. I don't want to be one of those people who goes home and says, "I hate everybody at work." I hang around with people I like, and I think they appreciate that more than they would a smidgen of stock.

Room to Innovate? Or Not?

PAM KELLEY: To get back to why there's so little innovation, it seems to me the superstores have a lot to do with it. What manufacturer can hold out against a Wal-Mart that's driving most of their business? How innovative can you be when Wal-Mart says, "This is what I want"?

TP: There's more to life than Wal-Mart. I love Wal-Mart. But to hell with Wal-Mart. Find distributors/customers who'll let you do what you do (assuming it's special) and forget Wal-Mart.

DICK FRIEDMAN: If I was in the Charmin business I'm not sure I'd want to forget Wal-Mart.

TP: It seems the world is going in two different directions. On the one hand, you see growing concentration in a few places; on the other hand, you see an explosion of specialists. For every Barnes & Noble that enters the fray, hundreds of independent booksellers spring up. The same is true on the book production side;

there's been a major consolidation among giant publishers and at the same time a record number of tiny houses specializing in, say, 18th-century Mexican cookbooks from the state of Chihuahua. You see these diametrically opposite trends.

PAM KELLEY: There will *always* be a market for the unique product.

BILL DAVIS: And the brilliant idea.

TP: Paradoxically, the bigger the biggies get, the more room there is for the little guy to squeeze in with something revolutionary.

ANTHONY HARNETT: That's what entrepreneurship is all about. Going for it with all you've got.

171

"Fate keeps on happening."
Anita Loos

ANTHONY HARNETT

LISTS!

172 The Turnaround Champs

Hundreds of corporate bosses have confronted monstrous change agendas in the past 10 years, but only a few have made a genuine about-face. To wit: Jack Welch at General Electric, the late Mike Walsh at Union Pacific Railroad and Tenneco, and Percy Barnevik at ABB Asea Brown Boveri. What do the three dynamos have in common?

■ **Frighteningly smart.** Most CEOs I've met are very bright. But Welch, Walsh, and Barnevik are almost in a league of their own. I, for one, am intimidated by each member of the trio. Don't try to blow smoke at this gang.

■ **Animal energy.** CEOs in general are an energetic lot. But these three are off the charts. *Fortune*'s Strat Sherman claims that Welch, whom he interviewed extensively, "just happens to have 2,000 percent more energy than the rest of us." Ditto Walsh and Barnevik. It's exhausting just to *watch* these guys.

■ **Irrational about action.** Though Welch, Walsh, and Barnevik are superb thinkers, they are also monumentally impatient. Like Ross Perot, they simply can't countenance, or even understand, procrastination. Normal barriers don't seem to exist for them, and they don't expect such hurdles to slow their underlings either. When you sign up for something, you do it — and intervening acts of God, nature, and competitors are no excuse for not getting it done on time.

■ **Distilled vision.** The turnaround trio has mastered "the speech." Though all three grasp nuance, they've boiled their message down to a handful of critical principles — with which they will ceaselessly bore frontline employees, senior executives, securities analysts, and, doubtless, their local fresh-veggie vendor. You have no trouble figuring out where this gang is coming from.

■ **Cut to the chase.** It was clear to Welch, Walsh, and Barnevik that the time for mincing half-steps was long past. They took the "big bath," as the accountants call it, all at once. They figured they had one brief opportunity to mount a real revolution, and they grabbed it. Though they took the time to build bridges with longtime disaffected employees, they nonetheless managed to compress years of work (by other chiefs' standards) into months.

■ **Disgust for bureaucracy.** Many CEOs, though impatient and action-oriented, are quickly captured by their bureaucracies. These three seem to be genetically averse to all forms of bureaucracy — and the wrath of the gods will be brought down upon anyone, very senior to very junior, who allows turf issues, the procedure manual, or "the way we [used to] do things around here" to interfere with progress.

■ **Performance freaks.** Welch, Walsh, and Barnevik slashed layers of bureaucrats, liberated the devil out of independent unit managers — and then they held the toes of the newly anointed chieftains very close to the fire. Sure, the world is ambiguous and changing fast. Nonetheless, you've been given a task to perform and given all the rope anyone could ask for and more. So perform. "Lead, follow, or get the hell out of the way" is Ted Turner's version of this.

> **"Lead, follow, or get the hell out of the way."**
> **Ted Turner**

■ **Straight shooters.** A local union leader told me that Pat Carrigan, the first woman to manage a General Motors assembly plant, "ain't got a phony bone in her body." Welch, Walsh, and Barnevik also have a visceral affinity for the truth. Bad news or good, they tell it to you straight. In return, they expect you to tell it to them straight. Period.

■ **Tomorrow is another day.** These execs think fast, decide fast. And they don't rehash yesterday's work. David Glass, CEO of Wal-Mart, said that the late Sam Walton's No. 1 skill was an ability to leave yesterday's cock-up behind and get on with the day's task. This ranks near the top for Welch, Walsh, and Barnevik as well.

■ **Half a loaf is no loaf at all**. "It ain't done till it's done" could be the Welch, Walsh, Barnevik joint motto. We've seen lots of half-turnarounds in recent times — Xerox, Kodak, Du Pont. Halfway is no way for these three.

■ **Driven individuals.** I'm no psychologist, but "driven" does not seem excessive when describing these bosses. They believe the impossible is possible, and are determined to prove it, then reprove it day after day. In short, I wouldn't want to stand between them and what they want to accomplish.

Are there other skills that mark large-scale turnarounds? Sure. For example, Welch, Walsh, and Barnevik can't match Michael Eisner's wacky brilliance, which was the right potion for launching bedraggled Disney on a sparky new trajectory. But GE, Union Pacific, Tenneco, and ABB needed to trash decades-old practices gone stale; and our heroes were the perfect chain-saw crew.

But they did more than cut. The three were also master rebuilders, if not quite Eisners. Mass destruction, I've concluded, must come first and fast at sagging corporations. Without the reconstruction, though, the pain is wasted.

Welch, Walsh, and Barnevik are fit for the Hall of Fame of corporate renovation. Emulating them is no small order. But even if you can't get an IQ or energy injection, the habits of mind that set them apart hold lessons for all of us — action, obsession, don't look back, no half-way, etc.

The "driven" believe the impossible is ....

Most of us meet life a little more than halfway. We try to eat right, exercise, recycle, be a good parent, spouse, citizen. We try our best, and if that's not enough — hey, we tried.

Then a medical crisis hits and we realize that life is, indeed, a life-or-death proposition. Other concerns screech to a halt, seem petty. Psychologists say these are the times when we really learn — and grow.

Many of you have no doubt been through a personal medical crisis, or one involving a loved one. Hopefully, the resolution was favorable. But once the dust settles, what can we learn from these harrowing experiences that might carry over to business?

■ **Perception is everything** — and extremely plastic. Time stops, or stretches out interminably. A three-day wait for lab-test results is the equivalent of three *months* of "normal life." I can recall each second, or so it seems, of a five-hour wait during my wife's 1991 surgery: Normally five hours go by in a flash.

Message: A second is not a second! And that has enormous consequences for everyday business practice. There is no one, true, inelastic reality — e.g., no certain measure of service, quality, or value. We invariably fail to give perception its enormous due. Our Western training implies that all phenomena are reducible to measurements about which "the reasonable man or woman could not disagree." What dangerous bunk!

■ **Acknowledge emotion.** About six long days after my wife's crisis arose, my system began to shut down from the stress. I got so dizzy that I couldn't drive. The condition lasted for days.

In business we try to hide emotions, especially in male-dominated operations. We downplay the care and feeding of relationships; we lament the time consumed in attending to feelings. Not even the most close-to-the-vest honcho, however, can deny the steamroller of feeling that overtakes us in times of crisis. We'd do well to remember that emotions are at work all the time — and *always* cry out for explicit recognition.

......possible, and are determined to prove it.

■ **A little TLC goes a long, long way.** Technically, the top doc plays the lead role in resolving a medical crisis. You literally put your life in her hands. Yet as the crisis passes, the most poignant memories are usually of the nurse who took an extra four minutes to give a back rub or explain why some postoperative awfulness is, in fact, normal as can be.

The business translation is obvious: Our top-gun designers, engineers, and marketers are pivotal players. But those whom we normally — and mistakenly — call "the supporting cast" (service providers, order-entry clerks, distribution teams) deserve equal billing. Deserved or not (and it mostly is deserved), they'll end up influencing customer perceptions even more than those top guns.

■ **We *can* handle change.** My wife left the hospital with a horrid catheter contraption. To our own amazement, she, I, and our friends adjusted to its presence within 48 hours, and it almost disappeared from our perceptual radar screen within 96 hours. We humans can cope with enormous dislocation — fast and with greater facility than we'd dare imagine.

There's lots of talk these days that workers aren't up to the overwhelming change the business agenda demands. Arrogant and mistaken assumption. Great as the changes transforming modern business are, they can't hold a candle to the personal traumas of illness, which most people — "workers" obviously included — get through quite well. The reality is that the true enemies of change are mainly managers fearful of losing power.

■ **The need for perceived control.** In medical emergencies, one hangs on every whisper, shred of overheard conversation between doctors, odd gurgle in the gut. And the curative power of information often equals that of our most potent medical palliatives.

This "need to know" is almost matched in everyday commerce. An informed colleague (customer, vendor) is a far less anxious one.

■ **Focus**. A hundred important "to do's" instantly drop by the wayside in the face of an emergency. That "make or break" meeting turns out to be anything but. Crisis demonstrates time and again just how focused we can be if we can ignore the extraneous.

Lesson: In the end, you will be remembered professionally for the two or three key projects where you made a difference. Though you'll doubtless have to perform endless routine tasks along the way (even the big CEO — Bill Clinton — does), the more you can focus on the central jobs, the better — for you, your teammates, and your enterprise.

Crises aren't fun. But they turn out to be pretty good teachers.

174

Q. I run a small-town chiropractic practice. Since I can't offer my staff of four high wages or big benefits, how can I keep them motivated?

A. First things first: Can you imagine reinventing your practice to attract customers from (fairly) far and (fairly) wide so that you could then offer toppish dollar and benefits (by local standards)? At first blush, your answer will probably be, "He doesn't understand Smalltown, U.S.A."

Maybe you're right. (Though I live in *very* Smalltown, U.S.A. — try a dozen folks — much of the year.) But why not, at least, gather your gang and flatly declare, "Look, I know we're small, but I personally dream of being a very desirable employer. Here are the economics of the business, no secrets left out. What can we do together to make this place scintillating?" Odds are you'll get an earful, if you're sincere and have the patience to hang tough through a lot of, at first, rambling discussions. Your newly empowered staff might even wind up bringing in those customers from (fairly) far and (fairly) wide.

175 Media as Customer

For 15 years now, I've been dealing almost daily with the press. I've been extolled, pilloried, quoted, and misquoted. The press has made me. And made me mad as hell.

Along the way I've learned a few lessons that, experience says, may have widespread applicability:

■ Tell the whole truth. The key word is "whole." Only a few business folks tell outright lies. Most, however, fail to acknowledge warts until confronted with photographic evidence. Reporters are by and large smart, and even the novices have first-rate B.S. detectors. "Truth" that goes only so far is most suspect of all.

■ Change your story when the story changes. **News flash:** Things aren't always as they seem, and time brings new facts to light. Sometimes yesterday's best effort at telling the truth deteriorates before your eyes. Sticking to your 12-hour-old or 12-day-old position isn't going to make the new, contradictory evidence evaporate.

■ Don't get worked up about out-of-context quotes. All of life is "out of context." Mary and her group prepare for weeks to make a complex, two-hour presentation to you. Passing Joe in the hall afterward, you reduce her argument to, "Mary says demand looks good for the spicy applesauce." Talk about taking somebody out of context!

Face it, the only story that will make you happy begins, "The brilliant Martin Mainman gave me an hour of his precious time last Thursday, and here's what he said . . . [a full transcript follows]." Guess what? It ain't gonna happen.

■ Return phone calls promptly. Reporters are always on deadline and being hounded by the petty tyrants (i.e., editors) who dominate their caves. If you can understand their "business needs," you'll have made a giant leap forward.

■ The media is your customer. In today's environment, with more competitors, more products, and more media, the press can be an important ally. (Just ask Virgin Group's Richard Branson or — circa 1982 — Apple's Steve Jobs.) Treat it as an ally and you're halfway home. Treat it as an adversary, and you'll get what you asked for.

■ Forget corporate guidance. Your plant has a toxic spill. Deal with the media on your own terms. Ignore the corporate flacks who are paid to be conservative and cover their bosses' backsides. (They'll typically have you act deaf and dumb.)

Be forthcoming. Be available. It's your plant, dammit, and if you want to be chairman someday, it will be because you rose to the challenge rather than quivered in the bushes and toadied to HQ wimps at moments like this.

■ Take the long-term view. It's repeat business that counts on the commercial side. And it's continuing relationships that count with your media stakeholders.

So you get roughed up unfairly (as you see it) on a story. What goes around usually comes around. Just as umpires have a way of correcting in the next game for a bad call in this one, so does the press. Get in a huff about today's undeserved whipping — and you're bound to get worse next time.

■ Know that there are jerks in the media. There are crummy customers. And malevolent reporters. Forming a global view based on one or two twits is stupid.

■ Cool it, you *are* fighting city hall. Business has generally given the press the back of its hand. The press is correct to be suspicious. You can't rewrite history (except locally, by carefully building goodwill with every 23-year-old rookie reporter who gets your business as his first beat).

■ Don't take your press releases seriously; the press doesn't. Don't be agitated if your press releases end up in the garbage can. Can you imagine what it's like to read such insipid puffery day after day? All press releases are discounted 90 percent — which, ordinarily, is as it should be.

■ Allow the media access to "real people." Most firms muzzle their frontline people. Mistake! "They," the folks near the action, are seen as far more trustworthy than the chief. Frontline people tend to speak in plain English understandable to their neighbors. So let the reporters have at your people. (Unless, of course, you *do* have something to hide.)

■ Say something fresh! Yes, "they" (the media) are looking for a sound bite. If you've got nothing new (and punchy) to say, don't be surprised when your blah, 30-minute interview gets cut in favor of an inflammatory one-liner by a disaffected former employee.

■ Try radio. Radio is a potent medium. Moreover, by its very nature you'll likely get 15 minutes to tell your story instead of 30 seconds on TV or one paragraph in the business pages.

Is all this too optimistic? I don't think so. Shoot straight and remember the long haul — and you'll have a mostly reliable ally (that will disappoint you from time to time, like all partners in all relationships).

176 "Dumb" Allen

Allen Puckett is the best consultant I ever worked with. The key to his success: Though one of the brightest people I've ever met, he asks the dumbest questions.

Bosses, high-paid consultants, and bright-eyed business school grads share one vexing problem: Most believe they're supposed to know the answers. Watch top brass wandering around a factory. You seldom hear them ask an interesting (dumb) question. They're afraid of tarnishing their (self-)image. They forget that it's a whole string of "What the hell is that?" queries that gets you to the nub of any problem. Workers on the line, like all of us, are delighted to talk about what they do. And, as fellow humans, they respect enormously the fact that you do have the gumption to ask those hopelessly naive questions.

So ask. Even if you think you know.
(Probably you don't.)    **THINK ABOUT IT!**

177 Presentation Secrets

So you're not always the life of the party. Nor did you captain your high school debate team. And figuring differential equations thrills you more than a crackling recording of Roosevelt's fireside chats.

None of this will block a sparkling career. But let's face it, if you could give somewhat scintillating presentations, you'd be better off. We all need potent persuasive skills to rope in supporters from time to time. Like it or not, then, a knack for communicating in "public" is vitally important.

Having long been a for-profit yakker, I offer this advice:

■ **Practice makes better.** Obvious as it sounds, too many ignore it. There are damn few natural composers, golfers, or race car drivers. And there are *no* natural speakers — at least I've never come across any. **Bulletin:** You get better at speaking by speaking, and speaking. It takes 10 years of tough training to become a journeyman physicist or carpenter, so why (he asked, speaking as a speaker) should *you* expect to pick up sophisticated presentation skills "by the seat of your pants"?

■ **Forget all the conventional "rules" but one.** Frankly, most laws of speechmaking — keep your hands out of your pockets, don't say "uh," lead off with a zinger — are garbage. But there is one golden rule: Stick to topics you deeply care about, and don't keep your passion buttoned inside your vest. An audience's biggest turn-on is the speaker's obvious enthusiasm. That's as true for a pitch to purchase a $200,000 computer system as it is for a plea to save the environment. If you're lukewarm about the issue, zip your lips.

■ **Stories, stories, more stories.** Charts and graphs have their place, and a pretty prominent one in many business presentations. Nonetheless, even an analytically inclined audience will remember one poignant comment from a survey respondent ("This company really doesn't give a shit about the likes of us") long after forgetting your Pagemaker 5.0-generated multicolor bar chart showing the firm's "openness to ideas" at 2.62 on a 7-point, sociometrically valid scale.

The best speakers, U.S. president or Ph.D. chemist, lavishly illustrate their talks with short, striking vignettes. In fact, the most potent speeches are often little more than strings of such vignettes, loosely linked by an outline and in support of just one or two big ideas.

■ **For heaven's sake, don't write it out!** If spontaneity isn't everything, it verges on it. That hardly means winging it. Paradoxically, careful preparation breeds comfort and thence spawns spontaneity. In short, never, ever write it out in full. If you do, you become a slave to your exact wording and inevitably lose 75 percent (make that 90, 95, 97 percent) of any emotional impact.

■ **Don't even think about getting it "right."** After decades of giving speeches, from five minutes to five days (with breaks!) in length, I've yet to be satisfied with one of them. But tomorrow is another day. Forget the "this is my only chance to shine" baloney. If you're worth a hoot, you'll get lots of chances to shine — and that one, 10-minute appearance in THE BOARDROOM, at age 28, won't decide your career. If you believe "this is it," you'll be so tight you'll swing before the pitcher even finishes his windup.

■ **Breathe!** I get flushed and breathless before any speech, to this day. Though I'm no pro when it comes to meditation, one answer is to close your eyes (or not), and take five or 10 deep breaths (even in front of others) before going up on stage to chair that big meeting.

■ **Get away from the podium.** You're probably not a stiff around the office, and almost certainly not at home. Why be a stiff when you're making an important presentation? Put your notes on index cards (written in bold letters if your eyes, like mine, ain't getting younger), so you won't be nailed to the lectern. Then wander — around the table, into the crowd, about the platform. Look comfortable, and your audience will be more comfortable, too. (Yes, this does take lots of practice — *but it works.*)

■ **Loosen up, you're not going to convince 'em anyway.** Speeches aren't about turning archenemies into cheering supporters. Martin Luther King's "I Have a Dream" speech hardly turned George Wallace into a champion of civil rights. Presentations are mainly opportunities to reassure those who already agree with you that you're a horse worth betting on. (King's speech roused his *supporters* toward greater efforts.) So try to relax, enjoy yourself, and come across as a passionate champion for your thing —

which is just what the audience wants you to do.

178 In Pursuit of Indigestion

There is an enormous arrogance in providing a reading list. Reading habits are hopelessly personal. Nonetheless, I'll dare to take the chance — and submit my perhaps unconventional picks for "good stuff" to school the new, or seasoned, manager or the would-be boss:

■ **Business history.** When I'm preparing for a seminar, reading the history of the industry that I'll be talking about is the single most valuable thing I do. Understanding the ups and downs, the shifts of dominant mentality, is priceless. Take retailing: *Land of Desire: Merchants, Power, and the Rise of a New American Culture*, by William Leach, was a revelation. Others on the business history list: *Money of the Mind*, by James Grant, a readable, raucous history of borrowing and lending in America over the last century-and-a-half; *Poor Richard's Legacy: American Business Values from Benjamin Franklin to Donald Trump*, by Peter Baida; *The World the Railways Made*, by Nicholas Faith; *The Whiz Kids: Ten Founding Fathers of American Business and the Legacy They Left Us*, by John A. Byrne; and *Hard Times*, by Charles Dickens.

■ **The real world of business decision-making**. All the entries here emphasize the messy, human way in which *real* decisions are made and *real* innovation takes place. They teach humility, if nothing else — and a hearty skepticism of grand designs. Truth is, I could construct a nifty business Ph.D. course around this little shelf of books alone: *Barbarians at the Gate: The Fall of RJR Nabisco*, by Bryan Burrough and John Helyar; *The Soul of a New Machine*, by Tracy Kidder; *Fast Forward: Hollywood, the Japanese and the Onslaught of the VCR Wars*, by James Lardner; *Final Cut: Dreams and Disaster in the Making of Heaven's Gate*, by Steven Bach; *The Nobel Duel: Two Scientists' 21-year Race to Win the World's Most Coveted Research Prize*, by Nicholas

Wade; *The Double Helix*, by James D. Watson; *National Defense*, by James Fallows; *Wide-Body: The Triumph of the 747*, by Clive Irving; *The Making of the Atom Bomb*, by Richard Rhodes; *Empire of the Air: The Men Who Made Radio*, by Tom Lewis; and *Tainted Truth: The Manipulation of Fact in America*, by Cynthia Crossen.

■ **Cross-cultural stuff.** Local and global concerns about deal-

ing with "others" are nobly (and readably!) charted in these books: *Interstate Commerce: Regional Styles of Doing Business*, by Clyde Burleson (the West Coast ain't the East Coast, etc.); *You Just Don't Understand: Women and Men in Conversation*, by Deborah Tannen; *Riding the Waves of Culture: Understanding Cultural Diversity in Global Business*, by Fons Trompenaars (see item No.147); *You Gotta Have Wa*, by Robert Whiting (Wanna understand Japan? Look at how they approach pro baseball!); and, for a really quirky way of getting at x-cultural issues, try *Pre-School in Three Cultures: Japan, China, and the United States*, by Joseph J. Tobin, Daniel Y. H. Wu, and Dana Davidson.

(There are also superb books on individual coun-
tries. Andrew Malcolm's *The Canadians* will astonish you with its insights about the next-door neighbor you thought you understood. Others in the same league: *The French*, by Theodore Zeldin; *The Germans*, by Gordon Craig; *An American Looks at Britain*, by Richard Critchfield. My friend Kenichi Ohmae, Japan's premiere management consultant, insists that James Clavell's *Shogun* is the best book on Japan for us gaijin.)

■ **Personality clashes and winning at office politics.** If you want to know what "office politics" can really be like, try *The War Between the Generals: Inside the Allied High Command*, by David Irving; and *Ike & Monty: Generals at War*, by Norman Gelb. For getting at least something done in a Byzantine bureaucracy, try

The Power to Persuade: How to be Effective in Government and Other Unruly Organizations, by Richard N. Haass; and *What They Don't Teach You at the Harvard Business School*, by Mark McCormack.

■ **Biography.** More garden-variety human drama, to help cure any lingering addiction to the Rational Model, can be found in the likes of *In All His Glory — The Life of William S. Paley*, by Sally B. Smith; *A Prince of Our Disorder: The Life* of T. E. Lawrence, by John Mack; *Charles De Gaulle*, by Don Cook; *Knight's Cross: A Life of Field Marshal Erwin Rommel*, by David Fraser; *American Caesar: Douglas MacArthur*, by William Manchester; and *A Streak of Luck: The Life and Legend of Thomas Alva Edison*, by Robert Conot.

■ **Innovation.** There are all too few good books on innovation (and the stifling thereof). These, though, are out and out winners: *The Rise and Fall of Strategic Planning*, by Henry Mintzberg (see item No.117); *Mastering the Dynamics of Innovation: How Companies Can Seize Opportunities in the Face of Technological Change*, by James M. Utterback; *The Competitive Advantage of Nations*, by Michael E. Porter; *The Republic of Tea*, by Mel Ziegler, Patricia Ziegler, and Bill Rosenzweig; *Doing Deals: Investment Bankers at Work*, by Robert G. Eccles and Dwight B. Crane; *Bureaucracy*, by James Q. Wilson; *The Age of Unreason*, by Charles Handy; *Further Up the Organization*, by Bob Townsend; *Out of Control: The Rise of Neo-Biological Civilization*, by Kevin Kelly; and *The Paradox of Success: When Winning at Work Means Losing at Life*, by John R. O'Neil.

■ **Education.** For a look at what education could be (for all ages, anytime, anywhere), peruse *School's Out: Hyperlearning, the New Technology, and the End of Education*, by Lewis Perelman.

■ **Selling stuff.** In first place, by a mile: *Customers for Life: How to Turn that One-Time Buyer into a Lifelong Customer*, by Carl Sewell and Paul B. Brown. Also: *The One-To-One Future: Building Relationships One Customer at a Time*, by Don Peppers and Martha Rogers; *Beyond MaxiMarketing*, by Stan Rapp and Thomas L. Collins; and *Ogilvy on Advertising*, by David Ogilvy.

■ **Economics.** Start and stop here: *The Fatal Conceit*, by F. A. Hayek. The brief last work of the Nobel laureate in economics, edited by W. W. Bartley III, is a life-altering (it altered mine) tribute to free markets.

There's lots more that "should" be on this list (a lot of my friends and fellow writers will be offended by the omissions), but you can decide for yourself among the conventional and "hot" management books. These picks, I can almost guarantee, will wake you up and shake you up. That's the point, isn't it? (OK, so I *am* a secret agent, on the take, for Maalox. So what?)

179 Surfacing Tacit Knowledge

We each have a different cognitive style, so maybe what I'm about to suggest applies only to a certain kind of mind — i.e., mine, for one.

The topic: Lists.

Not "to-do" lists (good things, if not overdone), but something more fundamental.

Let's say I've done my homework on a topic (a speech to bankers, for example). I've got stacks of articles, hundreds of pages of interview transcripts, a half-pound of 3x5 notecards scattered on the table and floor around me; perhaps they're roughly sorted into categories. But I'm overwhelmed. The issue: What do I *really* think about all this mass (mess) of material?

The answer: Go off to another room or to another desk, sit back for 10 minutes or so, maybe turn out the lights, then make a list. Not an orderly, tidy, logical, rational list. But just a series of disjointed, numbered statements/thoughts that come from somewhere deep inside. (E.g., "The local bank that tries to be all things to all people, and loses its distinction and fails to be 'a close friend to community,' is doomed when a big guy alights next door.")

Incidentally, such was the genesis of *In Search of Excellence*. I had a 700-page report(!) on our research at my fingertips, but I didn't really know what it meant. (It did have sections with titles, but still. . . .) The next week I had to give a big-deal 45-minute speech on the findings to PepsiCo's top 100 execs.

So one morning in May 1980, I literally did tilt back in my desk chair, and close my eyes for a few minutes; then I leaned forward and wrote eight phrases on the top sheet of a yellow legal-length pad. The phrases/items, with a few modest edits ("Do it, fix it, try it" metamorphosed into "A bias for action"), became the eight basic elements of the subsequent popular book.

The philosopher of science Michael Polanyi tells us this all makes sense. He wrote extensively about "tacit knowledge" in science. In short, we know a lot more than we think we know, a lot more than the data tell us directly. My lists (I probably use this tactic once a week) help surface that tacit knowledge and break the bonds of drab, linear thinking (take the cards, put them in orderly piles, etc., etc.). And even if the lists don't bear much resemblance to what ultimately emerges (presentation, newspaper column, speech, book), they often take me a big step forward. Forget "often." Make that *always*.

Next time you're stuck, try it!

180 In Praise of Naps (Etc.)

A student in New Zealand recently wrote, asking me to reveal my time-management secrets. My first instinct was to ignore the request — the topic irks me. I get irritated when people pull out fat "organizer" kits. Time-management "consultants" really bug me. My reaction is doubtless defensive. I have no time-management secrets. In fact, I consider myself a crappy time manager.

Still, I like to respond to student requests. Besides, I figured I must have an implicit time-management model. I came up with five strategies:

■ **Focus and reject.** Over the years, when something gets really serious, I "switch on" the issue at hand and "switch off" everything else. To switch off is more important that to switch on. Mail, phone calls, dinner parties, the leaky barn roof — later, ace.

SWITCH ON Issues at hand	←→	SWITCH OFF Mail Dinner parties Phone calls Leaky roofs

Such intensity of focus involves risk — alienating superiors and subordinates alike, maybe even quitting a job. It means that "available you/good ole Joe" ain't available for the next month, the next year.

■ **Use your day "right."** Understanding your metabolism is critical. I can work creatively from about 4 A.M. to 11 A.M. and work reasonably intelligently for another three hours. After that, forget it. It took me *decades* to figure that out. But now I'm religious about paying attention to my inner clock.

■ **Rest and/or frolic.** Winston Churchill invariably took a long afternoon nap — even while he was England's prime minister during World War II. I like that idea, and practice a variant while working on books. I write from about 4 A.M. to 7:30 A.M., nap until about 8:30, then go at it again. I'm always surprised at how refreshed I feel after an hour's pillow time. Everyone goes through daily doldrums. Knock off — nap, isometrics, meditation — and recharge.

Beyond that, a couple of weeks (or months) of rest and frolic in the midst of a daunting task is enormously stimulating. (I *try* to take at least a few weeks off between drafts of a book.) Woe betide the "pluggers" who pride themselves on never taking breaks: Dullness is their just dessert.

■ **Pursue "mindless" interruptions.** Studies suggest the most effective bosses thrive on unscheduled interruptions; the least effective chiefs program their days down to the minute. Practical translation: Allow for (plan for!) productive diversions. Take occasional off-the-wall calls that just might provide a highly profitable insight: "I thought you ought to know that your top-of-the-line product has a fatal flaw, though I'm sure your engineers must have told you." Ho. Ho. Ho. No, they had not.

I worry when the infotech gurus promise we'll soon be able to get our news (papers, magazines, etc.) tailored to "detailed informational needs." Yuck! I often find more useful information about "life" in Section D of *USA Today* than in the *Wall Street Journal*. Most bursts of inspiration come from the quirky juxtaposition of information. The weekly TV ratings may suggest more about consumer trends than the $200,000 market research you just commissioned. A night at the opera may be more help with a personnel problem than three hours with a human resources staffer — or reading some damn bestseller on e-m-p-o-w-e-r-m-e-n-t.

■ **Be true to yourself.** While I hope this brief recitation helps stretch your imagination, it is not a to-do list. We all have different rhythms. Your "time-management strategy" must fit you.

But can you get away with strategies like mine? I can tell you I've been practicing these sometimes antisocial habits since I was a young Navy ensign in Vietnam (my first real job). When faced with a challenge, like designing a bridge to be built out of the scraps at hand, I'd sometimes disappear for several days. In subsequent jobs, I'd evaporate for weeks and, in one case, months. In the latter instance, I was subsequently fired. It was the biggest career boost ever. (It gave me the space to focus on what was important.)

181 Just Do It

Each new day brings not only the rising sun and the rooster's crow (or the subway's rumble), but new competitors, new technologies, newly obsolete products — and new meaning to the term "survival of the fittest." Gone are the days when companies could afford a potbelly or a sluggish pulse. I always marvel when I see film of the mountain goat, effortlessly leaping from ledge to ledge at 10,000 feet — a machine perfectly engineered to survive in a most precarious environment. There's no room up there for the declawed, overfed tabby. The message is clear

— shape up or you will not survive. Here then, in short form, is my "must do" fitness regimen:

■ Within 90 days, quadruple spending authority throughout the firm, from the mail clerk to the division general manager. (**Hint:** Start with the mail clerk.)

■ Insist on a maximum of *two* levels of management between the "bottom" and the "top" in any division-size unit (e.g., 1,000 folks).

■ In every facility, review detailed operating results with all hands each week. (Each week = once every seven days. Sorry, just trying to be helpful.)

■ Look at training as *the* research-and-development expenditure (no matter the accounting conventions); fund it with at least 4 percent of gross revenues. (That goes for burger flippers as well as multi-media geeks.)

■ Almost all business can be done in virtually independent operating units of 250 or fewer people (with their own boards of directors, including outsiders — really). Reorganize accordingly within the year.

■ Within the next nine months, eliminate ALL frontline supervisors. (A-L-L, a bitsy three-letter word.)

■ Within the next year, devolve one-third of all staffers at the division level or above to customer-focused operating units, then another third the following year. Within five years, reduce headquarters staff to a maximum of 10 people per billion dollars in revenue (and no hiding "temporary assignees" stolen from a division around the corner); and . . .

■ Require remaining members of all "central" (corporate, division) staffs to sell their services to line units at market rates. Allow those line units, in turn, to buy any and all services from anybody, anywhere.

■ Make evaluation by subordinates a key component of *all* bosses' performance appraisals.

- Eliminate all job descriptions. NOW. (Today.)

- Destroy all organizational charts. NOW. (Today.)

- Have all top corporate/divisional managers pledge two days per month to customer visits (puny, really), two days per month to supplier and distributor visits.

- Make sure that every person in the organization makes at least two customer visits a year.

- Publicly traded companies: Within the next three years, sell substantial minority interest in half your business units to the public.

- Aim for one-third employee ownership of the corporation within five years.

- Chief executive officers and division general managers: Within the next 12 months, promote to a position of significant responsibility at least one rabble-rouser who doesn't like you or agree with you (on much of anything).

- Aim to have women occupy at least 30 percent of vice president/division general manager slots within five years. (Or 50 percent — hey, what if business *did* mimic life? Or, as one female correspondent suggested, 80 percent.)

- Make the words *glow*, *tingle*, *thrill*, *dazzle*, *delight* — and, of course, *WOW* — the primary bases for evaluating the quality of all your products and services. I.e., do customers "like" your service (bad), or are they "gaga" over it (good, great, fantastic!)?

- Each year, have customers systematically evaluate every one of your quality and service measures.

- The 10 senior members of corporate management: At the next industry trade show, demo the most sophisticated product your outfit makes.

- Finance and accounting staff: Spend at least two days per week in the "field" with internal customers (half your performance appraisal should be based on evaluations designed and executed by "customers").

- Make a *weekly* award in every unit, starting with work teams, to the person who discovers the stupidest thing the company is doing.

■ Subcontract at least 25 percent of R&D, half to organizations no more than one-tenth your size. (This applies to both $10 million and $10 billion companies.)

■ Base a third (half?) of executive incentive compensation on the share of revenue from new products and services introduced within the past 24 months. (*Really* new — remember, no electron microscope.)

■ At the division level, identify the top 15 "horizontal" processes (e.g., product development), map them carefully, and undertake a total revision of each one within the next three years.

■ Reduce total cycle time for everything by one-third in the next two years, another third in the following two years. (How about *two*-thirds in each instance? No kidding. E.g., who says a new car model can't be developed in *one* year?)

■ Sell off every piece of executive and boardroom furniture costing more than $500.

■ Vacate all facilities more than three stories high.

■ *Physically* integrate all functions within the next 18 months. (This is a B-I-G deal.)

■ Unless you are a local service company (restaurant, etc.) or your revenue is under $3 million, achieve a significant *international* market presence within three years. (There's really no reason to let the $1.5-million company off this hook, come to think of it.)

■ Make sure that at least 25 percent of attendees at your next offsite meeting are "outsiders" (customers, vendors, etc.).

■ In companies of $100 million revenue or greater, add corporate vice president positions (solo, no "assistants to" or other staffers including secretaries) for the following: knowledge management, perceived quality and brand-equity management, innovation, design.

Sweating yet?

ATTAINING PERPETUAL ADOLESCENCE

182   The Luscious Fringe

Have you noticed?

Most good (neat, innovative, wild, woolly) "stuff," large and small, happens in the boondocks, far, far from corporate headquarters, corporate politics, and corporate toadying.

It's no small point. In *Out of Control: The Rise of Neo-Biological Civilization*, Kevin Kelley makes this sweeping observation about biological processes, "Maximize the fringes. . . . Diversity favors remote borders, the outskirts, hidden corners . . . and isolated clusters. . . . A healthy fringe speeds adaptation, increases resilience, and is almost always the source of innovation."

So how healthy is your fringe? How loony are its inhabitants? ("CUTE, TOM," YOU MUTTER TO YOURSELF. CUTE, HELL. THIS IS ONE OF THE MOST IMPORTANT POINTS IN THIS BOOK. OK?)

183   Heroes for the Times

During a 1994 trip to the Copper Canyon, in Chihuahua, Mexico, I met Carl Franz, author of *The People's Guide to Mexico*,

nine editions old and the bible for serious travelers to that
ordinary country. Carl has created a niche for himself

(though he'd never use such a word) and found a
way to follow his quirky bliss — and simultaneously to make a difference and a life.

I quickly added him to my short list of heroes.
I won't embarrass the others by naming them,
but among them are authors, a performing artist,
a farmer, a politician, a plumber, a couple of big-

CARL FRANZ

company CEOs, entrepreneurs, and a military
leader. But no Gandhis or Roosevelts, since, on such a personal
honor role, I can't sensibly include people I don't know. In fact, I
guarantee that you wouldn't recognize more than four names
on my 12-person list. These folks more or less share 13 traits that
amount to a pretty good guide to success in general:

■ **Self-invented.** "I am an American, Chicago-born," begins Saul
Bellow's novel *The Adventures of Augie March*, ". . . and go at
things as I have taught myself, free-style, and will make the
record in my own way." All my Mount Rushmore nominees
have chiseled their masterpieces from the granite of life in a distinct, unusual fashion. Standard career path? Forget it. One job,
one company? Not even close.

■ **Ever-changing.** I don't think any of my dandy dozen has a
split personality in the clinical sense of the term; but surely all
are chameleons, not bound by consistency. They've tried on a
Nordstrom-full of outfits while remaining desperately and pas-
sionately committed to whatever they are pursuing at the
moment.

■ **Battered and bruised.** My heroes have screwed up things at
least as often as they've gotten them right. "A road without potholes is not a road worth traveling" could be their collective
motto. Failures don't seem to faze them; if anything, setbacks
amuse and motivate them.

■ **Inquisitive.** No question goes unasked for this squad of
achievers. Sometimes I think there's literally nothing that does

not interest them. They are determined to get to the bottom of any topic they touch — on or off the job. (*Job*? They are what they do; "job" is not part of their vocabulary.)

■ **Childlike, naive.** This gang refuses to grow up. Their appetite for exploration mimics, even in their seventh decade (in one instance), a four-year-old's.

■ **Free from the past.** The hell with Newton and his apple: Gravity has no meaning for this group. They are not weighed down by history. In a flash they'll thumb their noses at what only yesterday they were fervently espousing.

■ **Comfortable, even cocky in a way.** My grand gang members are at ease with themselves, unperturbed by the idea of life as an ever-elusive, moving target — an adventure to be relished, mostly for its detours.

■ **Jolly.** These people laugh — a lot. They marvel at human intrigues, and their appreciation of the absurd stokes their marvelous sense of humor. All of them have wrinkles (you know the kind) that can be attributed only to habitual laughter.

■ **Audacious and a bit nuts**. They'll try anything, from learning a new language to starting a new career, with what seems like no more than a moment's hesitation. Moreover, by the standards of the majority, they view the world through decidedly crooked glasses.

■ **Iconoclastic.** For my pilgrims, conventional wisdom is like a red cape to a bull. I sometimes think they're only happy when they're on the "wrong" side of an issue or truism.

■ **Multidimensional.** We're not dealing with saints. All members of this tribe have flaws, often as pronounced as their strengths. But, then, when was the last time you observed an desiccated soul accomplishing much of anything?

■ **Honest.** It's not that they always tell the truth or are above pettiness. Hey, we're all human. It's just that this set is attuned to reality and especially their own foibles. They are consummate and often quixotic truth-seekers, with little time for those who aren't as confused as they are.

■ **Larger than life.** My Band of Twelve are all heroic. That is, they paint their canvases, large and small, with bold brush strokes. They are fearless in their own fashion. They embrace the circus of life, rather than shrink from it.

Embrace the circus of life. That's the ticket. Some splash in small ponds. Some in oceans. But the water where they play is always frothing. And their ways can be yours. No doubt of it in my mind.

184

Fun Company of the Year Award goes, hands down, to Ben & Jerry's, the premium ice cream maker based in Waterbury, Vermont. What other company would have the flair, the spirit, the sheer chutzpah to turn a negative — the stepping down of its popular founder — into a multimillion-dollar bonanza of sensational publicity. (And perhaps a corporate rebirth.)

By holding a contest inviting their customers to send in a lid from a container of their favorite flavor along with a short essay on why they would make "a great CEO," blue-jeaned founder Ben Cohen has — once again — demonstrated the zany talents that quickly took his "just-an-ice-cream" company from an abandoned gas station to $154 million in sales.

It's only the latest in this innovative company's string of close-to-the-customer, keep-it-fresh moves. Extensive environmental programs, tours of the factory complete with free samples (you should see the lines), paying family farmers higher than market rates for their milk, buying nuts from imperiled rain forest tribes, and contributing 7.5 percent of its profits to an employee-controlled charitable foundation, all add up to a company image that's equal parts social conscience and just plain off-the-wall fun.

While Mr. Cohen is the first to admit that the company has

hired an executive search firm for
the serious business of actually
finding someone from among the
lid-top applicants to replace him,
what a wonderful, smile-inducing

> **BEN'S SUCCESS RECIPE**
>
> **Mix equal parts of social conscience and just plain off-the-wall fun.**

way to tell the world he's turning over the reins. (And attract
candidates who'd clearly elude the typically staid recruiters'
nets.) It's pure inspiration, the kind of inspiration that builds
rock-solid customer loyalty, that makes picking up a pint of Ben
& Jerry's more than picking up a pint of fantastic ice cream —
you're taking home a small slice of this man's zesty, caring spirit, his unbridled entrepreneurial joie de vivre.

185

Joie de vivre. That's what an ordinary day at work ought to be
about. Why not, eh?

186

"Crazy . . . you want crazy? But what about discipline?"

Oddly, crazy and discipline do mix. And mix well.
Thoughtful studies of successful entrepreneurs show that they
are masters at avoiding risks. Sure they exited their on-the-rise
14-year career at Hewlett-Packard or Kellogg. (And that sounds
risky as hell to most of us.) But then they work like mad — literally — on every little detail of their start-up plan; that is, they
routinely log 14-hour days aimed at reducing risks. (E.g., proof-
reading the invitations to the restaurant launch party for the
17th time at 1 A.M. at the printers, finally catching the awful
misspelling that had eluded them — and their professional
proofreaders — during the first 16 looks.)

In fact, all the "crazies" I've touted over the years are cut
from this mold. Crazy in their passion for their dream. Crazy in
the unconventional dimensions of that dream. But utterly
Prussian in pursuit of the details that make dreams come true.

Companies go into tailspins, failing to comprehend that the world around them has changed dramatically. Examples? Kodak, American Express, IBM, Westinghouse, GM, Sears, maybe Disney . . . and yes, someday, *even* Wal-Mart.

It's true that corporate culture does bind, especially — and ironically — in proud firms with long records of success (see the list above). But there's something missing in that analysis. Dig deeper and "culture" is the sum of individuals — particularly individuals in positions of responsibility. (Not just CEOs and VPs, but hundreds, perhaps thousands, of managers.)

So it's not just some amorphous "they" or mindless corporation that gets stuck. It is, to be blunt, thee and me.

Stop. Consider exactly what you'll do at work today: How fundamentally different will that be from what you did six months ago? A year ago? Write down your four biggest accomplishments of the past six months: Do they amount to at least the beginning of a significant change of direction? Be very honest. Your professional life could depend on the answers you give.

Which brings me to what I call the little r vs. BIG R gulf. The r (or R) stands for renewal; more precisely, personal renewal. No topic is more important.

So-called little-r renewal is something most people understand. It's constant improvement: A steady diet of reading, seminar going (even week-long seminars), three-week vacations, regular customer visits, etc. These are not things that everyone else does (far from it) and, therefore, to be commended — solid entrants in the better-than-nothing category.

But such activities are a far cry from the BIG R. BIG R really reverses your spin — profoundly altering a career, dramatically shifting perspectives, and fending off staleness that most of us don't see overtaking us. (And staleness always stalks us, closer than most of us are willing to acknowledge.) BIG-R ideas include:

■ Taking a *six* month sabbatical, learning something completely new

- Better yet, spending a *year* working in the inner city or Third World

- Signing up for two years in the Peace Corps, age 38 or 58 (yes, they take 58-year-olds)

- Grabbing a three-year (not one-year) lateral assignment/demotion to a geographical or vocational area totally foreign to you (*do* interrupt a fast-track career at age 34 for this)

- Upping the tempo of a major hobby (photography, gardening, woodworking, painting) to achieve genuine excellence at something other than your chief professional pursuit

- Earning a degree in a new area

- Making a major commitment to hand work or outdoor labor

- Taking off two hours in the middle of the day, at least three days a week, to do whatever (as long as it is contrary to your normal professional discipline)

- Seeking new friends who have interests that are, by and large, antithetical to yours; then hanging out with them, working on projects with them

- Quitting a good job with nothing particular in mind for a next step (i.e., drift for six months to a year)

> **You probably can't afford to do the more drastic things on the list . . . but can you afford not to?**

But I'm not rich, you rejoin. Or I've got kids to support. Etc.

Yes, I know. What I'm suggesting isn't easy. You probably can't "afford" to do the more drastic things on the list. But can you afford not to? Do you have the moxie to consider a radical restructuring of your affairs (which could end up refreshing your family, rather than punishing it)?

In record numbers, CEOs, senior managers, middle managers, and frontline employees are getting sacked, gulping pills, screwing up families, abusing colleagues, and basically resisting fundamental change — because they "can't afford" the sort of disruptive suggestions I've offered here. Believe me, little-r renewal is simply not enough.

The deeper underpinning for this uncompromising screed is the frightening fact that virtually all leaps forward — and we all need to be in the leaping business these days — are made by people who are naive, who literally don't understand "the rules" or the "way things have always been done." Objective No. 1, then, for the perpetual self-renewer is to attempt to get naive again; to learn to look at the world with some of the dewy-eyed innocence normally reserved for the very young. Fact: You can only look at "things" through naive eyes when you are, well, naive.

OK, let me come clean: I am simply stunned by the depth of the ruts in which I drive. *I think I am fresh. I am not.*

Am I getting through? Do you still think my BIG-R list is outrageous? Please don't answer in haste.

188

"A psychologist was once summoned for a delicate interview with a top executive who had been acting oddly. Every Wednesday afternoon, this hard-charging company man would leave his office for a 3:00 P.M. appointment and did not return. He never told anyone where he went, but because he was observed entering a nearby apartment building, it was assumed he must be visiting a mistress.

"The executive explained his habit to the psychologist quite easily. Inside Apartment 2B waited, not a luscious blonde, but a professional woodworking shop that he had set up, where he labored happily to turn out furniture and knick-knacks.

"He kept his special appointment with himself faithfully because it was his retreat from the demands he fulfilled so punctiliously day in and day out. He needed this chance to be alone with himself, engaged in an activity that took his mind far from the job and focused his attention in a calming way. The psychologist pronounced him eminently healthy. It was his retreat."

John R. O'Neil
The Paradox of Success

189

This GOOD thing........................breeds this MONSTER

This GOOD thing	breeds this MONSTER
Confidence	Sense of infallibility
Quickness	Overhastiness
Sharp wit	Abrasiveness
Alertness	Narrow focus
Dedication	Workaholism
Control	Inflexibility
Courage	Foolhardiness
Perseverance	Resistance to change
Charm	Manipulation
Thriftiness	False economy
Commitment	Blind faith

John R. O'Neil
The Paradox of Success

190

"Pity the leader who is caught between unloving critics and uncritical lovers. Leaders need . . . advisers who will guide them lovingly but candidly through the minefields of arrogance, overweening pride, fixed ideas, vindictiveness, unreasoning anger, stubbornness, and egoism."

John Gardner
executive, teacher,
leadership guru

191

A creative (and effective) business acquaintance called himself a "former hippie" in a conversation we had at a seminar. I planned to use that self-generated label in a little piece I was writing about his activities. I ran it by him, and he panicked. "That will seriously hurt my standing with top management," he said. (And he emphasized the "seriously.")

How sad. His big company is in a real competitive horse race in a volatile industry. It needs all the spark it can get — more than it has, I'd judge. The fact that execs can't handle "former hippie" (and even if they can handle it, a key employee *perceives* that they can't — same thing) speaks to the presence of a deadly disease: i.e., a lack of energy, enthusiasm, spirit, curiosity, and a sense of humor. Could the world of big corporations still be this sick? Yup. Hey, this is not the first time I've run across a story like my friend's.

(Incidentally, I'm sorry he stays where he is. He's better than such nonsense.)

192 By the Numbers?

I had dinner with an old friend and talented consultant about a week after he started a new assignment. We ended up talking past one another.

He'd spit out nonstop statistics, demonstrating how his client wasn't keeping up in this or that market segment, etc. Then I'd interrupt with something like, "But who's doing something *interesting* in the industry? . . . Didn't I read about a weird new product that . . . ?"

In short, he's a "quant jock," as we used to call the numbers-enthralled at McKinsey & Co. I'm a "cases" kinda-guy, who wants to know: "Who's doing something neat?"

Both approaches are important. (In fact, my training is mostly on the "quant" side, and to this day I pride myself on so-called hard skills.) Still, I worry — a lot — about folks who instinctively go for the numbers and ignore the odd way the real world unfolds. That's especially true these days, when, by the time you've got "it" (whatever) pinned down quantitatively, the market's scurried off in another direction.

193

In explaining legendary *Washington Post* editor Ben Bradlee's secret to success, and his habit of breaking the mold, reporter

Roger Rosenblatt writes, "Twelve is about Ben's real age." Bradlee himself admitted to "compulsive spontaneity" and "advanced immaturity."

In a market groaning under the weight of uninspiring products and services, perhaps we need to scrap the latest management fads, and simply go out in search of compulsives who promise they won't grow up!

194

"If people never did silly things, nothing intelligent would ever get done."

L. Wittgenstein

Right on, Ludwig.

195

RE-READ NO. 194 ABOVE.

196

My average seminar participant comes dressed in a drab suit, uses drab language — and noticeably quivers when I suggest that the most likely path to career salvation is to try to get fired.

Do you know how depressing and disheartening it is to look out at a sea of cookie-cutter clean- cut faces? (Even at my obscene rates, it's discouraging.) I often have to fight an urge to throw away my notes and scream, "Ye gads, wake up! Breathe! Go down swinging. Try something. Try *anything*. Be A-L-I-V-E, for heaven's sake!"

To wit, the greatest musician of this century. . . .

LEONARD BERNSTEIN LIVE — AND ALIVE — AT TANGLEWOOD, CONDUCTING
THE FIRST MOVEMENT OF MAHLER'S NINTH SYMPHONY

Diane Peters of Rosenbluth International, the travel-services growth star and giant, says that company recruiters often interview job candidates while they are driving a car. The reason: It's tough, she says, to put on a act or be someone other than who you really are when you're behind the wheel in city traffic.

Interesting.

199 A Dose of Strong Medicine

Chairman Stan Shih calls it a "disintegration business plan" — and, paradoxically, its aim is to vault the sales of Taiwan-based Acer Inc. from $2 billion to $8 billion in the short period between now and the year 2000, according to *The Economist*.

Shih plans nothing less than splitting his diverse computer company into 21 independent businesses. To underscore their independence, a majority share of the ownership in each will be sold to local investors (in Taiwan, Mexico, Malaysia, Singapore, the United States, etc.). First on the block will likely be Acer Peripherals, with sales of $340 million.

By going public in manageable, comprehensible (to securities analysts) bites, Shih is confident he can raise more money for investment than he could by keeping the information-systems conglomerate tied together; he can also give a sizable number of talented employees a big stake in the (local) action. Shih's also confidently betting that the loosely linked bits can respond faster to their volatile, discrete markets if they are mostly left on their own.

However, he's not abdicating responsibility. The holding company, he told *Business Week*, will be run as a "federation" — a term Shih likes. It'll retain responsibility for developing the Acer brand and for overall technical parameters.

Interestingly, Shih is moving in precisely the opposite direction from IBM. Lou Gerstner, the new CEO, has reversed the radical move toward decomposition mounted by his deposed predecessor, John Akers. He's now recentralizing the $70 billion monster. Who would you bet on? Sorry, Lou, the answer is Stan Shih. (It's not even a tough call.)

200

Laughter helps. (Lots.) We all make mistakes. All the time. If we get into the regular habit of openly discussing our most bone-headed plays — and sharing a B-I-G chuckle over them — then others will feel more comfortable doing the same. At the weekly company meeting, the boss of a small firm gives an award for recounting the grossest muck-up. (He frequently wins.) This is not to suggest sloppiness. The point is air-clearing laughter at small (and not-so-small) mistakes — followed by a discussion of how we can keep the same thing from happening again.

> **PRAISING MISFITS**
>
> **The boss of a small firm gives an award for recounting the grossest muck-up. (He frequently wins.)**

But above all, it certifies the idea that life is a circus, in which you'll only star if you are constantly trying new things — and, thence, constantly mucking up.

201

Every job has customers. Have every employee identify who his or her customers are.

202   The 30-Second Vacation

You've heard about the one-minute manager. How about the 30-second vacation?

I'm not kidding. Though no student of Zen Buddhism (my wife, Kate, is), I do engage in the Zen-like practice of "following my breathing." It might well be classified a near-miracle.

Bugged by the direction of a contentious conversation? Trapped in a cab by slow-moving New York City traffic, and already late for a meeting? Stalled on any topic?

Follow your breathing, for 30 seconds, a moment, or 10 or 20 minutes. By which I mean tuning into the basic process of breathing; you don't need to intone some esoteric mantra (*Om ne pod me om*, or some such); just, very slowly, "Breathing in, two, three, four. Breathing out, two, three, four."

I know there's more to it, and I practice a number of variations. But, in short, it calls a complete halt to whatever overwrought tension is building inside me. Doing it on the highway when I'm behind, say, three or four crawling vehicles, my speed automatically drops by 10 or 20 miles per hour — and my disposition returns to equilibrium, at times approaching passivity (no mean feat, for a classic Type A, argumentative personality). In fact, I can do it so unobtrusively that my seat mate on a plane, or even at a meeting, would have no idea what I was doing, unless she or he were to look directly into my slightly out-of-focus eyes.

Try it. Try any damn thing that will keep you fresh. That's my message.

203

"Consistency is the last refuge of the unimaginative."

Oscar Wilde

204

Consistency may well be the last refuge of the unimaginative . . . but little odors reveal more about the big stink than you would imagine.

While heading to the airport the other day, I passed a small(ish)-town high school. The town is, if not finished, heading nowhere.

The sign board on the street outside the school said it all. (Unintentionally.) It was aging, with peeled, faded paint; and even a bit lopsided The press-on letters, announcing a school board meeting, were attached in a crooked, haphazard fashion.

In short, the sign board was a mirror of the school, which was a mirror of the town, which was coming apart. (I won't reveal the location: Why add insult to injury?)

I'm not saying that to fix the sign is to fix the school is to fix the town is to fix the kids' future. I wasn't born yesterday.

I am saying that if I were appointed principal, I might well start by fixing the sign.

While the "all-we-need-is-a-dash-of-self-esteem" approach often can't deliver the big results that are needed, this community (school, kids, etc.) is nonetheless in desperate need of a booster shot of enthusiasm. And the sign, visible to all (e.g., casual passersby like me but, more important, the people who live there), would at least be a start. Maybe more than a trivial start.

The good news for would-be turnaround kings and queens, of schools and factories and insurance agencies, is that there are a jillion (almost literally) inexpensive places to begin. So you *can* make a difference. Fast. *If* you wish.

Does your 25 or 250,000 square feet of responsibility reek of decay? Or pride? Why don't you put down this book — and take a look?

205 To Dress . . . or Not

I was shocked. . . . No, I wasn't really shocked. I was . . . hysterical. No, not quite in hysterics either.

But I was highly amused, let's put it that way, by *Industry Week*'s June 20, 1994, cover story, "The Casual Corporation" — a dead-serious review of dress code status (e.g., "dress-down Fridays") in corporate America.

I mean, good God, *what is all the fuss*?

I run a small business. And our dress code is clear: Hire great folks, and they'll do what's right about dress and everything else. *That's it.*

The idea of a dress code is laughable, appalling, or both. (Both.) If we have clients coming in the next day, we usually let people know — and if they choose, they can adjust their dress.

I'm the principal shareholder, and I usually show up, winter or summer, in shorts and a *very* carefully chosen T-shirt or sweatshirt, and baseball cap. My wife will tell you, it often takes me five minutes to select the right hat. What mood am I in today: San Jose Sharks? Pacific Mountaineer? North Melbourne Kangaroos ? (Australian Rules Football — I love it.) Don't ever say I'm not dress conscious!

One of my two partners is a suit or smart-casual guy. Which is great. I invariably wear very dull suits when I'm giving speeches — hey, if you're gonna tell 2,500 folks their careers are in jeopardy, you'd better not wear your Hunter Thompson outfit (much as I'd prefer to).

Sun Microsystems boss Scott McNealy was once quoted on the topic. "We *do* have a dress code," he said. "You must." Now that I can handle.

206

Trust. Make a list of the people in your life you trust. Really trust. I'd lay a wager they're the people you feel closest to, turn to when you need advice or solace. Think about why you've given the people on that list your trust. They probably earned it. Just as you've probably earned theirs. Trust. Trust. T-R-U-S-T. It's the single most important contributor to the maintenance of human relationships. And for a business, it can, quite simply, mean the difference between success and failure.

In a research experiment, two groups of executives were given identical information about a difficult policy decision.

One group was briefed to expect trusting behavior from each other and the other to expect untrusting behavior. Even in such an obviously trivial, "make-believe" setting, the "trust group" reported significantly better decisions. In addition, trust-group members were more open with their feelings, experienced greater clarity about the group's goals, and searched for more alternative solutions. They also reported greater levels of mutual influence and expressed more unity as a management team.

`Nuff said. (Actually, never `nuff said on this topic — *the* topic, *the* soft underbelly of corporate renewal.)

PARTING SHOTS

207　The New Order: Work Mimics Life

Many firms are moving almost all employees into self-managed, multifunction teams that schedule their own work, develop budgets, and deal directly with customers and vendors. Such skills have long been the province of the senior and middle ranks. So it's hardly surprising that many execs are asking: "Are workers up to the challenge?" To understand why in nine cases out of 10 (99 out of 100 is more like it) the answer is yes, just look at life *off* the job. "Managing" day-to-day affairs encompasses most so-called big-business challenges.

■ **Long-term view**. Corporate chiefs, not workers, are the ones who have a problem here! The chief may be a slave to next quarter's earnings, but the average "real person" understands investment. For instance, workers routinely turn their wallets inside out to buy a house — and often undertake steep, 20-year tuition-savings programs for their toddlers.

(On the job, the story is the same. For example, workers usually comprehend better than their bosses the value of buying quality goods from vendors.)

■ **Complex tradeoffs**. Family life *is* tradeoffs. Take that $250 bonus to the store and buy some new clothes? Put the bucks aside for a long-desired vacation? Or toward a new car? The conflicting demands confronting self-managed work teams can be no more complicated than such constant personal choices.

■ **Self-management.** Experts say the shift to self-managed teams takes *years* of training and preparation. Really? What's a family but a self-managed team? Complex "flex-time scheduling algorithms" for a seven-person work team pale beside the logistics of a family with two working adults (holding three jobs between them) and a pair of teenagers. There are potholes in the road to effective self-management at work, and, heaven knows, there are dysfunctional families. But the idea of "self-managed units" hardly arrived last year.

■ **No job descriptions.** Some bosses doubt their employees can get through the day without job descriptions and a policy manual. So tell me, how many families have job descriptions and manuals?

I'm all for making to-do lists, at work and at home. (I do it.) But face it, we juggle lots of balls and handle ambiguity and surprises at home (and in our community activities) without resorting to detailed written guidance.

■ **Budgets.** Some companies handle budgets well. Some don't. The same is true for self-managed work teams. *And families.* But there's nothing alien about budgeting to the average 26-year-old worker, let alone the 36-year-old. The budget tightwire act is about the same for families and work groups. (If budgets are more complex at work, it's usually because accountants have obscured the obvious in a blizzard of techno-babble aimed at enhancing their own status.)

■ **"Relationship management."** The bowling team is tied for first, and you're the anchor. The showdown's Saturday, at the same time your 13-year-old starts his first youth soccer-league game. What's your call?

"Investing in relationship development" is essential in fluid organizational configurations. Training professionals insist it's an arcane art that only they can untangle. Hogwash! It's true that lots of people make lousy decisions about managing relationships (hence our high divorce rate), but nothing about the process requires a Ph.D. in clinical psychology.

■ **Network management.** Yet another "complex" must. But new? Many workers lead fund-raising drives for their club or children's school; chair the church Building and Grounds Com-

mittee; coach Little League; lead a Brownie troop. That is, they can pass the basic test — and the advanced course — in working in networks with "outsiders" who participate only if they're self-motivated.

■ **Dealing with vendors and customers.** Suppliers and customers are part of many modern work teams. And, ho-hum, "special skills" must be acquired to handle the new setup.

Huh? The average adult routinely works with numerous "outside vendors" — plumbers, dry cleaners, orthodontists, and, occasionally, realtors, contractors, and car dealers.

■ **Projects.** Projects, rather than repetitive tasks, are now the basis for most value-added in business. But there's nothing mysterious about projects — except bosses' long-standing belief that workers can't deal with them.

Consider a typical weekend: Sam and Sally do their fall planting, attack a complex home-improvement project, work with their 14-year-old on first-year algebra. See my point?

■ **Constant improvement.** Listen up. It's the biggest shift since

the beginning of the Industrial Revolution — i.e., asking workers to use their heads. It may be the biggest shift *at work*. But
what else is the average day all about in the suburbs — or in the
ghetto for that matter — other than taking initiatives? Sure, we
may give in and watch the full slate of NFL games on Sunday. (I
occasionally do.) But mostly, truth be known, we spend our
time trying new stuff and coping with surprises, tiny and large.

There *is* a lot of change going on in the workplace. But, oddly
enough, the result is making work life look more, not less, like
real life. The new "at-work skills" are complex. But so is living!

208 Nation as Classroom

Lewis Perelman, author of the provocative *School's Out*, has
coined a *fabulous* word: *kanbrain*.

He takes it from the Japanese *kanban* (the just-in-time inventory management idea — where the part you need is delivered to
where you want it, when you want it). Imagine, then, education
of any kind, available to anyone. Anytime. Anywhere.

The hotel housekeeper who wants to learn the rudiments of
accounting should be able to do so. At home. At 3 A.M. Any
day. Via cable TV with a black control-box atop it; from a CD
disk slotted into her 12-year-old's Game Boy.

In fact, I envision — as competitive necessity — the United
States becoming one big school "room." Stan Davis, one of
America's most original management thinkers, says we should
think about education as K-80, not K-12. School for life.
Anywhere. Anyplace. Anytime. Any subject.

It's no pipe dream. Already, 6 percent of all college credits in
the U.S. are earned electronically — i.e., via some sort of com-
puter-enhanced distance learning. (A June 1994 Stanford
University master's degree graduate never set foot on campus.)
But there is a long, long way to go.

So . . . let's go.

Take management, religious, and political gurus (including yours truly) with a grain of salt. It's good for you and good for humanity, as the philosopher E. M. Cioran makes clear in his *A Short History of Decay*:

> In itself, every idea is neutral . . . but man animates ideas, projects his flames and flaws into them. . . . Idolaters by instinct, we convert the objects of our dreams . . . into the Unconditional.
>
> [Man's] power to adore is responsible for all his crimes: A man who loves a god unduly forces other men to love his god, eager to exterminate them if they refuse. . . . Once man loses his *faculty of indifference* he becomes a potential murderer. . . . We kill only in the name of a god or his counterfeits. . . .
>
> In every mystic outburst, the moans of victims parallel the moans of ecstasy. . . . Scaffolds, dungeons, jails flourish only in the shadow of a faith — of that need to believe which has infested the mind forever. The devil pales beside the man who owns a truth, his truth. . . .
>
> A human being possessed by a belief and not eager to pass it on to others is a phenomenon alien to the earth, where our mania for salvation makes life unbreathable. Look around you: . . . everyone trying to remedy everyone's life. . . . The sidewalks and hospitals overflow with reformers. Society — an inferno of Saviors!
>
> It is enough for me to hear someone talk sincerely about ideals, about the future . . . to hear him say "we" with a certain inflection of assurance — for me to consider him my enemy. I see in him a tyrant. . . .
>
> We mistrust the swindler, the trickster, the conman; yet to them we can impute none of history's

great convulsions; believing in nothing, it is not they who rummage in your hearts. . . .

In every man sleeps a prophet, and when he wakes there is a little more evil in the world.

Quite simply, these are as important as any words I've ever come across. They frighten me. They ring true. They are worth occasional re-reading.

Ah, the circus of life.

210

"There are more things in heaven and on earth than are dreamt of in your philosphy."

William Shakespeare

ACKNOWLEDGEMENTS

This book has been a lifetime in the making, and thence has many cooks. Including:

Tribune Media Services, which has energetically distributed my columns for the last 10 years, thence forcing me to generate 800 somewhat ordered words a week, come hell or high water; and the over 100 editors, from the United Arab Emirates to San Jose, California, who run the column—and the thousands of readers, the world over, who have written challenging letters. Challenge is the only basis for growth, and I owe a huge debt of gratitude to every participant at one of my seminars who's raised her or his hand—and expanded my thinking with the ensuing, often pointed question. Several conversations with busy business leaders are cornerstones of this book; I appreciate the no-holds-barred, on-the-record dialogues we had together.

As to pulling it all together, my partners in crime and co-creators from the start have been: libretto (words), Donna Carpenter, Tom Richman, Sebastian Stuart; score (design), Ken Silvia; and orchestral arrangement (e.g., getting a lot of folks organized to talk with me, plus performing a host of other tasks including fact checking), Erik Hansen. Of course, the six of us would never have begun had not it been for the strong support of my agent and friend, Esther Newberg, and my pub-

lishers (and friends), Sonny Mehta, Jane Friedman, and Marty Asher.

Our hearty band hardly did it alone. Donna C. and Ken S. were ably assisted by Maurice Coyle, Jessica Robison, Cindy Sammons, Mike Mattil, Martha Lawler, and Nancy Cutter. At Vintage-Knopf, Linda Rosenberg and Laurie Brown kept us on track, and Carol Carson Devine gave us a cover that will not soon be forgotten. Katy Barrett and Carl Lennertz are working like the devil to get and keep the book in the front of the stores; and Carol Janeway is urging the book into stores beyond the borders of North America. Back home in Palo Alto, Chris Gage did a lot of almost everything (again). Ian Thomson, partner and friend, kept me honest (again). And Paul Cohen, Liz Mitchell, Jayne Pearl, and Darlene Viggiano have worked with me on columns for 10 years—and have been researchers/co-authors of several stories which first saw the light of day in our newsletter. Kate Abbe (spouse, poet, publisher, pal) as usual provided the intellectual and emotional support that made all the difference—along with good humor that sometimes evaded me as yet another deadline neared.

Finally, Arthur, the donkey on our farm in Vermont, must get his due. When the alarm clock failed (as I made it do ever so frequently), his insistent, high-decibel braying was the real call to the writing desk that, finally, could not be ignored.

NOTES

"What recommends commerce...and pray to Jupiter": "Thoughts on the Business of Life," *Forbes*, September 12, 1994, p. 292.

STARTERS

PAGE

3   "Honor your errors...systematic error management": "Three Abridged Chapters from *Out of Control: The Rise of Neo-Biological Civilization*," *Whole Earth Review*, Spring 1994, p. 94.

4   "...their willingness to be attentive": Mary Oliver, "Mockingbirds," *The Atlantic Monthly*, February, 1994, p. 80.

4-5   "Consider research done...poor in quality": Richard C. Whiteley, *The Customer-Driven Company: Moving from Talk to Action* (Reading, MA: Addison-Wesley, 1991), pp. 9, 10.

5   "A year and...those in the other group": Ellen Langer, *Mindfulness* (Reading, MA: Addison-Wesley,1990), p. 1.

6   "It's not my...to *de*-motivate them": Terry Neill, Whittemore Conference on Hypercompetition, Amos Tuck School of Business, September 10, 1994.

8   "The only security...seat of our pants": *Whole Earth Review*, Summer 1994, p. 20.

8   "How do I work? I grope": "Tidbits," *Whole Earth Review*, Summer 1994, p. 7.

11   "What would you do...I think not": Robert Kahn, "There's Nothing Like a Typo," *Retailing Today*, April 1994.

19   "Ho-hum....Issue 200mn Credit Cards": *The Australian Business Asia*, Wednesday July 20 - August 2 1994, p. 3.

21   "Not so long ago...trillion bits of information": "Wonder Chips: How They'll Make Computing Power Ultrafast and Ultracheap," *Business Week*, July 4, 1994, pp. 86, 90.

22   "Cognetics boss...nondurable wholesaling": David Birch, Anne Haggerty, William Parsons, *Hot Industries*, Cognetics, Inc., 1994, p. 4.

23-4   "It carries TQM...these 'defects' graphically": Harry V. Roberts, *Selected Paper Number 73: Using Personal Checklists to Facilitate Total Quality Management*, The University of Chicago, Graduate School of Business, p. 3.

24   "*Now* I know...an attitude problem": "Fire When Ready," *Harper's*, August 1994, pp. 18-19.

GETTING THINGS DONE

31   "Eighty percent of success is showing up": (Woody Allen is also quoted as saying, "Eighty percent of *sex* is showing up.)

Notes

38   "In his first book...you've got a leg up": Harvey Mackay, *Swim With the Sharks Without Being Eaten Alive* (New York: William Morrow and Company, 1988).

MILK, COOKIES, AND MANAGING PEOPLE

55   Hal Rosenbluth and Diane McFerrin Peters, *The Customer Comes Second: And Other Secrets of Exceptional Customer Service* (New York: Morrow, 1992).

58   "Equilibrium is...dis-equilibrium": Kevin Kelly, "Three Abridged Chapters From *Out of Control: The Rise of Neo-Biological Civilization*," *Whole Earth Review*, Spring 1994, pp. 93, 94.

59   "What are the upper...customers by name": Echo Montgomery Garrett, "Branson the Bold," *Success*, November, 1992, p. 24.

59   "Antony Jay...a maximum of 12 hours": Antony Jay, *Corporation Man* (New York: Pelican Books, 1975), pp. 114-123.

60-61   "In most modern armies...to maintain cohesion": Robin Dunbar, "Why Gossip Is Good for You," *New Scientist*, November 21, 1992, pp. 28-31.

62   "Carl Schmitt is...cookies and milk": "Customer Service Quality—Key to a Successful Bank," Speech given at Robert Morris Associates Fall Conference, San Francisco, September 28, 1992.

65   "Peter Drucker hinted...distinctly new phenomenon": Peter Drucker, "The New Society of Organizations," *Harvard Business Review*, September-October 1992, p. 100.

65-66   "The grand viziers...temporary constituents benefit": R. Edward Freeman and Daniel Gilbert, Jr., *Corporate Strategy and the Search for Ethics* (Englewood Cliffs, NJ: Prentice-Hall, 1980) pp. 158, 160, 164, 165, 175.

67   "How dominant are...equals 96 percent": Brian Quinn, Whittemore Conference on Hypercompetition, Amos Tuck School of Business, September 10, 1994.

67   "The world's two...balance of services trade": *1994 World Competitiveness Report*, published by the World Economic Forum, Geneva, Switzerland.

68   "More U.S. workers...by the entire Fortune 500": National Foundation for Women Business Owners, Washington, DC.

79   "He even wrote a book about it": David Armstrong, *Management By Storying Around* (New York: Doubleday Currency, 1992).

72-73   "TGI Friday's wants...fellow job candidates": Nick Bryant, "Thank Goodness It's Fun Getting a Job at Friday's," *Daily Mail*, March 3, 1994.

79-81   "On October 21, 1993...in overall attitude": Srikumar S. Rao, "Welcome to Open Space," *Training*, April, 1994, pp. 52-56.

81   "Considering telecommuting...obstacles of tele-commuting": Patricia B. Seybold, "Summertime and Telecommuting Can Be Easy," *Computerworld*, July 25, 1994, p. 37.

90   "Reward people based...take serious breaks": Tim Stevens, "Creative Genius," *Industry Week*, July 4, 1994, p. 18.

92-93   "During the 1980s...pride and excellence": A version of this story appeared in *On Achieving Excellence*, September 1992, by Michele Moreno.

93   "To learn, fail...punish inactivity": Tim Stevens,"Creative Genius," *Industry Week*, July 4, 1994, p. 18.

93   "Education, technology...in the modern economy": Brian Quinn, Whittemore Conference on Hypercompetition, Amos Tuck School of Business, September 10, 1994.

PENS, TOILETS, AND BUSINESSES THAT DO IT DIFFERENTLY

96-97   "How about pallet-racking...global marketplace": Graham Gardiner, "Spacerack Uses Innovation to Win Asian Business," *Business Queensland*, Week of July 25, 1994, p. 11.

97   "Your company is wobbly...second best-selling car": Alice Rawsthorn, "Talent Needs Intelligence Too", *Financial Times*, Monday June 13, 1994, p. 16.

97   "Today, more stores...to be different": Mark Stevens, "Safe is Risky," *Profit*, September/October 1994, p. 17.

98-102   "It isn't every plumbing...66,000-person business": A version of this story appeared in *On Achieving Excellence*, March 1992, by Darlene Viggiano.

104   "David Maister is...Maister readily uses": David Maister, "Are You Having Fun Yet," *The American Lawyer*, June, 1994.

108   "The clothes seemed...what I didn't want": Ingrid Sischy, "Some Clothes of One's Own," *The New Yorker*, February 7, 1994, pp. 45, 46, 47.

109   "European Union leaders...in public opinion": Edward Mortimer, "More Strategy, Less Small Print," *Financial Times*, Wednesday June 15, 1994, p. 13.

109   "The customer...guide to the future": Steve Lohr, "On the Road With Chairman Lou," *The New York Times*, June 26, 1994, Section 3, p. 6.

113   "Anything we do...don't wait for reasons": *Whole Earth Review*, Summer 1994, p. 66.

118-119   "Ten years ago...can be damned special": Editor: Nancee Weingarden, *PPS A Passion for Parking*, Summer Newsletter 1994. (A Passion for Parking is published quarterly by Professional Parking Services, Inc.)

119   "This is a business...never have to grow up": Michael Graham, "Citizen Pain," *Cincinnati*, June 1994, p. 92.

131   "John Martin...knows where I am": Rich Karlgaard,"ASAP Interview, Susan Cramm & John Martin," *Forbes ASAP*, August 29, 1994, p. 70.

133   "For years companies...to seduce them": Alice Rawsthorn, "Talent Needs Intelligence Too," *Financial Times*, Monday June 13, 1994, p. 16.

133   "Ludwig von Mises...leaps of faith": Michael Prowse, "'Austrian' Recipe for Prosperity," *Financial Times*, Monday February 28, 1994, p. 17.

Notes

Breaking the Mold

163   "In the 1930s...for us to be leaders": Walter Adams and James Brock, *The Bigness Complex: Industry, Labor, and Government in the American Economy* (New York: Pantheon Books, 1986), pp. 39-40.

163   "The same bug has bitten...'me-too' goods": Shunichi Otaki, "What Ever Happened to Sony?" *Tokyo Business Today*, August, 1994, pp. 20, 22.

164-166   Research on Southwest Airlines was conducted by Peter Karl, Char Woods, and Tom Peters, Summer 1994. Additional information was derived from *Fortune*, Kenneth Labich, "Is Herb Kelleher America's Best CEO?" May 2, 1994, pp. 46, 50.

166-173   All quotes in "Strategic Planning, R.I.P.,"are from *The Rise and Fall of Strategic Planning: Reconceiving Roles for Planning, Plans, Planners*, Henry Mintzberg (New York: The Free Press, 1994), pp. 13, 98, 99-100, 108, 131, 134, 139, 172, 195, 203, 221, 223, 234, 235, 238, 255, 258, 259-264, 266, 272, 287, 288, 299, 332, 363.

173   "Sometime during the...joy of creating": Peter Robinson, "Five Ways to Make Business Schools Into Useful Institutions," *The Red Herring*, April/May, 1994, p. 100.

174   "Once we have...wheels for changing terrain": Ian Fraser, "Retailer to the World," *Director*, June, 1994, p. 48.

174-175   "Some research by...unusually low costs": Myron Magnet, "Let's Go For Growth," *Fortune*, March 7, 1994, p. 72.

175   "George Roberts...their company's shares": Herb Greenberg, "Business Insider," *San Francisco Chronicle*, Friday, June 18, 1993, p. D1.

178   "The brilliant Supreme...service of their company": *U.S. Supreme Courts Reports*, "Concurring opinion for Whitney vs. California," Vol. 274, p. 376.

178   "I've watched even...disagreement with the chief": Anthony Lewis, *Make No Law: The Sullivan Case and the First Amendment* (New York: Random House, 1991), p. 70.

180   "Jack Hitt, writing...Dream on": Jack Hitt, "Original Spin: How Lurid Sex Fantasies Gave Us 'America'", *The Washington Monthly*, March 1993, pp. 25-27.

180   "Take the Rodney King...like a ballet": Patricia Greenfield and Paul Kibbey, "Picture Imperfect," *The New York Times*, April, 1, 1993, p. A1.

180-181   "Economist and Nobel...one of them boiling over": Michael Prowse, "'Austrian' Recipe for Prosperity," *Financial Times*, Monday February 28, 1994, p. 17.

181   "The late Richard Feynman...is no good": James Gleick, "Fermat's Theorem," *The New York Times Sunday Magazine*, October 3, 1993, p. 53.

182   "With many companies...after the event": William Burger, "Up, Up & Away: Peter Pan's Empire," *Newsweek*, June 13, 1994, p. 31.

182-183   "Are you regenerating...you flunk, you leave": Michael E. McGill and John W.

Slocum, "Unlearning the Organization," *Organizational Dynamics*, Autumn, 1993, p. 78. Published by the American Management Association, New York.

183-185   All quotes from *Shadows of Forgotten Ancestors: A Search for Who We Are*, Carl Sagan and Ann Druyan, (New York: Random House, 1992), pp. 26, 27.

185-186   All quotes from *Hypercompetition: Managing the Dynamics of Strategic Maneuvering*, Richard A. D'Aveni with Robert Gunther, (New York: The Free Press, 1994), pp. 10, 30-31, 35-36.

186-187   "Consider these words...let them compete": John Kavanagh, "AMP Rolls Up Its Sleeves," *Business Review Weekly*, October 29, 1993, p. 24.

187   "Call it testimony...two companies' leaders": Personal communications with the author.

187   "A pattern emphasized...sign of impending death": James M. Utterback, *Mastering the Dynamics of Innovation: How Companies Can Seize Opportunities in the Face of Technological Change* (Boston: Harvard Business School Press, 1994), p. xxvii.

189-190   "These days we...buy another Saturn": Alan Solomon, "Car is Big Wheel at Homecoming," *Advertising Age*, July 4, 1994, p. 12.

191   "Love to see...numbers were skyrocketing": "New Era of Human Migration Has Begun, Experts Say," *San Francisco Chronicle*, August 9, 1994, pp. A1, A6.

192   "Think Indonesia...fourth most populous country": Jim Abegglen, Whittemore Conference on Hypercompetition, Amos Tuck School of Business, September 10, 1994.

192   "The quality movement...That's absurd": Ronald Henkoff, "The Hot New Seal of Quality," *Fortune*, June 28, 1993, p. 117.

192-193   "Terry Neill...organizational focus": Terry Neill, Whittemore Conference on Hypercompetition, Amos Tuck School of Business, September 10, 1994.

193   "West Churchman...ethics and aesthetics": Quoted in *Paradox of Success: When Winning At Work Means Losing At Life: A Book of Renewal for Leaders*, John R. O'Neil (New York: G. P. Putnam's Sons, 1993), p. 48.

194   "How do I know...see what I say?": *Bartlett's Familiar Quotations*, 15th ed. (Boston: Little, Brown, 1980), p. 869.

194-196   All quotes in Section 142, "Leap, Then Look," taken from Michael Schrage, "The Culture(s) of Prototyping," *Design Management Journal*, Winter 1993, pp. 58, 62, 65.

195   "Incidentally, the 'sense'...hyperorganized planners": Behnam Tabrizi and Kathleen Eisenhardt, "Accelerating Product Development," *Study Paper, Department of Industrial Engineering and Engineering Management*, Stanford University, March 17, 1994.

196   "Most people die...are one's mistakes": *A New Dictionary of Quotations on Historical Principles*, Selected and Edited by H. L. Mencken (New York: Alfred A. Knopf, 1966), p. 796.

Notes

The Wacky World or (mostly), What Have You Done about Asia Today?

201-204   "Section 145...And, Now, India,": Most statistics in this section can be found in "Financial Times Survey: India," *Financial Times*, Thursday September 30, 1993.

204   "So which India...an economic power?": Barbara Crossette, *India: Facing the Twenty-First Century* (Bloomington, IN: Indiana University Press, 1993), p. 36.

204-205   "Textbooks laden with...cleaner streets and factories": "He Wants Your Job," *The Economist*, June 12, 1993, pp. 15-16.

205-206   "The tragedy of...more than the Belgian": Donald McCloskey, *Second Thoughts: Myths and Morals of U.S. Economic History* (Oxford: Oxford University Press, 1993), pp. 172-173.

206   "In an *Industry Week*...becomes immaterial": John Sheridan, "Reengineering Isn't Enough," *Industry Week*, January 17, 1994, p. 62.

207-212   "Section 147, People Are Different": All quotes from Fons Trompenaars, *Riding the Waves of Culture: Understanding Diversity in Global Business* (Originally published by The Economist Books, London, 1993; Revised Edition published by Irwin Professional Publishing, Burr Ridge, IL, 1994), pp. 1, 17, 36-37, 49, 67, 78, 85, 98, 194.

212   "And then along comes...year time horizon": Cathy Castillo, "Comparative Strategies in Marketing," *Stanford Business School Magazine*, June, 1994, p. 28.

212   "The biggest barrier...own gut as well": Jeffrey J. Ake, "Easier Done Than Said," *Inc.*, February, 1993, p. 96.

215   "The '*International*' Herald Tribune...big cities, too": *International Herald Tribune*, Thursday, September 29, 1994, p. 18.

216   "Asia is on...throughout the city": "Sitting Comfortably," *The Economist*, June 12th, 1993, p. 77.

217   "Light of the...creep eastward": Robert Hass, ed., *The Essential Haiku: Versions of Basho, Buson, & Issa* (New York: The Ecco Press, 1994), p. 101.

Tomorrow's Strange Enterprises

245   "Reengineering is the...environment shifts?": Tom Brown, "*De*-Engineering the Corporation," *Industry Week*, April 18, 1994, p. 20.

246-247   "*New York Times* reviewer...days old now": James R. Oestreich, "A Lesson in Humanity From a Master of It," *The New York Times*, January 25, 1994, p. C16.

249   "*Gentry* magazine...about 100 e-mail messages!": *Gentry*, June July 1994, p. 7.

249   "The basis of...its knowledge assets": S. Hedberg, "The Knowledge Edge," *CIO*, June 1, 1994, p. 78.

258-259   "There are two...do it or disappear": Geoff Lewis and Robert D. Hof, "The World According to Andy Grove," *Business Week/The Information Revolution 1994*, pp. 77-78.

259 "Sun Microsystems CIO...the Boeing 747": Rick Tetzil, "Surviving Information Overload: Lost in the Infobog? You're Not Alone," *Fortune*, July 11, 1994, p. 56.

259 "The three Rs...capacity for change": Speech by Fred Gluck, Merck/Manhattan College Lecture series, Princeton Club, October 21, 1992.

260 "When we see...learning meaningful things": Peter Senge, "Creating Quality Communities," *Executive Excellence*, June, 1994, p. 12.

261 "Distance learning'...they had ever taken": National Technological University Annual Report, 1992-1993, pp. 3, 7.

261-262 "Some have...internal service functions": Rochelle Garner, "A Tough Act To Follow," *Computerworld*, July 4, 1994, p. 72.

LISTS!

279 "*Fortune*'s Strat Sherman...energy than the rest of us": Personal communications with the author.

ATTAINING PERPETUAL ADOLESCENCE

301 "It's no small...source of innovation": Kevin Kelly, "Three Abridged Chapters from *Out of Control: The Rise of Neo-Biological Civilization*," *Whole Earth Review*, Spring 1994, pp. 93-94.

302 "I am an American...in my own way": Saul Bellow, *The Adventures of Augie March* (New York: Viking Press, 1965), p. 3.

304-305 "Fun Company of...joie de vivre": Geoffrey Smith, "Life Won't Be Just A Bowl of Cherry Garcia," *Business Week*, July 18, 1994, p. 42.

308 "A psychologist was...It was his retreat": John O'Neil, *Paradox of Success*, p. 165.

309 "This GOOD thing...Breeds this MONSTER": John O'Neil, *Paradox of Success*, p. 67.

309 "Pity the leader...stubbornness, and egoism": John Gardner, quoted in *Paradox of Success*, p. 222.

310-311 "In explaining legendary...'advanced immaturity'": Roger Rosenblatt, "The Old-Boy Network: Ben Bradlee and the Virtues of Advanced Immaturity," *Men's Journal*, September, 1993, p. 25.

314 "Diane Peters of...wheel in city traffic": Robert Gottliebsen, "People Power Back in the Growth Equation," *Business Review Weekly*, November 19, 1993, p. 26.

314 "Chairman Stan Shih...mostly on their own": "Inside the Box," *The Economist*, July 9th, 1994, p. 66; Pete Engardio, "For Acer, Breaking Up Is Smart To Do," *Business Week*, July 4, 1994, p. 82.

316 "Consistency is the...of the unimaginative": Robert I. Fitzhenry, ed., *The Harper Book of Quotations*, 3rd Edition (New York: Harper Perennial, 1993), p. 102.

Notes

317   "But I was...in corporate America": Daniel J. McConville, "The Casual Corporation," *Industry Week*, June 20, 1994, pp. 12-17.

PARTING SHOTS

324   "Lewis Perelman...*Anytime. Anywhere*": Lewis Perelman, "Kanban to Kanbrain," *Forbes ASAP*, June 6, 1994, pp. 85-95.

324   "In fact, I envision...Anytime. Any subject": Stan Davis and Jim Botkin, *The Monster Under the Bed* (New York: Simon and Schuster, 1994), p. 173.

325-326   "In itself...evil in the world": E. M. Cioran, *A Short History of Decay* (London: Quartet Books, Ltd., 1990), pp. 3, 4, 5, 6.

326   "There are more...in your philosophy": William Shakespeare, *Hamlet*, Act I, Scene V, Lines 166-167.

INDEX

Index

Index

Index

PICTURE CREDITS

A NOTE ABOUT THE AUTHOR

Tom Peters is the co-author of *In Search of Excellence* (with Robert H. Waterman, Jr.) and *A Passion for Excellence* (with Nancy Austin) and the author of *Thriving on Chaos, Liberation Management* and *The Tom Peters Seminar*. Though he is founder and chief of the Tom Peters Group in Palo Alto, California, he and his family spend much of their time on a farm in Vermont, thanks to the information technology revolution.